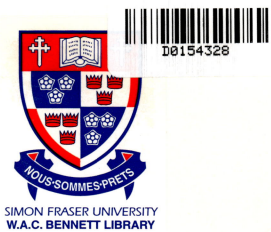

Innovation Systems in a Global Context
The North American Experience

The integration of national economies in a global economic system has become a central feature of contemporary political, social, economic, and cultural life. However, the mechanisms of such integration are not well understood. In this collection of essays, leading scholars in the area of evolutionary economics clarify the structure of innovation systems and discuss the role played by technological innovation in fostering economic growth and international integration.

Focusing on North America, *Innovation Systems in a Global Context* examines the nature of existing systems of innovation in Canada, Mexico, and the United States; the conceptual questions surrounding the analysis of such systems; trends towards the creation of supra-national systems in East Asia, Europe, and North America; and some of the ecological, cultural, economic, and social problems confronting these large-scale systems.

Robert Anderson, Theodore Cohn, Chad Day, Michael Howlett, Catherine Murray teach at Simon Fraser University.

Innovation Systems in a Global Context

The North American Experience

Edited by
ROBERT ANDERSON
THEODORE COHN
CHAD DAY
MICHAEL HOWLETT
CATHERINE MURRAY

McGill-Queen's University Press
Montreal & Kingston · London · Ithaca

© McGill-Queen's University Press 1998

ISBN 0-7735-1780-4

Legal deposit fourth quarter 1998
Bibliothèque nationale du Québec

Printed in Canada on acid-free paper

McGill-Queen's University Press acknowledges the
support of the Canada Council for the Arts for its
publishing program.

Canadian Cataloguing in Publication Data

Main entry under title:

Innovation systems in a global context: the North
American experience

Includes bibliographical references and index.
ISBN 0-7735-1780-4

1. Technological innovations–North America. 2. North
America–Economic integration. 3. International
economic integration. 4. North America–Economic
policy. Anderson, Robert, L. 1942-

HC79.T4I548 1998   338.9'26'097   C98-900635-2

Contents

Figures

Tables

Acknowledgments

The research upon which this book is based was supported by the Social Science and Humanities Research Council of Canada (SSHRC), the National Science Foundation (NSF) of the United States of America, and CONACyT of the Republic of Mexico.

We would like to thank the many participants of the 1994 Special Summer Institute on Competitiveness, Innovation and Sustainability in the North American Region held at Whistler, British Columbia, for their contributions to this volume. Thanks are extended especially to Nina Stipich of SSHRC, Ken Oye, Donald Barry, Teresa Guttierez, Robert Varade, and other members of the organizing committee for the trinational institute.

We are also grateful for research assistance in various forms supplied by Christine Massey and Bill Souder. Denyse Zenner, director's secretary in the School of Communication, Simon Fraser University, often acted as communication coordinator of this long project. Members of the Centre for Policy Research on Science and Technology (CPROST), including Richard Smith and Morley Lipset, aided in many aspects of the book preparation. A follow-up grant from SSHRC permitted us to prepare the papers collected in this volume for circulation and publication.

At McGill-Queen's University Press, Philip Cercone and Brenda Prince provided assistance and encouragement. Reviewers commissioned by the press provided invaluable comments and suggestions for improving the text. Judith Turnbull copy-edited the manuscript, and Anita

Mahoney of the Dean of Arts Office at Simon Fraser University typeset the manuscript.

We thank you all.

Innovation Systems in a Global Context

Introduction: Innovation Systems in a Global Context

ROBERT ANDERSON, THEODORE COHN,
CHAD DAY, MICHAEL HOWLETT, AND
CATHERINE MURRAY

The ever-increasing integration of national economies in a global economic system has become a central feature of contemporary political, social, economic, and cultural life. Yet the contours and mechanisms of such integration are not well understood (Gamble and Payne 1996). Does integration lead to economic prosperity? Is integration occurring more at the regional or global level (McMahon and Woodliffe 1996)? How does integration affect local or subnational economies and societies? What has been the impact of such activity on the environment, labour, women, and other groups marginalized by earlier periods and patterns of economic growth?

Answering these questions is a difficult task, for one must not only make a careful empirical analysis of existing social and economic trends but also rethink many social, political, and economic orthodoxies that have failed to explain contemporary developments (Archibugi and Michie 1997). One promising theoretical direction that can help address such questions is offered by evolutionary economics, or endogenous growth theory, pioneered by European, Latin American, and North American researchers. Endogenous growth theory delves into the question of the historical relationship between technological change and economic growth (Dosi et al. 1988).[1] Focusing on the manner in which social, cultural, and economic actors have tended to develop dense networks, or "systems of innovation," scholars working in this vein have begun to derive a set of propositions relating to the key role played by technological innovation in fostering economic growth and international integration.

This concern with innovation and its linkages with competitiveness and sustainability leads to a number of important research questions. To what extent are there "national communities" of innovators (Nelson and Rosenberg 1993)? How does technical advance affect international trade patterns, regional innovation systems, or environmental quality? How do we account for continuous but sharply uneven flows of product and process innovations in global or regional communities (Dosi and Soete 1991)? Is it more advantageous to import technical advances or to develop them domestically (Kamien and Schwartz 1982)? What types of policies are likely to encourage innovation and also comply with international trading principles and environmental standards (MacNeill et al. 1991)?

The essays in this book address these questions, expand on the elements of the theory of innovation systems, and examine the implications of the extension and deepening of such systems for economic growth and social and cultural change.

SYSTEMS OF INNOVATION

The Organization for Economic Cooperation and Development (OECD) has defined a *system of innovation* as a "network of institutions in the public and private sectors whose activities and interactions initiate, import, modify and diffuse new technologies" (OECD 1991). A substantial body of literature emerging in the early 1990s examined the factors that promote innovation and technological change (Lundvall 1992; Freeman 1995). Many of these studies focused on the national level and highlighted the importance of country-specific capabilities, skills, and knowledge in bringing about technological change (Nelson 1993). It was found that nation-states differed in their methods of adopting innovations, in their sectoral strengths, and in their overall ability to produce change (Archibugi and Michie 1995). Many countries, concerned with their ability to remain competitive and prosperous, began to question their policies towards science and technology and expanded their notions of the significance of such policies (Niosi 1991b).

The reshaping of national systems of innovation (NSI)[2] is now of major concern to many countries. However, the direction and targets of policymaking have varied greatly in geopolitical terms. While all countries have examined this issue on the national level, some have focused a great deal of attention at the subnational level and others have concentrated on the supranational, continental, or multi-state regional level. Some countries, in turn, have focused on the sectoral level, while others have attempted more integrated multi-sectoral strategies (Edquist 1997; de la Mothe and Paquet 1996).

Although the nation-state and national economy are, and will continue to be, central actors in systems of innovation, the emergence of large-scale, supranational, regional trading blocs and the growth of international interdependence inevitably raise questions about the development of innovation systems above the national level. This edited volume focuses on the national systems of innovation in North America and how they are changing and adapting as a North American system of innovation begins to develop.[3] To address this issue, the essays in this book examine the nature of existing systems of innovation in Canada, Mexico, and the United States, the conceptual questions surrounding the analysis of such systems, trends towards the creation of supranational systems in East Asia, Europe, and North America, and several of the ecological, cultural, economic, and social problems confronting these large-scale systems.

OUTLINE OF THE BOOK

The first section of this volume addresses several of the conceptual and methodological questions raised above with respect to innovation systems and the concept of subnational, national, and supranational innovation systems. In chapter 1, Charles Davis discusses the links that exist between technological innovation, the sustainability of social and ecological systems, and economic competitiveness. Noting the trend towards the creation of a continental system of innovation in North America, Davis warns against the tendency sometimes displayed by adherents of evolutionary growth theory to assume that such developments are necessarily benign or providential. Care must be taken by governments to ensure that their policies in this regard address the entire spectrum of social, cultural, political, economic, and environmental concerns raised by closer continental integration.

Our current understanding of innovation is based on outmoded linear and sequential assumptions, which do not take sufficient account of the close linkages between innovation and competitiveness. According to this traditional sequential model, universities produce basic knowledge, government laboratories contribute applied pre-commercial knowledge, and private firms conduct commercially applied research and development using the two kinds of knowledge and specially trained personnel. Studies indicate, however, that innovation in fact results from competition, cooperation, and other types of interactions. Furthermore, inflexibilities and information gaps in the innovation system may lead to inefficiencies that impede global competitiveness.

Davis not only examines innovation and competitiveness, but also attempts to assess the potential effects of economic activity on long-term sustainability (Redclift 1987). The World Commission on Environment and Development, or Brundtland Commission, defined *sustainable development* as economic growth that "meets the needs of the present without compromising the ability of future generations to meet their own needs" (World Commission on Environment and Development 1987). The growth of environmentalism in advanced industrial states results partly from the attention given to quality-of-life issues in affluent societies. However, it also reflects an awareness that serious ecological problems pose a threat, not only to long-term economic growth, but also to the survival of the planet. While specialists on competitiveness and innovation only rarely address sustainability issues, Davis stresses the fact that the linkages among these three issues must be addressed.

While Davis examines the movement towards supranational innovation systems, Gilles Paquet in chapter 2 focuses upon the continued existence of significant sectoral and subnational systems. He points to the paradox that increased large-scale integration often relies on the intensification of local or meso-level systems. Paquet, like Davis, urges governments to be aware of these linkages when they formulate and execute any policies directed towards enhanced or increased levels of supranational integration. In some instances, a focus on multinational innovation systems has led to a tendency to overlook the fact that some national innovation systems also involve subnational systems.

In Canada, the United States, and Mexico, the *centralized-mind syndrome* looms large. Little attention has been paid to the new powers that state or local governments have acquired as international integration has progressed. These may not be of equal importance in every country, but there is already evidence that subnational regional features interact with specific sectoral and industrial organizations to create an organization-location-technology nexus that plays an important role in explaining the dynamics of innovation. In other words, in the case of some countries, production and innovation are highly dependent on regionally specific sets of actors and agents. The question of how such subnational systems are integrated into multinational systems deserves careful study and analysis.

In chapter 3, the third essay in this section, Sidney Weintraub also takes up the question of the challenges to further integration in North America. The American agenda in the next round of World Trade Organization (WTO) negotiations for opening markets and reducing regulatory barriers has met with obstacles from a number of parties. Also, the short-term prospects for either broadening or deepening the North American Free Trade Agreement (NAFTA) are unclear, partly because the U.S. Congress has delayed in renewing the "fast-track approval" requirement for the inclusion of other countries, such as Chile. Weintraub asks how U.S. policy immobilism and a lack of regional leadership in innovation networks affect regional integration and the development of intraregional innovation systems.

Weintraub argues that North American integration must deepen well beyond the removal of border barriers to trade and foreign investment. It is also necessary to establish compatible industrial standards, upward harmonization of environmental standards, and more control over national regulations that serve as disguised trade barriers. Such deepening of integration is necessary if the NAFTA countries are to benefit from innovation at the regional level. This involves locating research and production facilities on the basis of economic rather than protectionist factors, and establishing plants of sufficient scale, through co-production and vertical integration, to service the needs of the North American market and compete more effectively globally.

Deeper integration will also lead to the spread of technology from the United States to the two economically weaker NAFTA countries, particularly Mexico. The spread of process innovation to Mexico, according to Weintraub, not only will increase North American competitiveness, but will also ease concerns about deeper integration. Mexican wages are highest in manufacturing sectors where process innovations are most extensive, and the closing of the technology gap with Mexico should therefore lead to a narrowing of the wage gap in North America. As the wage gap decreases, the United States and Canada will become less concerned about the benefits that Mexico derives from "cheap labour." On the other hand, the closing of the technology gap should ensure Mexicans that they will not lose industry because of higher productivity in the United States and Canada.

The second section of the book deals with the existing national systems of innovation in the three countries of North America. In some parts of North America, as in many industrial or newly industrialized countries, the state is the dominant element in the national innovation system. As Jorge Niosi sets out in chapter 4, more than 50 per cent of the national R&D effort is financed directly or indirectly by government in Canada. Government targets that effort towards some civilian and a few military priority areas, and it regulates the intensity and organization of R&D through its many policies and agencies.

Canada's NSI is composed of some 3,500 to 4,000 private companies conducting R&D, 30 research universities, and 150 government laboratories, mostly federally funded and controlled. Included as well are federal departments such as Industry Canada and its provincial counterparts, the Federal Development Bank, and the small venture capital industry. The success of Canadian innovation is reliant upon both the effectiveness and efficiency of each innovating agent as well as upon that of the system as a whole.

There are important questions in the Canadian context, as Niosi's chapter indicates. Is Canada providing adequate financial support for innovation? Is the university system producing the numbers of scientific, engineering, and management personnel that the private sector requires? Is industry benefiting from university and government research? Are university technology transfer programs and provincial policies encouraging the development of new innovative firms? How does the invisible input of foreign technology affect Canadian industries? How can new industries involved with advanced materials and processes be built upon the foundation of the knowledge of traditional industries that use natural resources and raw materials?

With growing global integration of the world's economies, resource-based, newly industrializing economies (NIEs) like Mexico's must move towards a future based on goods and services with a higher information content. As Kurt Unger and Carlos Ramírez argue in chapter 5, this change is required if NIEs are to compete in an increasingly integrated and competitive global marketplace, characterized by highly mobile capital and investment flows and decreasing barriers to trade and investment. Moreover, the economic and social development needs of rapidly industrializing economies are such that greatly expanded trade and investment flows are necessary merely to maintain present inadequate growth rates.

Mexico's decision to join the General Agreement on Tariffs and Trade (GATT, renamed the World Trade Organization) in 1986 and to confederate in forming the NAFTA indicates its awareness of the need to respond to the forces of integration. However, as Ramírez and Unger argue, the initial results of these moves have been dispiriting, as most industries have seen their technological level decrease, drawing into question the entire continental integration strategy of recent Mexican administrations.

In the United States, the most advanced economic and technological system in North America has been undergoing intensive changes in the post–Cold War period. As Henry Etzkowitz outlines in chapter 6, the United States has begun restructuring its research and development networks as its military-industrial complex is downsized. Competition in many markets and sectors from East Asian newly industrializing countries (NICs), Japan, and Germany has also been escalating.

The United States is moving into a new environment for innovation in which universities and other knowledge-producing organizations play a much stronger role. Local, regional, and national governments play a more prominent role in industrial policy. International and multinational authorities are also involved. Even the older, larger firms are revising the way that they develop technology, entering into horizontal and vertical strategic alliances to develop and market new products. The emergence of a new group of science-based technologies, together with the need to renew older technologies, has revived issues related to the source and diffusion of innovation in the late twentieth century

In response, U.S. governments have attempted to bolster the "triple helix" of links between industry, universities, and governments in knowledge creation and technological development. This effort occurred outside of the former military direction of research. Armed with new intellectual property rights legislation established under the 1980 Bayh-Dole Act, Etzkowitz argues that U.S. governments have provided incentives for university-based research and development activities that have promoted significant hi-tech, productive outcomes. Combined with NAFTA-based initiatives in technology transfer across nations, this has led to a "new politics of innovation" in which intense linkages across actors and nations are encouraged and developed by local, state, and national U.S. governments.

The third part of the book examines the trend, apparent in recent years, towards national innovation systems being supplanted or transformed into large, supranational, regional, or continental systems. In chapter 7, John Alic builds on the observations of Niosi, Ramírez, and Unger, and Etzkowitz in their national case studies and specifically addresses the development of a supranational innovation system in North America. Developments over the past decade have seen the economies of Canada, the United States, and Mexico move away from national regulation of markets and towards their international regulation. Codified in the terms of agreements such as the Canada–U.S. Free Trade Agreement, the North American Free Trade Agreement, and the World Trade Organization, these movements at the macro-level are reducing barriers to trade and easing the entry of international firms into domestic markets.

In the North American context, Alic notes, the United States is clearly the dominant player. It has, of course, by far the largest economy and leads the other two countries in any measure of technological development. In the emerging North American integrated system, Alic argues, U.S. policy is central. At the present time, U.S. policymakers face two possible choices for the future development of the North American region. They could retain their central position and take advantage of the lower wage rates and plentiful resource and energy supplies of their NAFTA partners, but such a strategy might result in lower wage rates and living standards for U.S. workers and citizens. The alternative would be to support higher wages and productivity growth in Canada and

Mexico so that all three countries might continue to advance and grow together.

Just as in North America, recent developments in Asia have seen the establishment of the basic elements of a regional system of innovation. Tied to agreements such as the Asia-Pacific Economic Cooperation (APEC) forum and the Association of South East Asian Nations (ASEAN), the economies of the NICs, along with more established economies such as Japan's and the economies of developing countries such as China and Indonesia, have featured increasing integration of the regional economic space. This has generated profound consequences for national participants, the region, and other emerging regional systems.

At first sight, the regionalization of production in East Asia might appear to be adequately explained merely by reference to changing patterns of comparative advantage in international trade as indicated in the movement in relative factor prices. As John Ravenhill argues in chapter 8, however, such an account is incomplete. The changing geopolitical context and technological developments have also played an important role in this process.

Ravenhill notes that the regionalization of production in East Asia has its foundations in the Japanese colonial period. Japanese production in Taiwan, Korea, and Manchuria was an integral part of the pre-1945 Japanese Empire. The postwar roots of interfirm alliances in East Asia date back to the direct investment in Taiwan by Japanese firms in such industries as electronics and machinery manufacturing in the late 1950s. These investments aimed at establishing a Japanese presence in the local market. They were followed by a series of equity and non-equity alliances between Japanese and local enterprises in response to local ownership and content regulations promulgated by the Taiwanese government. The same pattern was replicated, to a lesser extent, in Korea in the aftermath of the signing of the Japan-Korea Normalization Treaty in 1965. In the last decade, such networks have undergone an important spatial extension. Malaysia, Thailand, and coastal China have all become linked to production in Northeast Asia, so that we may now speak of regionalized manufacturing activity in a number of industries.

As in North America, Ravenhill notes, the future direction of regionalization in East Asia depends to a great extent on the policy of a single country, in this case Japan. While smaller countries in the region have benefited from the creation of ASEAN and APEC in terms of their ability to develop apart from Japan, these countries continue to face challenges in terms of their contribution to technical advance in the region. Capital mobility threatens to increase losses in manufacturing and production to low-cost suppliers such as China. Whether Japanese firms will extend the same technology transfers to the region as they did to Korea, and to a lesser extent Taiwan, in the 1970s and 1980s is the critical question facing this emerging regional innovation system.

The innovation component of the European Union (EU) has always been front and centre in European integration. Cross-national efforts such as Airbus and other defence, transportation, and communication initiatives have been accompanied by regionalized production and product development, university-industry transfer centres, and firm-level and sectoral strategies. Unlike North America and East Asia, Europe does not have a single lead actor in its innovation system. As Luc Soete notes in chapter 9, the continuous integration process in Europe has meant that the policies of individual European countries have a much reduced ability to effect major regional change, while the need for flexible adjustment of supraregional policies has grown in the information economy.

Soete examines the important distinctions that are made between core, less-favoured, and peripheral subregions in the framing of EU economic and social policies for the "Information Society." While the potential decentralizing effects of information communication technologies (ICTs) may allow regions to overcome historic locational disadvantages, Soete notes the continuing significance of core regional clusters such as Baden-Württemberg, Emilia-Romagna, or London within the European Union. Sophisticated labour markets, localized input-output linkages, tacit knowledge diffusion, or networks of social capital are not easily amenable to interregional transfer. Indeed, he argues, physical proximity remains very important for complex innovation activities, such as strategic management, research, design, and development.

Soete questions the utility of generalized information or innovation policies in regional integration, suggesting instead that these should be targeted towards those areas where benefits of liberalization are unlikely to filter through. Information policies, for example, should be designed to overcome disparities in access to information infrastructure. They should be focused on peripheral regions, with less emphasis on universal minimums in technical standards across regions than on functionality and alternative technologies to accelerate investment. And equally if not more important to sustainable regional growth, in his view, is investment in human capital – the development of human resources and institutional structures that support regional innovation and learning organizations.

After the third section's comparative examination of the emerging North American innovation system, the fourth section devotes attention to several key social, economic, and environmental problems that policymakers will face in the coming decades. In chapter 10, Richard Harris looks closely at the disparities between the U.S., Canadian, and

Mexican economies and discusses the consequent difficulties for further integration. Although there is considerable controversy over definitions of competitiveness, a definition proposed by the U.S. President's Commission on Industrial Competitiveness has received fairly wide acceptance. Competitiveness, in the commission's view, is "the degree to which a nation can, under free and fair market conditions, produce goods and services that meet the test of international markets while simultaneously maintaining or expanding the real income of its citizens" (Hart 1992, 5). As Harris notes, while scholars have traditionally included productivity, comparative advantage, and terms of trade as important factors determining competitiveness, even more important is the entire complex system of institutions and organizations involved in the evolutionary growth of national economies.

Harris clearly demonstrates the linkages between trade, competitiveness, and innovation in a North American context and, like Weintraub, argues that deeper integration is necessary if the three NAFTA partners are all to benefit. According to Harris, the diversity of the three North American countries has often heightened concerns about the effects of integration; for example, Mexico and Canada fear U.S. domination, Canada and the United States have concerns about Mexican advantages as a result of cheap labour, and Mexico worries that its manufacturing sector will be obliterated by higher productivity in the industrial North. Harris argues, however, that this diversity should be viewed as a source of strength rather than weakness for the three North American countries. He emphasizes that deeper North American integration will improve the region's trade competitiveness, since the three countries will benefit from their complementarity in resource endowments and in their differences in labour costs, savings patterns, and structures of demand.

In chapter 11, Stephen Cohen and Paolo Guerrieri take up this question of trade and competitiveness but examine it in the context of links between the North American and East Asian systems. The *new international trade theory*, also called *strategic trade theory*, takes issue with the neoclassical approach to understanding why countries trade.[4] It argues that this static analysis has limited explanatory value in the current climate of dynamic change. Much of world trade now takes place between countries with very similar factor endowments; indeed, many goods and services require similar factor proportions, regardless of the location in which they are produced or are available. Many countries have now achieved a level of economic development that can support a wide range of industries and services. It is also evident that the competitiveness of a particular national economy can, and frequently does, change over time. These empirical observations have led to the development of theoretical analyses of strategic trade and industrial policies that focus on the role of economies of scale and the dynamics of technological innovation as additional sources of gain from trade beyond differences in factor endowments.

While formal governmental agreements, such as the European Union and NAFTA, have played an important role in integration in Europe and North America, regional integration in East and Southeast Asia has been firm- and production-led. Asian governments have played a facilitating role, but there is to this point no regional integration agreement in Asia comparable to the EU and NAFTA. Plans of the Association of South East Asian Nations and the Asia-Pacific Economic Cooperation forum for future free trade agreements have yet to be realized.

Cohen and Guerrieri show that a considerable amount of integration has occurred in East and Southeast Asia on an informal basis and that this has contributed positively to innovation and trade competitiveness in the region. Nevertheless, neo-mercantilist policies combined with the lack of formal regional integration agreements have also contributed to considerable asymmetry between Japan, on the one hand, and its Asian economic partners on the other. Thus, Cohen and Guerrieri present data to show that Japan has had a large and growing trade surplus with other Asian states. Indeed, Asia's cumulative trade deficit with Japan increased to about U.S.$163 billion in the period from the second half of the 1980s to the early 1990s. This asymmetry within the region has contributed to a triangular trade pattern in which Asian countries – especially the East Asian NICs – have depended on substantial trade surpluses with the United States and Europe to offset their trade deficits with Japan. Cohen and Guerrieri believe that to counter asymmetrical relations within Asia and to avoid a protectionist reaction by North American and European countries to their large trade deficits with Asia, moves should be made towards stronger regionalism in Asia. Such moves, according to the authors, would contribute to the development of "a dynamic regional domestic market more able to absorb Asian production and exports." By alleviating tensions with North America and Europe, this "could make multilateral agreement easier rather than more difficult to achieve."

The emerging regional system of innovation in North America must also deal with the extreme labour market discrepancies among the three partners in the system, as well as with a wide range of attitudes, opinions, and practices related to labour force issues and gender roles. Internally, innovation systems can be affected by a wide range of factors, including the educational process, the organizational structure of the producer, the technology of production, labour-management relations, and other related elements of the production process. Competitiveness and innovation are also affected by factors related to social mores and cultural attitudes, such as those concerning the participation of women in the labour force and family life.

The question of labour adjustment entails a large set of factors. These are addressed in the chapter on the Mexican experience (chapter 12) by Diana Alarcón and Eduardo Zepeda. Confirming Ramírez and Unger, the authors demonstrate that the period since NAFTA came into effect has seen weak productivity growth in Mexico, a decline in employment conditions, and the persistence of high levels of unemployment or underemployment, which have weakened aggregate demand. Foreign-owned export plants, known as *maquiladoras*, have made an undeniable contribution to exports and job creation, in their view, but with a high cost. The national input content of *maquiladora* production has remained unchanged at 2 per cent on average, and linkages to indigenous medium and small enterprises have not been forged. Alarcón and Zepeda dispute certain assumptions of trade-led growth theories. The export sector, showing the greatest growth in Mexico after the NAFTA signing, has tended to be concentrated in certain capital- and technology-intensive sectors. Beyond this elite group, the link between indigenous technology development and access to export markets is not clear.

While Mexico has adopted far-reaching economic reforms to speed North American integration, the authors suggest that serious problems remain. Macro-economic policies that emphasize stabilization rather than structural reform may actually block innovation and decrease competitiveness. The Mexican innovation system needs to promote job development and labour adjustments by integrating domestic medium-sized firms with the *maquiladoras*, stimulating exports in agriculture, and developing broader access to capital and investment in technology. To do this effectively, Mexico requires support from its North American partners. Competitiveness, innovation, and harmonization of labour standards have sharply different meanings in the three countries in North America because of their different stages of development.

Students of regional innovation systems are left to ask, "What do transregional production chains mean for the power of capital?" Given changing sectoral patterns of employment and the changing nature of the work relationship, what should be the appropriate organizational model for labour? In the 1930s, craft unions were replaced by industrial unions. Today's "new workplaces" and "new workers" present a similar challenge: large industrial unions are trying to organize fast-food production workers together with bank and clerical workers, but with limited success. Clearly, there has been insufficient analysis of the importance of new labour practices or social constraints in regional innovation systems.

It is now well understood that ecological constraints on human activity exist at various levels. These range from local limitations on the assimilative capacity of airsheds, for example, through to regional problems of resource depletion in fisheries, to the global effects of climate change or ozone depletion. While some of these constraints are subject to "technical fixes" of various kinds, the fact remains that human processes and alterations of the biosphere may be approaching the physical limits of natural processes at the planetary level.

As Roberto Sanchez argues in chapter 13, the final contribution to the book, there may be ecological limits to the physical scale of human activity in North America. With continued extensive economic growth, human society in North America may approach and exceed the region's ecological carrying capacity. The remedy involves levels of constraint that go beyond localized responses and technical fixes; it raises questions about patterns of consumption and economic development in general. But Sanchez, like Davis, argues that endogenous growth theorists have not been quick to address the relationships between competitiveness, trade, and sustainability in innovation systems. Nor have policy analysts identified the adjustments necessary at the level of political regimes, or the utility of parallel environmental accords in trading regimes, to promote more sustainable production with less use of natural resources or consumption of energy. Sanchez asserts that the transition to sustainable development should be taking place within NAFTA at the present time but that in each of the nations the political will to make it happen is lacking. Institutional limitations within Mexico, budget cuts to environmental agencies in Canada, and conflicts with a business community that lobbies for less stringent standards in the United States all make it questionable whether advances in environmental protection won during the 1970s and 1980s can be sustained and improved in the 1990s and beyond.

CONCLUSION: MAKING THE MOST OF NORTH AMERICAN INTEGRATION

The chapters in this volume all illustrate that significant changes in the structure and behaviour of innovation systems are occurring throughout North America and most of the world (Dosi 1982; Etzkowicz 1994). They also show how the emerging North American system has distinct characteristics that its European and East Asian counterparts do not share.

The European system, for example, has adopted more of a Keynesian approach to regional economic integration, widely influenced by the French tradition of *étatisme*, which has created a wide range of institutional arrangements to address economic and social issues. European economic integration involves "an attempt to build an administrative framework that takes into account the economic efficiency and collective security needs of the community, by means of the creation of a genuinely mixed economy at the regional level, when it seemed no longer viable on a national level" (Deblock and Rioux 1993, 32). While new theorists like Soete question the utility of such pan-regional innovation policies in alleviating intraregional disparity, new attention is being paid to macro- and micro-innovation policy networks.

In contrast, the North American and East Asian systems largely concentrate on removing barriers to the movement of goods and capital and have few mechanisms to promote positive social adjustment to integration. The short-term costs of this approach have been high. As the Mexican contributors to this volume argue, the period since NAFTA was initiated has witnessed such a deterioration in social conditions in their country that a fundamental question must be raised. What can national governments or regional partners do in their efforts to promote trade or competitiveness through the development of complex innovation systems to accommodate induced social change?

As several authors in this volume argue, the North American system of innovation, if it is to provide optimal benefits to the three member countries, must deepen well beyond the removal of border barriers and even the unimpeded flow of direct investment. Innovation, competitiveness, and sustainability policies can be raised from the national to the supranational regional level, but this would involve a degree of political support and policy coordination that is currently lacking. Deepening the North American system requires the establishment of common or compatible systems, as has already been accomplished in Europe. These include industrial standards, especially for inputs into final products; agreed-upon non-restrictive standards for the provision of technical and professional services; upward harmonization of environmental and sanitary standards; compatible requirements for transportation and communication links; rapid customs clearance; and the ability of each country to penetrate the regulatory processes of the others to monitor and prevent import restrictions in the guise of regulatory activity. Investing in human capital and forging the triple helix of industry, government, and university are two ways to begin to address a part of the non-economic, intangible side of regional innovation systems.

The essays in this volume reveal much about the idea of innovation itself – its utility as a counterweight to trade-led models of economic growth and as a putative policy paradigm. It is evident that no single discipline or method is sufficient to allow us to understand or explain what goes on in innovation. The competition, cooperation, and occasional conflicts that fuel innovation occur simultaneously. Information gaps, inflexibilities, and asymmetries reveal themselves as difficult to resolve. Successes in innovation, like failures, can be understood only with recourse to the particular economic and social history of a place, the development of science and technology knowledge systems there, and its history of international relations and global capital and commodity flows. No single discipline seems to provide this explanatory power: conversely, research on the incremental integration of systems of innovation helps pull together a rich mix of different perspectives.

The complexity of the innovation process demonstrates the value of generating communication between researchers from different fields, and from different countries, as was begun at the 1994 meeting of the Tri-National Institute on Trade, Innovation, Competitiveness and Sustainability in Whistler, British Columbia. That meeting, which was jointly sponsored by the research councils of Canada, Mexico, and the United States, inspired this collection. As the essays in this volume show, the three countries involved in the emerging North American regional system will have to decide whether the advantages of greater policy coordination outweigh the losses to national sovereignty and territorial control that are involved in the system's construction.

NOTES

1 Given the key role played by innovation and cycles of economic growth and decline related to innovation, this approach is sometimes termed "Neo-Schumpeterian," after the Austrian economist and long-time Harvard University scholar Joseph Schumpeter. See Nelson and Winter (1974, 1982), Anderson (1994), and Schumpeter (1928, 1939, 1947).
2 The term "national system of innovation" (NSI) was probably first used by Bengt-Ake Lundvall (1992), although the idea of national factors related to innovation can be traced back to the nineteenth-century German political economist Friedrich List (1966). See Niosi and Bellon (1994).
3 There is widespread academic consensus that governments and other organizations in the three North American societies have begun to change in order to adjust and adapt to the changing continental trading and production environment (Spender 1997; Casas and Luna 1997; Langford, Langford, and Burch 1997).
4 The classical approach going back to Adam Smith and David Ricardo emphasizes trade based on comparative advantage and relative cost efficiencies. In the 1920s and 1930s, most neoclassical economists supported a more elaborate theory to explain a country's comparative advantage (the Heckscher-Ohlin theorem), based on the relative abun-

dance and scarcity of factors of production, such as capital, labour, and resources (de la Mothe and Ducharme 1991; Krugman 1992; Harris 1993; Scherer and Belous 1994).

REFERENCES

Aicholzer, George, and Gerd Schienstock, eds. 1994. *Technology Policy*. New York: De Gruyter.

Anderson, E.S. 1994. *Evolutionary Economics: Post-Schumpeterian Contributions*. London: Pinter.

Archibugi, Daniele, and Jonathan Michie. 1995. "Technology and Innovation: An Introduction." *Cambridge Journal of Economics* 19:1–4.

– 1997. *Technology, Globalisation and Economic Performance*. London: Cambridge University Press.

Casas, Rosalba, and Matilde Luna. 1997. "Government, Academia and the Private Sector in Mexico: Towards a New Configuration." *Science and Public Policy* 24 (1): 7–14.

Deblock, Christian, and Michèle Rioux. 1993. "NAFTA: The Trump Card of the United States?" *Studies in Political Economy* 41:7–44.

de la Mothe, John, and Louis Marc Ducharme, eds. 1991. *Science, Technology and Free Trade*. London: Pinter.

de la Mothe, John, and Gilles Paquet, eds. 1996. *Evolutionary Economics and the New Political Economy*. London: Pinter.

Dosi, Giovanni. 1982. "Technological Paradigms and Technological Trajectories: Suggested Interpretation of the Determinants and Directions of Technical Change." *Research Policy* 11:147–62.

Dosi, Giovanni, and Luc Soete. 1991. "Technological Innovation and International Competitiveness." In Niosi (1991b, 91–118).

Dosi, Giovanni, Christopher Freeman, Richard Nelson, Gerald Silverberg, and Luc Soete. 1988. *Technical Change and Economic Theory*. London: Pinter.

Edquist, Charles. 1997. "Systems of Innovation Approaches – Their Emergence and Characteristics." In C. Edquist, ed., *Systems of Innovation: Technologies, Institutions and Organizations*. London: Pinter.

Etzkowitz, Henry. 1994. "A Sociological Paradigm for Economic Development." In L. Leydesdorff, ed., *New Developments in Technology Studies: Evolutionary Economics and Chaos Theory*. London: Pinter.

Freeman, Chris. 1995. "The 'National System of Innovation' in Historical Perspective." *Cambridge Journal of Economics* 19:5.

Gamble, Andrew, and Anthony Payne, eds. 1996. *Regionalism and World Order*. London: Macmillan.

Harris, Richard G. 1993. "Globalization, Trade and Income." *Canadian Journal of Economics* 26 (4): 755–6.

Hart, Jeffrey A.. 1992. *Rival Capitalists: International Competitiveness in the United States, Japan, and Western Europe*. Ithaca, N.Y.: Cornell University Press.

Kamien, Morton L., and Nancy Schwartz. 1982. *Market Structure and Innovation*. New York: Cambridge University Press.

Krugman, Paul. 1992. "Does the New Trade Theory Require a New Trade Policy?" *World Economy* 15 (4): 423–42.

Langford, Cooper H., Martha W. Langford, and Douglas R. Burch. 1997. "The 'Well-Stirred Reactor': Evolution of Industry-Government-University Relations in Canada." *Science and Public Policy* 24 (1): 21–8.

List, F. 1966. *The National System of Political Economy*. New York: Augustus M. Kelley; originally published 1841.

Lundvall, B.A. 1992. *National Systems of Innovation: Towards a Theory of Innovation and Interactive Learning*. London, Pinter.

MacNeill, Jim, et al. 1991. *Beyond Interdependence: The Meshing of the World's Economy and the Earth's Ecology*. New York: Oxford University Press.

McMahon, John A., and J.C. Woodliffe. 1996. *Regionalism and World Trade*. London: Books International.

Nelson, R.R., ed. 1993. *National Innovation Systems: A Comparative Analysis*. Oxford: Oxford University Press.

Nelson, R.R., and S.G. Winter, Jr. 1974. "Neoclassical vs. Evolutionary Theories of Economic Growth: Critique and Prospectus." *Economic Journal* 84 (4): 886–905.

– 1982. *An Evolutionary Theory of Economic Change*. Cambridge, Mass.: Belknap/Harvard University Press.

Nelson, R.R. and N. Rosenberg. 1993. "Technical Innovation and National Systems." In Nelson (1993, 3–27).

Niosi, J. 1991a. "Canada's National System of Innovation." *Science and Public Policy* 18 (2): 83.

– ed. 1991b. *Technology and National Competitiveness: Oligopoly, Technological Innovation, and International Competition*. Montreal and Kingston: McGill-Queen's University Press.

Niosi, J., and Bertrand Bellon. 1994. "The Global Interdependence of National Innovation Systems: Evidence, Limits and Implications." *Technology in Society* 16 (2): 173–97.

OECD Organization for Economic Cooperation and Development). 1991. *Technology and Productivity: The Challenge for Economic Policy*. Paris: OECD.

Redclift, Michael. 1987. *Sustainable Development: Exploring the Contradictions*. London: Methuen.

Scherer, F.M., and Richard S. Belous. 1994. *Unfinished Tasks: The New International Trade Theory and the Post-Uruguay Round Challenges*. British–North America Committee, Issues Paper no. 3. Washington, D.C., May.

Schumpeter, J.A. 1928. "The Instability of Capitalism." *Economic Journal* 38 (151): 361–86.

– 1947. "The Creative Response in Economic History." *Journal of Economic History* 7 (2): 149–59.

– 1939. *Business Cycles.* New York: McGraw Hill.

Spender, J.C. "Publicly Supported Non-Defense R&D: The USA's Advanced Technology Program." *Science and Public Policy* 24 (1): 45–52.

World Commission on Environment and Development. 1987. *Our Common Future.* Oxford: Oxford University Press.

PART ONE

Conceptualizing Innovation Systems

1 Competitiveness, Sustainability, and the North American Regional System of Innovation

CHARLES DAVIS

INTRODUCTION

Over the past decade, several broad sets of issues have attracted the attention of researchers, policymakers, and business people in North America with interests in the ways that scientific and technical resources are created and deployed. The first of these concerns international economic competitiveness, and the second, social and environmental sustainability. What does each mean in terms of science, technology, and innovation management and policy?[1]

Competitiveness and *sustainability* both work as a metalanguage, each with its own set of assumptions, problems, and agenda of prescribed actions. Each agenda shares a sometimes millenarian language to describe the apocalyptic consequences of failure to attain competitiveness or sustainability, which are held as imperatives that challenge nations at the deepest levels. The sustainability agenda is comprised of a recent "green technology" thread in management thinking and a broader concern with the consequences of technological innovation for employment, health, and the quality of life. The competitiveness and sustainability agendas do not often refer to each other, and in many respects talk past or contradict each other. Typically there have been few overlaps or linkages between the sustainability and competitiveness policy networks and interest groups. However, both agendas are sensitive to issues of technological innovation, and both hint at the necessity or the inevitability of a new "techno-economic paradigm" upon which the next century's peace and prosperity can be based. In one formulation that has been strongly advocated for over a decade by some technology policy advisory agencies and more recently by some prominent management researchers and business associations, a strategic course of technological innovation provides the only way to reconcile the two conflicting goals, the first of which is to reduce levels of pollution and resource deterioration and the second to achieve major, sustainable increases in economic activity. In other words, a particular course of action regarding technological innovation can provide an intersection between the competitiveness and sustainability agendas.

A third set of issues concerns the accelerating North American *economic integration*, crowned by the North American Free Trade Agreement (NAFTA). What implications do regional economic integration and the particular North American trade regime have for national and subnational science and technology policies, for the innovatory activities of firms in the North American economic space, and for the attainment of sustainability or competitiveness?

The fourth set of issues comes from the concept of *systems of innovation*, a concept that has been increasingly employed by researchers studying technological change. Because innovation involves groups of actors (firms as well as non-economic actors), new forms of learned institutional behaviour, and interactivity with some regularity and structure, the concept of innovation systems is attractive. It has been promoted by some of the most influential science and technology policy agencies in the world, notably the Organization for Economic Cooperation and Development (OECD), which in 1994 launched a policy-oriented research project on national systems of innovation.[2] Various national and subnational policy actors are increasingly employing an innovation systems approach. In North America, in addition to many efforts to trace out configurations of national, local, or sectoral innovation systems, certain questions naturally arise: What are the characteristics of the North American regional system of innovation and what kind of innovation is it producing?

These questions can lead to sensitive issues about the geographic division of labour in North America. For a number of years, participants in symposia on North American economic integration were treated to enthusiastic speeches, usually by Americans, proclaiming that with Canadian natural resources, Mexican cheap labour, and U.S. know-how, the North American economic region could recover its prosperity. But in Canada and Mexico, the peripheral countries or "spokes" of North America, the obvious question was how countries that specialized in cheap labour or the production of industrial staples could hope to raise their standard of living in the emerging North American "knowledge economy." The dilemma in Canada and Mexico is that neither has been able to chart a development course based on sustained selective investments of national wealth in science and technology; further, few of their national firms are able to produce or exploit advanced technologies. At the same time, neither country can afford hindrances to access to the U.S. market. The emergence of a formal North American trade regime has meant that a large number of technological second-stringers found themselves in the Olympics, not just fat and complacent businesses that had enjoyed their protected market for too long but also peasant communities, small family-owned firms, and peripheral regions without the skills and infrastructure to attract footloose investments. The economic disruptions caused by adjustments to the new rules of the trade game have challenged national governability and social peace far more in Canada and Mexico than in the United States, the regional hegemon.

This chapter explores some of the issues bounded by innovation, competitiveness, sustainability, and North America. I will try to be explicit about its assumptions.

First, I use the term "competitiveness" to refer to the ability to offer products or services successfully in an open trading system, in exchange for income, despite others who offer similar products or services, thus maintaining or expanding access to the life choices that income can purchase. Competitiveness is a frequently cited rationale for and objective of innovation policy measures in Canada. I use the term "sustainability" to refer to development that does not pass on undue or irreversible environmental costs to succeeding generations.[3] The term "innovation" usually refers to the first commercial application of a product or process by a user.[4] This definition of innovation is close to what is commonly understood as "technological progress," and it focuses attention on increases in efficiency and productivity. About one-third of U.S. economic growth between 1929 and 1982 can be attributed to innovation of this sort (Denison, 1985). However, a broader definition of innovation than that encompassed by efficiency and productivity issues is required to address the competitiveness and sustainability agendas, because the larger the increment of technological change, the more likely that organizational or social innovation is involved. Understanding innovation at the managerial, organizational, social, or cultural levels requires not just that a host of conceptual and measurement problems be solved, but also that such values as social justice and environmental stewardship be addressed.

Second, I claim that two of the most consistent (and increasingly explicit) policy agendas of our times, the competitiveness and sustainability agendas, are committed to stimulating, guiding, or directing science and technology to achieve their ends. Each agenda attempts to influence technological and industrial innovation in the narrow sense, and each ponders the broader issues of institutional and social innovation. This interest in the instrumental rationality of science and technology naturally raises the question of how to guide and direct innovation and for whose benefit. Governance of science, originally the exclusive prerogative of alpha silverbacks of the Republic of Science, is passing from peer-adjudicated and command models to market-allocated and club models of decision making. How well can these models of resource allocation steer the innovation system to goals of competitiveness or sustainability?

Third, innovation takes place in "systems" of public and private institutions defined by their interactions and the rules and routines of their behaviour. Innovation research uses notions such as systems of innovation (Niosi et al. 1993; Nelson 1993; Edquist 1997) to describe the social institutions of innovation. The set of distinctions among minor and major forms of technological change employed by evolutionary economists helps to address the level-of-analysis problem encountered when searching for the boundaries of a system.[5]

Fourth, I inquire about the utility of a "systems of innovation" approach in the North American region. The existence of a North American system of innovation may be surmised on the basis of the considerable degree of economic integration that has taken place among the United States, Mexico, and Canada. The contours and dynamics of this system have never been well described. Instead, typically the "national systems of innovation" of the United States, Canada, and Mexico are described separately, without analysis of the regional interactions.

Fifth, the section on innovation and sustainability focuses mainly on green technology issues. Issues of natural resource management, energy, transportation, sustainable cities, sustainable livelihoods, or sustainable agriculture need to be examined from an innovation perspective.

Neither competitiveness nor sustainability, however defined, is imaginable in the absence of innovation. As North American economic integration proceeds, science and technology policies and private management strategies will respond to the emerging conditions of innovation in the region. Subregional patterns of economic activity will change, and successful social mastery of new configurations of production will be an important skill to acquire. The greening of technology policies and management practices and the persistence of innovation-related social issues present new challenges in the context of regional trade liberalization, heightened intra- and interregional competition, increased mobility in factors of production, and the declining propensity of public institutions to organize collective action in the general interest.

A NORTH AMERICAN SYSTEM OF INNOVATION

The notion of systems of innovation can be put into operation in terms of financial flows, legal measures, policy linkages, standards, and flows of information, science, technology, and people (Niosi et al. 1993; OECD 1997). Among the legal and policy measures that are contributing to an integrated North American innovation system are the NAFTA rules governing investment, intellectual property, and technical standards. Among the financial and technology flows is the huge volume of bilateral trade between the United States and its two neighbours, especially intrafirm trade. Among the flows of science are the innumerable research and scholarly linkages between Canada and the U.S. on the one hand and the U.S. and Mexico on the other.

A regional system integrator is an actor that interacts with regional members to align and integrate their economic and technological systems, including bilateral and multilateral trade, direct investment, official development assistance, non-market technological collaboration (for example, military), political relationships, provision of services, establishment of trade rules, export of production technology, and export of the "software" of technological development, such as management beliefs, social science paradigms, administrative and technical curricula, information, publications, and symbolic reward systems (Yamashita 1991). These linkages help spread patterns of growth and institutional and technical change into related economies. In Asia, the Japanese role of regional integrator may represent "an enlargement of the parent-subcontract industrial relation" to include newly industrializing countries (NICs) (Yamashita 1991, 4). In Europe, the role of systems integrator is played by a supranational institution, the European Union, through its multitude of programs and policies, and by the networks of firms and institutions within the regional economic space. In North America, large U.S. firms, the huge and influential American scientific and technical community, the powerful U.S.-based communications and media forces, and the regional trade rules are the principal innovation system integrators in North America.

The North American international system is characterized by a hub-and-spokes pattern of interchange in which the United States' neighbours entertain extensive interactions with the U.S. but very little with each other. The hub-and-spokes communication structure is found in economic transactions, political communication, patterns of migration and subsequent patterns of ethnic and linguistic affiliation, and patterns of scientific communication. To take the latter example, co-authored U.S.-Canada and U.S.-Mexico scientific publications accounted for about 12 per cent of Canadian scientific output and about 16 per cent of Mexican output, respectively, in 1990. However, these publications only represent about 2 per cent of American scientific output (Davis, Dufour, and Halliwell 1993, 277). The United States accounts for 40 per cent of Canadian co-authored articles and 45 per cent of Mexican co-authored articles, while Canada accounts for only 11 per cent of U.S. co-authored articles (Leclerc and Gagné 1994). There is thus an asymmetry in which the quantitative importance of the bilateral relationship with the hub scientific community is disproportionately great in the spoke scientific community. Qualitative factors such as reputation and institutional credibility are present as well. Furthermore, the amount of bilateral Canada-Mexico scientific publications and trilateral Mexico-Canada-U.S. publications is negligible, reflecting the paucity of scientific interchange between spokes and the relative absence of trilateral or transnational institutions to support scientific research at the regional level.[6]

In contrast to trends in Asia and Europe, science, technology, and innovation have never been prominent considerations in the discussions about the North American region's future. Before the present decade, neither Canada, nor the United States, nor Mexico tended to see itself as a member of a North American community or system. Most attention focused instead on the extensive bilateral relationships between Canada and the U.S., and between Mexico and the U.S., with a particular fascination for border regions. That North America as a region has not received much intellectual attention is explainable by the apparent interchangeability of "United States" with "North America," the low level of interaction among all three NAFTA members, and the absence of what might be regarded as a North American agenda (Letouche 1991). Even under the NAFTA, few would suggest that North America might evolve into a region possessing a specific, shared identity with significant institutions on a continental scale.

However, regional economic integration is certainly reshaping the North American economic and social landscape. The North American Free Trade Agreement establishes a framework for a trade regime encompassing one of the largest (about 360 million people) and richest (about U.S.$6 trillion) regional markets in the world. NAFTA sets trade rules for a regional economy that has already undergone substantial integration. Canada and the United States have the world's largest bilateral trade relationship, and the United States is Mexico's largest trading partner. NAFTA includes provisions for the reduction and eventual elimination of most tariffs affecting commerce among Canada, the United States, and Mexico in commodities, manufactured goods, and services. However, NAFTA goes beyond tariff elimination to establish rules governing trade and investment. The three countries agree not to discriminate against each other's goods and services and to eliminate most tariffs over a decade. Customs procedures and temporary entry for business travellers are simplified. Mexican import licensing procedures are immediately eliminated. The chapter on rules of origin sets out formulae by which Mexican, American, or Canadian products incorporating third-party materials or components can qualify for preferential access to each other's markets. Under the net cost formula, most products qualify for preferential treatment with 50 per cent North American content. In the case of light vehicles, the figure is 62.5 per cent. This provision is designed to discourage new transplants from using Mexico to supply the U.S. automotive market. The rules for determining North American content can be complex in practice, and their primary implication for manufacturing is in sourcing practices. NAFTA extends national treatment to member countries' suppliers of goods and services to public markets. NAFTA signatories agree not to impose offsets or performance requirements in public procurement. Improved tendering and dispute resolution procedures are specified. The rules governing public procurement are broader than those in the GATT procurement code, and NAFTA, in its extension of procurement rules to subnational governments (states, provinces, and municipalities), goes well beyond the Canada-U.S. Free Trade Agreement (CUSFTA). The net result is to liberalize a North American public market estimated at about $70 billion.

NAFTA sets rules regarding control over foreign investments. It establishes the principle of national treatment for all three parties regarding investments, establishment of new businesses, acquisition and sale of businesses, and the conduct and operation of businesses. No minimum levels of equity may be imposed on purchases or ownership. No performance requirements (for import substitution, local sourcing, export targets, foreign exchange generation, production sharing, product mandates, hiring of nationals in management positions, or technology transfer) may be imposed on investments from any of the three countries or on any investments from any third country (Article 1106). However, governments may offer "advantages" to firms in exchange for commitments regarding research and development, training, expansion, or location of production facilities.

Canada retains the investment-screening regime established under CUSFTA (the right to review direct acquisition of Canadian-controlled firms valued at more than Can$150 million). No restrictions may be placed on the patriation of profits and transfer payments. Mexico retains a range of investment prohibition privileges in the energy and communication sectors. Unlike CUSFTA, NAFTA contains a chapter setting out rules for intellectual property. Chapter 17 applies standards regarding sound recordings, literary and artistic works, software, data, designs, copyright, trademarks, and patents. It makes provisions for enforcing intellectual property rights, and it restrains the parties' latitude to permit compulsory licensing of patents.

NAFTA also contains provisions governing energy, natural resources, agriculture, financial services, technical standards, telecommunications, cultural industries, and transportation services. Like the agreement's provisions discussed above, the general thrust is to deregulate and liberalize trade in these industries within North America and to specify special cases in which governments retain rights to discriminate. Two "side agreements" cover labour and environmental issues. However, the penalties envisaged by these two agreements in case of non-compliance are weak (Shrybman 1993; Martin 1992). Continental market liberalization necessarily modifies the options available to policymakers to structure national or subnational economic development, and reduces the range of policy instruments available. Because NAFTA establishes new rules for the game of regional trade, it has been called an "economic constitution for North America."

What are the implications of NAFTA for innovation policy and management? In the first place, NAFTA clearly restrains governments from imposing performance requirements on foreign investors, North American or other, and considerably reduces governments' latitude to screen foreign direct investment (FDI).[7] Also, under NAFTA, although governments cannot impose performance requirements, they can negotiate some kinds of innovation-related performances with firms in exchange for incentives.

In the second place, like CUSFTA, NAFTA contains no rules governing subsidies, one of the most difficult issues on the trade policy agenda. Many kinds of government assistance have been labelled subsidies in U.S.-Canada trade disputes, including grants, tax credits, low-interest loans, and unemployment insurance. The subsidy issue was not resolvable during CUSFTA negotiations. In the case of NAFTA, the subsidy issue was referred to the GATT, where the Dunkel text contains rules governing publicly supported R&D and other kinds of subsidies. Since NAFTA does not cover subsidies, the rules of the game are unclear regarding direct or indirect public involvement in initiatives that help create advantage in the private sector. Given the uncertainty about subsidies, policymakers in Canada and Mexico will surely pay close attention to innovation policy practices in the United States in the belief that American practices will set a *de facto* standard in the region, especially since the Clinton administration adopted a more vigorous approach to promotion of industrial innovation than the two preceding administrations.

In the third place, NAFTA is clearly intended to cover the activities of subnational governments insofar as the respective federal governments are empowered to commit subnational governments through international agreements. NAFTA will thus have much the same effect on state and provincial innovation policies as it will on national policies in North America. Many states and provinces have developed quite extensive programs and institutions in support of innovation. Similarly, many American cities offer substantial industrial incentives. Tax and subsidy competition among localities is widespread in North America.

European and North American regional trade arrangements shield regional economies from offshore competition. However, the two regional arrangements are based on quite divergent philosophies. Europe has adopted a Keynesian approach to regional economic integration, creating a wide range of institutional arrangements to address economic and social issues. European economic integration involves "an attempt to build an administrative framework that takes into account the economic efficiency and collective security needs of the community, by means of the creation of a genuinely mixed economy at the regional level, when it seemed no longer viable on a national level" (Deblock and Rioux 1993, 32). In contrast, NAFTA, like the Canada-U.S. Free Trade Agreement it superseded, largely concentrates on removing barriers to the movement of goods and capital. NAFTA is a "negative" approach to regional economic integration. It is concerned largely with removing tariff and non-tariff barriers to movements of goods, services, and capital. It has no mechanisms to promote positive adjustment to economic integration. Problems of adjustment are largely left to the national governments to resolve.

A regional trade agreement provides preferences among member countries and fosters intraregional trade at the expense of interregional trade. Continental trade liberalization is precipitating wide discussion in North America about jobs, the environment, and national sovereignty. What are the implications of economic continentalization for science and technology strategies in the region, considering the increasingly integrated continental production system into which the two smaller countries have opted, and considering also the constraints placed by NAFTA on the use of a wide range of traditional instruments of industrial and economic policy?

The rationale for trade liberalization is well known. Manufacturing firms require economies of scale to compete in global markets, and production efficiencies are determined by relative size of market. Under tariff protection, inefficient, subcritical plants produce short runs of excessively diverse product lines. Access to a large market and increased competition should lead to rationalization and accelerated R&D

investments (Daly and MacCharles 1986). Trade liberalization is inducing manufacturers in Canada to rationalize production within the North American market, decreasing unit costs and reducing the productivity gap with the United States (ECC 1988). One expects increased competition to improve the technical and allocative efficiency of firms (Globerman 1990). Thus, economic gains from trade liberalization are principally realizable in the presence of productivity growth via attainment of economies of scale, increased internal R&D investments, and a higher rate of technological diffusion within firms and their supplier networks. As for the reorganization of production in North America, the simplest assumption is that of segmented production, with resource extraction, mass assembly operations, and higher R&D and management functions all sited in different locations. However, a much wider range of organizational responses is available to firms, such as just-in-time production (and its implications for proximity to suppliers), strategic alliances, multi-locational production strategies, flexible specialization, and the like (Eden 1991, 1994). Concern is being voiced that the North American trade regime provides strong incentives for manufacturers "to respond to market competition with a low-wage strategy, which will lower incomes and productivity over the long run, rather than [take] the more difficult path of producing quality products more efficiently." This would create downward pressures on social and environmental standards in North America.[8]

While the objective pursued by conventional trade policy is to increase the *allocative*, or Ricardian, efficiency of the economy, the rationale of development-oriented innovation policy is to increase the *growth*, or Schumpeterian, efficiency of the economy (Dosi, Zysman, and Tyson 1990, 25). A major task facing policymakers, practitioners, and innovation researchers in North America is to identify plausible routes to technological learning in open economies and assemble a collection of policy instruments that are relatively effective (i.e., likely to induce technological spillovers into the economy), efficient (i.e., do not entail disproportionately high costs), and acceptable under the prevailing trade regime.

INDUSTRIAL INNOVATION AND CANADIAN COMPETITIVENESS

Canada is a trading nation. Approximately 30 per cent of Canada's gross domestic product (GDP) is generated through international trade, and the combination of imports and exports amounts to half of Canada's GDP. Germany is the only one of the Group of Seven (G-7) countries in which international trade contributes a higher proportion of GDP. Although much of the discussion about innovation in Canada has been pitched in terms of adjustment to globalization, Canada's international trade is mainly continental. About three-quarters of Canadian trade is with the United States, and more than half of this is intrafirm trade. Furthermore, Canadian international trade is highly concentrated. About 70 per cent takes place through about fifty firms, half of which are of Canadian origin.

The striving for competitiveness has created an eager market for indicators, yardsticks, and report cards in Canada. These provide sometimes paradoxical views on the state of Canadian competitiveness. According to the United Nations Human Development Index in 1992, Canadians enjoy the highest quality of life in the world. According to the OECD, Canada recently had the fastest increase in employment among the G-7 countries and the second highest growth rate. But the World Competitiveness Report's 1993 survey ranked Canada eleventh among twenty-two industrialized countries, down from fourth place just four years earlier. The World Competitiveness Report gave relatively high marks to Canada's financial system (third place) and infrastructure (fifth place), but low marks to Canadian science and technology strategies (sixteenth place), quality of production technologies (fifteenth place), trade diversification (twentieth place), quality of management (fourteenth place), and investment in new equipment (twenty-first place). Of all countries surveyed, only Britain's manufacturing base had deteriorated more dramatically than Canada's. Canada has lost an estimated half million manufacturing jobs since 1989, with manufacturing's share of overall employment falling to about 15 per cent. The unemployment rate is about 11 per cent, and by the mid-1990s the net public debt/GDP ratio will have climbed to about 75 per cent – up from about 30 per cent at the beginning of the 1980s. Canada is carrying one of the highest per capita public debts among advanced countries.

Canadian competitiveness has been dissected and debated in an avalanche of reports and studies.[9] Many believe that Canada's overall technological effort is too modest – and R&D expenditures too heavily dependent on the public sector – to help realize Canada's aspirations to maintain an advanced economy. To get to the bottom of the competitiveness question, in 1990 the federal government and the Business Council on National Issues commissioned Harvard Business School strategist Michael Porter to apply his renowned "diamond" analysis to Canada. In *The Competitive Advantage of Nations* (1990), Porter says that a nation's goal is to improve the standard of living by increasing the growth of industry through raising industrial productivity and through shifting resources to higher-productivity segments. This normally happens when firms work to reduce unit costs and differentiate products.

However, firms will not choose to do so unless faced with competition (rivalry) and opportunities for innovation in their markets. Nations are competitive if their firms can engineer not just cost improvements but also differentiation. Normally, international rivalry pushes firms down product streams towards highly differentiated products, requiring constant innovation on the part of the firm. Internationally competitive firms create a virtuous cycle in which successful competition provides a surplus that is reinvested, driving further growth through innovation and learning. Mass production strategies are abandoned to less-developed countries. The most appropriate national innovation strategy is one that encourages firms to compete at the high end of the market through innovation, product differentiation, and service delivery, in contrast to one that relies solely on traditional cost-cutting, productivity-enhancing measures.[10]

Porter's thesis is that national competitive advantage is embedded in a "competitive diamond" of four essential attributes: (1) factor conditions (labour, land, natural resources, infrastructure, labour skills, and services to industry); (2) demand conditions (the quality and strength of home-market demand for local industrial output – Porter attaches considerable importance to the presence of knowledgeable, demanding local customers); (3) related and supporting industries, especially the presence or absence of internationally competitive suppliers; and (4) firm strategy, structure, and rivalry, which constitute the conditions in which companies are created, organized, and managed.

Porter says that firms have a "home base" where the key strategic decisions are taken and where the core product and process technologies are maintained. If firms do not use their national home base in this way, they don't contribute to the competitiveness of the national economy. Porter's Canadian report, with the ominous title *Canada at the Crossroads*, argues that Canada is not doing so well in the new competitive environment (Porter 1991). Five trends indicate underlying weaknesses: low productivity growth, high unit labour costs, persistently high unemployment, lagging investment in skills and technology upgrading, and an unencouraging macroeconomic climate for productive investments. Porter observes that Canada is deficient in vigorous export industries. Most Canadian exports are in natural resource industries (materials and metals, forest products, and petroleum and chemicals), with some other successful export in transportation (mainly automobiles and avionics) and food and beverage industries (Porter 1991). In other words, Canada specializes in exports of unprocessed or semi-processed commodities. Many of the sales of the relatively higher value-added export, such as chemicals or autoparts, go to a very small number of parent firms in the United States. Porter concludes that in

Canada natural resource factor advantages are more important than innovation-related "created advantages," and that an abundance of natural resource–related factors does not necessarily lead to new factor creation. Instead, it leads to specialized resource firms. One might expect an indigenous capital goods industry to service the resource industries, but this has not happened in Canada as it has in certain other countries, such as Sweden or Finland, which have experienced a greater degree of successful natural resource–based industrialization.

Furthermore, Canadian domestic demand plays a minor role in the development of internationally competitive Canadian firms; the American market and American suppliers predominate. Domestic rivalry is usually not significant in internationally competitive Canadian industries, nor do these industries develop local clusters of upstream and downstream linkages. Canadian regional development policies prevent geographical concentration of firms, and foreign direct investment in Canada has reduced the importance of supporting industries through intrafirm transactions or vertical integration. Moreover, Porter notes that few non–North American firms have developed a home-base–type relationship with Canada.

Porter irked defenders of continental economic integration when he suggested that high levels of foreign direct investment in Canada are an impediment to international competitiveness. Canada has one of the highest levels of foreign ownership of industrial assets of any advanced country, raising the question of "the extent to which foreign ownership inhibits the development of a national innovation system and, indeed, whether a national innovation system is necessarily preferred to integration into an international system" (McFetridge 1993, 320).

Porter's analysis provoked a debate about the appropriateness for "small countries" of the national diamond competitiveness framework. Canada's home-country diamond "does not have the answers to explain Canada's international competitiveness," say D'Cruz and Rugman (1992), who are concerned with the strategic behaviour of multinational corporations (MNCs) operating from small, open economies. To be applicable to Canada, the Porter model needs to be corrected "for the nature of foreign direct investment in Canada, the value added in Canada's resource industries, and the relevance of Canada's home country diamond in an integrated North American economic system" (D'Cruz and Rugman). In a stream of publications, Rugman and D'Cruz put forward a series of critiques of the Porter model in particular and of the more generally held belief in Canada that policies to promote indigenous manufacturing or high-technology firms are critically important.

The D'Cruz-Rugman analysis of Canadian competitive advantage is based on the recognition that most Canadian firms are concentrated in sectors or production phases in which cost reduction is the primary competitive strategy. Canada's ten leading export industries are automobiles, pulp and paper, vehicle components, commercial vehicles, nonedible agricultural products, non-ferrous metals, crude oil, cereal products, natural gas, and motors, turbines, and pumps. With the exception of the automotive sector, Canadian export performance "is not determined by an ability on the part of its manufacturing sector to compete in international markets. It depends instead upon the output of the natural resource sectors" (D'Cruz and Rugman 1992, 21).

Also, Rugman and D'Cruz take issue with Porter's selection of strategic industrial clusters. In *Fast Forward: Improving Canada's International Competitiveness* (1991), they identify ten subregional clusters accounting for the bulk of Canadian GDP and note that seven of the ten clusters are in the resource sector or in wage-sensitive production phases of manufacturing.[11] They view competitiveness in these industries as largely determined by productivity growth, which in turn is driven by factor costs, especially wage and capital costs. In other words, indigenous advanced-technology development is not regarded as important in these sectors' competitiveness.

The problem of staples-driven economic development is the central theme of Canadian economic history. Trade in primary products is a very slowly growing segment of world trade. This is partly because barriers to entry are relatively low, encouraging exports from the Third World and soon from the former Soviet Union. Of equal concern is the phenomenon of *dematerialization of production*, in which information-rich, highly engineered components such as optical fibres, ceramics, or high-strength composites replace simple commodity-based components. Because of competition and dematerialization of production, the long-term trend for commodity prices is down. In 1992 The *Economist* "reported that real commodity prices were at their lowest level since the magazine began calculating an all-item index in 1845" (Pestieau 1993, 2). Canada has specialized its international trade in a small range of slow-growth commodities concentrated in the North American market. Canadian resource firms typically develop firm-specific process innovations that provide competitive advantage. They maintain technical currency through procurement of foreign machinery, licences, patents, and foreign producers, and when they do undertake R&D, it is frequently abroad. Thanks to their cultural or geographic proximity to American and British technology markets, Canadian multinationals "are probably among the fast 'technology followers'" (Niosi 1983, 189). However, compared to their competitors in other countries, Canadian firms distinguish themselves by choosing to compete more on the basis of cost than on the basis of innovation. For example, a recent study of innovation strategies in the Canadian non-ferrous metals sector found that R&D spending had declined in the 1980s, remaining at less than 1 per cent of sales, while R&D spending in comparable Japanese and European firms had doubled to more than 2 per cent of sales (SCC 1992b). This behaviour reflects deliberate strategy, not just costs of production. According to Japanese and Finnish managers of mining companies quoted in the study, conventional business operations generating half or more of total revenues received only a small fraction of the R&D budget, while research on higher value-added activities – new materials and new products – received up to 90 per cent of the R&D budget.[12]

A second key shortcoming of the Porter model when applied to small, open economies, according to Rugman and D'Cruz (1993), is that one cannot measure the international competitiveness of smaller countries in terms of export shares because "much of the business of smaller countries is conducted abroad (through foreign direct investment) within the larger triad markets of the United States, E.C. and Japan – where the action is." Porter does not count overseas sales by the subsidiaries of Canadian-owned multinationals in export share data, giving the impression of poor Canadian export performance. Dunning (1993) points out that there are three kinds of cross-border commercial interactions: arm's-length trade, interfirm cooperative agreements, and foreign direct investment. He argues that Porter has substantially underestimated the importance of globalized production, especially the cross-border value-added activities of transnational firms, much of which takes place as intrafirm trade.

Canada is an important exporter of capital. Canadians invest abroad almost as much per capita as Americans. Between 1987 and 1991, about $5.4 billion was invested in the country annually, while about $6.6 billion was invested outside the country each year. In 1990 the foreign direct investment stock in Canada stood at $125.3 billion and the Canadian direct investment stock abroad stood at $86.7 billion (UN 1993). Even the resource industries are footloose. Between 1980 and 1990, incoming foreign direct investment stock in the primary sector in Canada increased only slightly, from $4.6 billion to $5 billion, while Canadian outward direct investments in the primary sector increased from $2.7 billion to $5.7 billion. The largest increases in outward FDI in the past decade are not in the primary sector, however, but in low value-added segments of the secondary sector and in parts of the tertiary sector. In the former, the Canadian outward FDI stock increased from $17.3 to $46 billion between 1980 and 1990, with huge increases in FDI stock in food and beverages ($2.3 to $5.8 billion), paper ($2 to $10.5 billion), coal and petroleum products ($0.9 to $6.5 billion), metals ($5.5 to $14.2 billion), and other manufacturing ($0.9 to $3 billion). Canadian outward FDI in the tertiary sector increased from $7 billion to $34.9 billion, with the largest increase in the financial and insurance industries ($3.7 billion to $24.7 billion between 1980 and 1990). In 1990 Canada had $86.7 billion of FDI outside the country, of which 61 per cent was in the U.S., 21 per cent in Western Europe, and 13 per cent in developing areas (UN 1993).

Porter's model raises questions about how two-way FDI contributes to a small country's competitive advantage, and this is no doubt a critical issue for small countries. In the past, incoming FDI has been considered much more significant than outward FDI in discussions of Canadian economic competitiveness. This is especially true in the context of understanding the accumulation of technological capability. A long debate within Canada has weighed the pros and cons of incoming FDI and, in particular, its effects on domestic innovatory capability. Porter believes that outward FDI is valuable in creating competitive advantage, but that foreign subsidiaries are not sources of competitive advantage and that inward FDI is "not entirely healthy" (as cited in Rugman and D'Cruz 1993). The opportunity to centralize operations and rationalize production in a regional market is especially attractive to manufacturing MNCs in mature or price-sensitive industries that "are among the leading proponents of the strategy to narrow product mix and expand production runs" (Litvak 1990, 118). However, a closer look at the often conflicting pressures towards globalization and localization shows that the strategic consequences of these pressures are not identical across industries. Some firms develop multinational or global highly rationalized structures, and others develop transnational structures or purely local structures (Crookell 1990; Eden 1991). Multinational firms respond to changes by examining ownership advantages, internalization advantages, and locational advantages; new information-based manufacturing technologies and trade policy changes also influence locational decisions (Eden 1991). Because of these factors and the importance of the U.S. market, the Canadian diamond is not necessarily of primary significance to Canadian firms. They also must take into account the U.S. diamond, and for this reason small trade-dependent countries like Canada, Denmark, and New Zealand must look at their competitive advantages in terms of the domestic diamonds of their principal markets. This requires a "double diamond" strategy (Rugman and D'Cruz 1993).

The diamond debate is not just about the sources of competitive advantage in a small economy that must export into a larger regional market, but also, and primarily, about the sources of competitive advantage in a resource-based economy. The debate raises the enduring issue of the causes of arrested industrialization or (from less of a teleological perspective) the issue of the sources of technological learning. Porter's study confirmed that Canada has "never developed an innovation system in which there are sufficient creative and stimulating links (or effective competition) between firms to cause high rates of development, adoption, or modification of processes or technologies" (Britton et al. 1996). No other major country has such a highly extroverted system of innovation or one that is so highly dependent on that of a single other country. The upside of this situation is that there is no better system of innovation with which to have an affiliation than the U.S. one. It is dynamic and culturally proximate, and observers from the "spokes" will find in the United States a microcosm of the world. Peripheral North American countries will find that the only way to ensure interactive learning with elements of the core North American innovation system is through continued maintenance of their own scientific and technological infrastructure, at their own expense.

"GREEN" INDUSTRIAL INNOVATION

Although alarms about global environmental degradation have been sounded for the past three decades, the environmental situation today is different in four new ways (Rath and Herbert-Copley 1993, 7). Rapid increase in the scale of pollution has accelerated loss of soil, species, clean water, and natural environments. Tens of thousands of synthetic chemicals, most of which are untested as to toxic or environmental effects, are replacing natural pollutants. The transboundary impacts of environmentally disturbing human activities require international or transnational remedies that could be complex and take a long time to put in place. Because "the various environmental threats are inextricably linked, both in their causes and effects," none of them can be addressed or solved in isolation from the others.

There is growing acceptance of the precautionary principle and the *clean production paradigm* in environmental management. The precautionary principle, which was endorsed by the Earth Summit at Rio de Janeiro in 1992, discourages attempts to establish environmental management strategies based on a calculation of the pollution carrying capacity of the environment, with investments in improved technologies aiming at waste management and production of end-of-pipe pollution abatement techniques. Instead, the precautionary principle advocates reduction to zero of all emissions of substances that are "persistent, toxic and liable to bioaccumulate ... even where there is no scientific evidence to prove a causal link between emissions and actions" (Jackson 1991, 8). The clean production paradigm advocates such approaches as product life cycle assessment and closed-cycle industrial ecological design to foster across-the-board prevention of pollution in industrial systems (Dethlefsen, Jackson, and Taylor 1993; Hirschhorn, Jackson, and Baas 1993). The principles of clean production are precaution (reduction of anthropogenic inputs into the environment), prevention (extension of the analysis of environmental implications of production as far upstream as possible), and integration of environmental protection measures across system boundaries (integration of protection measures into the production process) (Jackson 1993b).

The U.S. Environmental Protection Agency defines pollution prevention as "source reduction" that eliminates or reduces pollutants through improvements in equipment, technology, processes or procedures, redesign or reformulation of products, substitution of raw materials, and "improvements in housekeeping, maintenance, training and inventory control." Recycling, reuse, and end-of-pipe pollution control are excluded. The Technology Innovation and Economics Committee of the U.S. National Advisory Council for Environmental Policy and Technology advocates a hierarchy of technological approaches to environmental improvement; in order of desirability, these are as follows: technologies that prevent pollution (including waste minimization and source reduction technologies), recycling technologies, environmental control (i.e., end-of-pipe) technologies, and clean-up (i.e., remedial) technologies (EPA 1991).

The distinctions between minor and major forms of technological innovation suggest ways of distinguishing between tactical and strategic approaches to eco-technological change. Tactical interventions aim to accelerate the incremental improvement of the environmental efficiency of existing industry by reducing wastage and increasing recycling. They would put in place policy and economic incentives and disincentives, management paradigms, and investment and training strategies to produce many small improvements on a broad front. Strategic interventions would aim to innovate substantially improved technologies, radically improved technological systems, or new techno-economic paradigms.

This concept of technological distinctions between innovations of minor and major magnitude is being taken up by national and international policy and program agencies. For example, the OECD advocates a three-pronged transition to the "fourth industrial revolution," the clean industrial production revolution comparable to the steam, steel-electricity, and electronics revolutions. The first thrust is to induce incremental improvements in industrial performance by acting to identify, deploy, and implement existing cleaner technologies through provision of information, removal of barriers to trade and implementation, government purchasing programs, and so on. The second thrust is to accelerate technical and technological change by acting to promote innovative development and widespread implementation of new generations of cleaner technologies, through enunciation of coherent goals and policies such as Japan's New Earth 21 Plan or the Netherlands' National Environment Policy Plan Plus, which set long-term environmental quality goals. The third thrust is to sustain environmentally sound industrial innovation by acting to ensure that cleaner technologies become and remain the basis for economic development in the long term through, for example, education, collective action, and continuing innovation of cleaner technologies (OECD 1993, ix–x).

The conjunction of innovation policy and environmental policy is relatively recent. Environmental sustainability has not been a major consideration among mainstream innovation policy and management researchers. Winn and Roome (1993) searched the core R&D management literature of the 1970s and 1980s for work on environmental issues and identified only nine articles. Clarke and Reavely's (1993) 10,000-item bibliography of core science and technology management literature contains references to only thirty-one documents that focus explicitly on environmental issues. Similarly, the literature on green innovation policies is relatively small and dispersed among the literatures on environmental management, environmental economics, risk assessment, and economics of innovation.

As in any policy area, one wishes to know what the policy objectives are and what they should be, which instruments are deployed and why, and what are their effects, including costs and benefits; one also wishes to understand the policymaking process. Key environmental policy instruments for industry are regulations, technical assistance to firms, economic instruments such as tax and liability arrangements, consensus-building processes such as round tables, and international agreements.[13]

A comprehensive pollution prevention environmental policy regime should include (1) technical assistance programs; (2) education and training; (3) financial incentives; (4) increased use of liability regulations; and (5) "regulations specifically requiring the development of waste reduction plans and the submission to governments of regular reports on their progress in waste reduction" (Baas et al. 1992, 14; Yakowitz and Hanmer 1993). Of growing interest is research on the effects of environmental regulation and standards on the rate and direction of innovation. Regulation is the most widespread mechanism of public control of industrial environmental performance. Most research on the effects of environmental, health, and safety regulation is designed to determine its effects on productivity and profitability. In a review of this research, the Office of Technology Assessment (1994) concludes that environmental regulation was responsible for 10 to 15 per cent of the productivity slowdown in the U.S. in the 1970s, but that "other factors (such as technology changes, investment, and training) were more important" (p. 325).

Promotion of acquisition of environmentally improved industrial technology is becoming an important environmental policy goal. The structure of incentives and disincentives to invest in minor or major forms of industrial innovation having some relation with environmental sustainability is clearly a key issue. The design of environmental policy from an innovation policy perspective must ensure that counterproductive policy measures from other domains, such as subsidies for energy, water, or local raw materials, are detected and dealt with. The traditional approach to control of industrial pollution is through implementation of end-of-pipe technologies, the main effect of which is to displace the pollution charge from one medium to another. Concomitant with this approach to environmental industrial technology policy are regulatory regimes based on concepts of environmental assimilative capacity or critical pollution loads.[14] Historically, "technology diffusion has played a limited and subordinate role to regulation, permitting, and compliance in the regulation-based environmental management system" (EPA 1992, 15). This is because the regulation-based environmental policy systems of the 1970s encouraged investments in pollution control technologies rather than in environmental improvement of processes, products, housekeeping, and materials handling. Permitting and compliance regulatory frameworks created a demand for add-on pollution abatement techniques, a demand reflected in national science and technology policies. In the former West Germany, for example, governmental support for R&D on clean technologies focused largely on invention of end-of-pipe pollution abatement techniques (Bongaerts and Heinrichs 1987). Once investments have been made in end-of-pipe pollution control technologies, there is little incentive to adopt the more comprehensive pollution prevention management paradigm. Furthermore, suppliers of pollution control solutions may resist movement towards a precautionary policy regime: "experience in the U.S. has shown this to be a significant issue, because the end-of-pipe approach has advocates and a large industry selling the hardware of pollution control (e.g. scrubbers, incinerators, waste treatment plants)" (Hirschhorn 1992, 11).

End-of-pipe innovation does not enhance productive efficiency, it just lowers the cost of compliance. Improvements aimed at eco-efficiency that deal with the products of processes, on the other hand, can create "innovation offsets" exceeding the costs of compliance (Porter and van der Linde 1995, 101). Long-term solutions to environmental problems "require a move toward radical innovations in product design and in the process technologies used by companies" (Geffen 1995, 321). Regulations "must be explicitly designed with technological considerations in mind – that is, they should be fashioned to elicit the type of technological response desired" (Ashford 1993, 296). The regulatory design "should combine an assessment of the innovative capacity of the possible responding industrial sectors with levels and forms of regulation tailored to that capacity. The entire process should reflect a realistic evaluation of the best possible achievable technological goal" (ibid., 289). The EPA's National Advisory Council for Environmental Policy and Technology emphasizes that disincentives to technological innovation and adoption of environmentally improved technologies must be removed from regulatory permitting and enforcement (EPA 1992, 1991).

Technical assistance to firms for improvement of environmental performance is another public policy instrument that has led to recent institutional innovation in Canada and the United States. Technical assistance institutions can be classified on a four-point scale of increasing involvement in a firm's decision making (Doyle 1992). At level one, the technical assistance institution provides information and networking services. There are many public and private environmental technology databases and referral services available, including the International Cleaner Production Information Clearinghouse (ICPIC). At level two, in addition to providing information, the technical assistance institution brokers specialized in services such as business planning, market assessment, and identification of financial sources. Many chambers of commerce and business innovation centres operate at this level. At level three, the technical assistance institution provides technical and financial infrastructure support, including (for example) operation of incubators, prototyping services, technical services, and arm's-length financial assistance. This is a hands-on technical assistance role that requires proactive behaviour on the part of the institution. An example of a level three institution in the United States is the National Environmental Technology Applications Corporation (NETAC). NETAC provides business evaluations, technology evaluations, regulatory and intellectual property assistance, training, and technical services such as testing and demonstration. It also has a product evaluation centre that specializes in bioremediation technologies. At level four, the institution participates directly in the firm through equity investments and close technical and management ties. An example is the Finnish National Fund for Research and Development (SITRA), an independent public fund of about U.S.$100 million with the mission to take research to market. It supports new ventures through minority equity participation (Doyle 1992). Overall, "an important lesson from the United States is that cleaner production outreach programmes can take many different

forms. There is considerable variation in the pollution prevention programmes managed by the 50 states. The programmes are located in a
variety of institutions and provide a diverse array of services" (UNIDO/
UNEP 1992, 7). Transition to cleaner production can begin with a waste
audit, the "first step in an on-going programme designed to achieve
maximum resource optimisation and improved process performance.
It is a common sense approach to problem identification and problem
solving" (UNEP/UNIDO 1991). The waste auditing procedure advocated
by the United Nations agencies defines sources, quantities, and types of
wastes being generated; collates information on unit operations, raw
materials, products, water usage, and wastes; highlights process inefficiencies and areas of poor management; helps set targets for waste reduction; permits the development of cost-effective waste management
strategies; raises awareness in the workforce regarding the benefits of
waste reduction; increases management's knowledge of these processes;
and helps to improve process efficiency (UNEP/UNIDO 1991, 3–4). The
result of a waste audit is the development and implementation of an
action plan to reduce waste and improve production efficiency, which,
if implemented, can provide significant economic benefits to the firm,
as indicated by the findings of the Dutch PRISMA program.

The PRISMA waste-auditing procedure identified about 200 pollution prevention options among a group of corporate participants. Only
30 per cent of these options implied technological modifications; 30
per cent implied improvement in housekeeping procedures; 30 per
cent implied changes in materials and raw materials; and 10 per cent
implied product modifications (Dieleman and de Hoo 1993). Taken
together, housekeeping procedures, material inputs, production technologies, and product parameters constitute *industrial practice.* Significant benefits can be gained from incremental improvements in existing
industrial practice, especially in relatively backward subregions of North
America where the stock of equipment and the skill sets of workers and
management are all likely to be farther from good practice than in
technologically dynamic subregions. The precautionary principle and
the clean production paradigm hint that they can move towards major
changes of technology systems through many incremental improvements
in production and transformation of management philosophy. Also of
interest is the development of new R&D-based production systems in
which eco-efficiency is a critical design parameter. The capacity to create technologies has never been greater in industrialized countries.

The world is currently on the brink of a new techno-economic paradigm based upon information and imaging technologies, biotechnology, new materials, and a range of improved energy technologies. The
technical characteristics of radically different technologies for long-term

environmental sustainability are still largely speculative, and the environmental implications of various configurations of the emerging techno-economic paradigm are only beginning to be explored (OECD 1991; Freeman 1992). It is not so simple to identify the kinds of "clean" or environmentally sound technologies that should be promoted widely. Since no currently known technologies are perfectly clean or entirely environmentally sound, cleanliness and environmental soundness are relative. The key characteristic of cleaner technologies is that they are cleaner than prior technologies with respect to materials flow, energy efficiency, or toxicity. Cleaner technologies

- extract and utilize natural resources and prepare products as efficiently as possible;
- use as little energy and raw materials as possible per unit of product output and per unit of utilization (useful lifetime) of the product;
- generate products with reduced or no potentially harmful components and minimize releases to air, water, and soil during fabrication and use of product;
- ensure that any residua of production and use that are generated are managed in an environmentally sound manner;
- ensure, for non-perishable goods, that product durability and lifetimes are maximized insofar as practicable; and
- ensure that, after the useful function is ended, products or their key components are recoverable insofar as possible (OECD 1993, 2).

These characteristics can apply to many techniques and practices across the entire range of industries. As a World Resources Institute (WRI) report observes, "today the climate for innovation seems uniquely rich, poised between technological revolutions in progress and others just emerging" (Heaton, Repetto, and Sobin 1991, 7). A huge reservoir of untapped technological potential in biotechnology, materials, and informatics exists that could increase energy efficiency and reduce waste production. The WRI report proposes environmentally critical technologies for the United States[15] and environmental technology policy initiatives that would include a federal institute for environmental technology, new funding arrangements to support environmental technological innovation, new missions for national laboratories, new patterns of R&D cooperation, new arrangements for international cooperation, regulatory reform, and reorientation of existing programs (Heaton, Repetto, and Sobin 1992).

Most industrialized countries have taken measures to stimulate innovation of new generations of environmentally sound technologies. The Japanese are probably the most ambitious in this respect. Their New

Earth 21 plan aims to develop a new industrial paradigm to restore the earth's natural functions over the next century by returning the emission of global-warming gases to pre-Industrial Revolution levels. They have established RITE, the Research Institute of Innovative Technology for the Earth, for the development and global promotion of next generation environmental technologies. RITE is applying advanced technologies to problems of renewable energy, energy efficiency, new manufacturing processes, and capture and fixation of carbon dioxide. Germany, the Netherlands, Italy, and Canada are other industrialized countries that have established national initiatives to support development of strategic environmental technologies.

The precautionary principle is increasingly incorporated into frameworks for environmental action. Simonis (1990), for example, identifies three strategic elements of environmental modernization of industrial society: ecological structural economic change (notably actions to delink growth from environmentally relevant input factors); preventive environmental policy; and ecological orientation of environmental policy. An eco-industrial policy includes ten priorities: establish a strategic vision, manage structural change, shift to circular industrial ecosystems, design products for needs, build human capacity, ensure corporate accountability, use market mechanisms for industrial transformation, guide technological development, foster sustainable livelihoods, and build global partnerships.

Shifts in businesses' thinking about the strategic importance of eco-efficiency are becoming apparent (Davis and Smith 1995). In one recent survey of 200 senior executives in the United States, 90 per cent said that environmental considerations were part of their strategic planning process. In a survey of 250 European companies, almost three-quarters were found to have specific plans to improve environmental performance. A 1991 report from the Canadian Federation of Independent Business states that 99 per cent of its members are concerned about the state of the natural environment and that 60 per cent have made, or are about to make, significant changes to their businesses to respond to environmental concerns. The ISO14000 series of environmental management standards was approved in 1996.

CONCLUSION

The sustainability and competitiveness agendas are addressed by specialized actors in policy networks, lobbies, research institutions, government agencies, and some non-governmental not-for-profit organizations. Ultimately, attainment of the twin goals of environmental sustainability and economic competitiveness may require a much deepened understanding of these complex issues by the public. This is partly because movement towards sustainability and competitiveness requires a multitude of behavioural changes among citizens and partly because the magnitude of necessary changes requires well-informed voters in democratic political systems. While most of the discussions about sustainability and competitiveness focus on policy and economic incentives, the roles of the public – as consumers, as voters, as civic actors – are important as well. The competitiveness agenda makes a strong set of demands on social values and the business culture. If Canada and the United States develop what has been called a "high growth, low employment" economic trajectory, successful social adjustment to technological change will require new social and political skills. The sustainability agenda is analogous. North American consumers say they want to preserve the environment, but green marketing does not always elicit the expected responses and citizens are "wary of the environmental costs they might have to pay as taxpayers, consumers, or workers" (MacEvoy 1992). With the exception of markets, mechanisms and instruments of deliberate social choice, especially ones that are feasible under regimes of democratic governance, are a relatively unknown part of the selection environment that might lead to eco-efficient industrial innovation. For example, the notion of cleaner production does not rest upon a narrow doctrine of technical efficiency, but on a deeper ambition to gauge the social appropriateness of products (Jackson 1993b). Philosophers of industrial metabolism and industrial ecology are attempting to locate principles of extrafirm regulation in efficient systems of transactions among firms, while another research trend attempts to locate the principles of a strong, socially determined selection environment in processes of social negotiation of technical change.[16] Freeman (1992) points out that the issue of eco-efficient industrial production hinges on estimates of the feasibility with which an "accelerated orientation of the science-technology system in the desired direction can be brought about." As far as common resources are concerned, "sustainability of the system will depend more on social institutions controlling access than on production technologies" (Lynam and Herdt 1989, 396). But we have decreasing degrees of freedom as we move from the scientifically conceivable to the technologically feasible, and from there to the economically viable and the socially acceptable (Perez 1983).

In this chapter, I have tried to address the competitiveness and sustainability issues in terms of the North American system of innovation, which is constituted largely of flows of trade, people, technology, and investment across North America, bilateral scientific relations between the major regional power and the two smaller countries, and trade policy rules embodied in a formal agreement. Formal scientific or technical collaboration at the trilateral North American level is modest. The contours of the North American innovation system remain to be mapped. Undoubtedly the nodes of the regional innovation system are in technologically dynamic metropolitan areas. For the "smaller" countries of the region, integration into a regional innovation system has particular advantages and disadvantages. Two outstanding questions have to do with business strategy in the new North American economic space and the scope, aims, and ambitions of innovation policy within or pertaining to this space. A number of other issues remain to be addressed, such as the technological dimensions of regional economic security, the special problems of less-developed regions of North America, the regulation of competition and monopolies at the regional level, the promotion of eco-efficient industrial innovation, and the degree to which eco-efficient industrial production is competitive in the North American or global context.

Some observers believe that a convergence of political culture, economic beliefs, and, possibly, core values is taking place among the three North American countries. If so, it is primarily occurring among élites – political, economic, military, and scientific – whose assumptions are "liberal, market-oriented, competitive, and homogenizing," on the one hand, and based in North American middle-class styles and material culture, on the other. With respect to the latter, "it may be more accurate to see it as a technological culture, created by the mass media, which has forced the abandonment of traditional U.S. culture as surely as of Canadian and Mexican cultures" (Cross 1992, 305). While élites may share views about the appropriate economic and political rules of the game and the tools and techniques to deal with them, the restructuring of economic relations in North America is giving rise to an often remarked upon decentralization of decision making that challenges the three federal systems of North America. Joel Garreau's prescient *Nine Nations of North America* (1976) foresaw the eventual disintegration of North American space into nine distinct entities, based on history, economics, and culture. Clough (1997) believes that at least twenty metropolitan "nations" are being born in the United States, each with its élites, economic and cultural interests, and crucial foreign linkages. But even this rendition does not do justice to the impressive proliferation of identities in the North American space. Automobile- and media-enabled cultural innovation drives hyperconsumerism and promotes proliferation and dispersion of interests and identities ranging from consumer cults to resurrection of ancient affiliations with local or ethnic networks. The World Wide Web is the most recent metamorphosis of North American technological creativity: despite its name and its origins in Switzerland, about 85 per cent of Web users are North Americans. The pioneers were affluent, technically skilled males in their twenties, but educational institutions, public programs, and advertisements have stimulated a high level of new recruitment into use of the Web in North America, that is, among older and younger persons, females, and somewhat less affluent persons (Kehoe and Pitkow 1996). Increasingly densely networked firms, individuals, and communities are one of the distinguishing features of the North American system of innovation. However, Web connectivity hastens the redundancy of national or North American identities by enabling electronic microcultures, the cyberspace equivalents of the diminishing civic realm in real life, each with a language and a shared narrative ranging from the sublime to the ridiculous. How these electronic microcultures and the interactivity that enables them add up to the much sought after social capital that is said to lubricate innovation systems remains to be seen.

NOTES

1 In this chapter, the terms "science policy and management," technology policy and management," and "innovation policy and management" are used interchangeably.
2 The OECD innovation systems website is at http://www.oecd.org/dsti/ stp/nis/ . The OECD project is focusing on developing indicators for mapping innovation systems, developing analytical approaches, and exploring the implications of *systemic approaches* to innovation policy.
3 The issue of social sustainability cannot be so simply specified. Insofar as poverty breeds environmental degradation and environmental degradation breeds poverty, linkages between environmental and social sustainability are evident. High levels of consumption also breed environmental degradation. In some "traditional" societies with extensive knowledge of the natural environment, social and environmental sustainability are closely linked.
4 In contrast, "invention" refers to an original or novel creation.
5 Freeman (1992) distinguishes among innovation at the level of the firm, the production system, the technology system, and the techno-economic paradigm. These distinctions identify progressively larger increments of change in current practices of production and progressively wider groups of organizations and behaviours taken as reference points. Incremental innovations are minor cumulative changes continuously occurring in firms that can add up over time to significant improvements in productivity and efficiency. Radical innovations are discontinuities in the production system. Changes in the "technology system" are the result of clusters of radical innovations that create "far-reaching changes in

technology, affecting several branches of the economy, as well as ultimately giving rise to entirely new sectors." Technological revolutions, or changes of the techno-economic paradigm, are "new technology systems that have such pervasive effects on the economy as a whole that they change the style of production and management throughout the economy" (Freeman 1992).

6 For descriptive statistics on the state of science in North America, see Nichols and Ratchford (1996).

7 The issue is not whether unencumbered inward and outward FDI confers important benefits. The issue is whether selective intervention to affect the terms of investments and takeovers in specific cases of strategic importance is warranted (Lipsey 1991) and, if it is, the extent to which it is feasible in an open trading system.

8 Faux and Lee (1993, 244); see also the discussion in Herzenberg (1993) and Eden (1994).

9 The issues on the competitiveness agenda range from human resources, science, finance, and policy processes to cultural values and rules of international trade. Forty-five competitiveness reports and studies are described in Prosperity (1992) and SCC (1992a). Some Canadian competitiveness grey literature is analysed in Davis and Smith (1995).

10 Porter proposes a four-stage model of national competitiveness development in which capacity to construct advantage grows progressively greater: (1) factor-driven countries draw most of their comparative advantage from basic factors of production; (2) investment-driven countries compete on the basis of standardized products based on foreign technology that has been acquired and adapted; (3) innovation-driven countries appropriate and improve foreign technologies and also create their own – at this stage, local clusters of industries become "wider" and "deeper"; and (4) in wealth-driven countries, substantial outward financial investments lead to a loss of domestic clusters and loss of market share.

11 The clusters are western forest products, Alberta energy, prairie farming, metal mining, Ontario automotive, Ontario manufacturing, Toronto financial, eastern forest products, Montreal aerospatial, and Atlantic seafood. Missing in this rendition is "Silicon Valley North," the Ottawa-based telecommunications and microelectronics complex that was inadvertently incubated through public labs and public procurement in the national capital region.

12 Similar trends were found in other sectors in Canada. The Canadian pulp and paper industry spent about four times less on R&D than its major American and European competitors. In the forest products industry, which is the largest source of Canada's trade surplus, relative levels of R&D spending were about half that of major competitors. Only

two forest products firms conducted in-house R&D on solid wood products. Industrial R&D staffing fell from 600 in 1980 to 500 in 1990 (SCC 1992c). On the Canadian resource sector's limited propensity to use technology as a competitive weapon, see Hayter (1996) and Wallace (1996).

13 Ashford (1993). A more comprehensive taxonomy of innovation policy measures that might be applied to environmentally sustainable industrial innovation is provided by Rothwell and Zegvold (1985).

14 On attempts to found environmental management regimes on scientific understanding of the behaviour of various pollutants in the environment, see Chadwick and Nilsson (1993).

15 These are energy capture (photovoltaics, geothermal, solar thermal electricity, nuclear fission); energy storage and application (batteries, superconductors, hydrogen storage, heat storage, fuel cells); special energy end-uses (transportation, buildings); agricultural biotechnology; improved agricultural techniques; manufacturing monitoring, modelling, and control; catalysis; separations; precision fabrication; materials design and processing; information, communications, and computing; and contraception.

16 For example, Irwin and Vergragt (1989). Radical social innovation for environmental sustainability is especially problematic. Massive changes in lifestyles and consumption require social engineering, coercive policies, or extremely rapid social learning on an unprecedented scale. On the efforts (largely in northern countries) to define frameworks for green political action, see Eckersley (1992) and Dobson (1990). On the question of the politics of the social transition to sustainability, see, for example, Kassiola (1990).

REFERENCES

Ashford, Nicholas A. 1993. "Understanding Technological Responses of Industrial Firms to Environmental Problems: Implications for Government Policy." In Fischer and Schot (1993, 277–307).

Baas, L.W., M. Van der Belt, D. Huisingh, and F. Neumann. 1992. "Cleaner Production: What Some Governments Are Doing and What All Governments Can Do to Promote Sustainability." *European Water Pollution Control* 2 (1): 10–25.

Boardman, Robert, ed. 1992. *Canadian Environmental Policy: Ecosystems, Politics, and Process.* Toronto: Oxford University Press.

Bongaerts, Jan C., and Dirk Heinrichs. 1987. "Government Support of Clean Technology Research in West Germany: Some Evidence." *R&D Management* 17 (1): 39–50.

Britton, John N.H., ed. 1996. *Canada and the Global Economy: The Geography of Structural and Technological Change.* Montreal and Kingston: McGill-Queen's University Press.

Britton, John N.H., James M. Gilmour, William Smith, and Guy P.F. Steed. 1996. "Technological Change and Innovation: Policy Issues." In Britton (1996, 433–44).

Chadwick, M.J., and J. Nilsson. 1993. "Environmental Quality Objectives: Assimilative Capacity and Critical Load Concepts in Environmental Management." In Jackson (1993a, 29–39).

Clarke, Tom, and Jean Reavely. 1993. *Science and Technology Management Bibliography 1993.* Ottawa: Stargate Consultants.

Clough, Michael. 1997. "Birth of Nations." *Los Angeles Times,* 27 July.

Crookell, Harold. 1990. "Subsidiary Strategy in a Free Trade Environment." Working paper 1990-II, Investment Canada, Ottawa.

Cross, Michael S. 1992. "Towards a Definition of North American Culture." In S. Randall, H. Konrad, and S. Silverman, eds, *North America without Borders? Integrating Canada, the United States, and Mexico,* 303–6. Calgary: University of Calgary Press.

Daly, D.J., and D.C. MacCharles. 1986. *Canadian Manufactured Exports: Constraints and Opportunities.* Montreal: Institute for Research on Public Policy.

Davis, Charles H., Paul Dufour, and Janet Halliwell. 1993. "La collaboration scientifique et technologique en Amérique du Nord: un point de vue canadien." *Études internationales* 24 (2): 269–96.

Davis, Charles H., and Richard Smith. 1995. "Management of Technology and Technological Change in Canada." In K. Minden and P.K. Wong, eds, *Developing Technology Managers: Comparative Pacific Rim Strategies,* 15–61. Armonk, N.Y.: M.E. Sharpe Publishers.

D'Cruz, Joseph R., and Alan M. Rugman. 1992. *New Compacts for Canadian Competitiveness.* Toronto: Kodak Canada.

Deblock, Christian, and Michèle Rioux. 1993. "NAFTA: The Trump Card of the United States?" *Studies in Political Economy* 41:7–44.

Denison, E. 1985. *Trends in American Economic Growth, 1929–1982.* Washington, D.C.: Brookings Institute.

Dethlefsen, V., T. Jackson, and P. Taylor. 1993. "The Precautionary Principle." In Jackson (1993a, 41–62).

Dieleman, Hans, and Sybren de Hoo. 1993. "Towards a Tailor-Made Process of Pollution Prevention and Cleaner Production: Results and Implications of the Prisma Project." In Fischer and Schot (1993, 245–76).

Dobson, Andrew. 1990. *Green Political Thought.* London: HarperCollins.

Dosi, Giovani, John Zysman, and Laura D'Andrea Tyson. 1990. "Technology, Trade, and Schumpeterian Efficiencies." In de la Mothe and L.-M. Ducharme, eds, *Science, Technology and Free Trade,* London and New York: Printer.

Doyle, Denzil. 1992. "Building a Stronger Environmental Technology Exploitation Capability in Canada." Unpublished report prepared for Environment Canada and Industry, Science and Technology Canada, Ottawa.

Dunning, John H. 1993. "Internationalizing Porter's Diamond." *Management International Review* 33 (2): 7–15.

ECC (Economic Council of Canada). 1988. *U.S.-Canada Productivity Gap, Scale Economies, and the Gains from Freer Trade.* ECC discussion paper no. 357. Ottawa.

Eckersley, Robyn. 1992. *Environmentalism and Political Theory: Toward an Ecocentric Approach.* Albany: State University of New York Press.

Eden, Lorraine. 1991. "Multinational Responses to Trade and Technology Changes: Implications for Canada." In McFetridge (1991, 133–71).

– 1994. *Multinationales en Amérique du Nord.* Calgary: University of Calgary Press.

Edquist, Charles, ed, 1997. *Systems of Innovation: Technologies, Institutions and Organizations.* London and Washington: Pinter.

EPA (United States Environmental Protection Agency). 1991. *Permitting and Compliance Policy: Barriers to U.S. Environmental Technology Innovation.* Washington, D.C.: EPA and National Advisory Council for Environmental Policy and Technology.

– 1992. *Improving Technology Diffusion for Environmental Protection: Report and Recommendations of the Technology Innovation and Economics Committee.* Washington, D.C.: EPA and National Advisory Council for Environmental Policy and Technology.

Faux, Jeff, and Thea Lee. 1993. "Implications of NAFTA for the United States: Investment, Jobs, and Productivity." In Grinspun and Cameron (1993, 235–49).

Fischer, Kurt, and Johan Schot, eds. 1993. *Environmental Strategies for Industry.* Washington, D.C.: Island Press.

Fletcher, Joseph F. 1992. *Canadian Attitudes toward Competitiveness and Entrepreneurship.* Ottawa: Industry, Science and Technology Canada

Freeman, Christopher. 1992. "A Green Techno-Economic Paradigm for the World Economy." In C. Freeman, ed., *The Economics of Hope: Essays on Technical Change, Economic Growth and the Environment.* London and New York: Pinter.

Garreau, Joel. 1976. *The Nine Nations of North America.* New York: Houghton Mifflin.

Geffen, Charlotte A. 1995. "Radical Innovation in Environmental Technologies: The Influence of Federal Policy." *Science and Public Policy* 22 (5): 313–23.

Globerman, Steven. 1990. "Trade Liberalization and Competitive Behavior: A Note Assessing the Evidence and the Public Policy Implications." *Journal of Policy Analysis and Management* 9 (1): 80–9.

Grinspun, Ricardo, and Maxwell Cameron, eds. 1993. *The Political Economy of North American Free Trade.* Montreal and Kingston: McGill-Queen's University Press.

Hatzichroniglou, Thomas. 1991. "Indicators of Industrial Competitiveness: Results and Limitations." In J. Niosi, ed., *Technology and National Competitiveness: Oligopoly, Technological Innovation, and International Competition,* 177–221. Montreal and Kingston: McGill-Queen's University Press.

Hayter, Roger. 1996. "Technological Imperatives in Resource Sectors: Forest Products." In Britton (1996, 101–22).

Heaton, George, Robert Repetto, and Rodney Sobin. 1991. *Transforming Technology: An Agenda for Environmentally Sustainable Growth in the 21st Century.* Washington, D.C.: World Resources Institute.

– 1992. *Backs to the Future: U.S. Government Policy toward Environmentally Critical Technology.* Washington, D.C.: World Resources Institute.

Herzenberg, Stephen. 1993. "Continental Integration and the Future of the North American Auto Sector." In M. Appel Molot, ed., *Driving Continentally: National Policies and the North American Auto Industry,* Ottawa: Carleton University Press.

Hirschhorn, Joel S. 1992. "Pollution Prevention Implementation in Developing Countries." Unpublished report prepared for the U.S. Agency for International Development.

Hirschhorn, Joel, T. Jackson, and L. Baas. 1993. "Towards Prevention: The Emerging Environmental Management Paradigm." In Jackson (1993a, 125–43).

Irwin, Alan, and Philip Vergragt. 1989. "Re-thinking the Relationship between Environmental Regulation and Industrial Innovation: The Social Negotiation of Technical Change." *Technology Analysis and Strategic Management* 1 (1): 57–70.

ISTC (Industry, Science and Technology Canada) 1992. *Canada's Business Culture.* Ottawa: ISTC.

Jackson, T. 1991. "The Principles of Clean Production: Concepts and Principles for Guiding Technological Choice towards Sustainable Development." Seminar digest paper, Stockholm Environmental Institute.

–, ed. 1993a. *Clean Production Strategies: Developing Preventive Environmental Management in the Industrial Economy.* Boca Raton: Stockholm Environmental Institute and Lewis Publishers.

– 1993b. "Principles of Clean Production: Developing an Operational Approach to the Prevention Paradigm." In Jackson (1993a, 143–64).

Kassiola, Joel Jay. 1990. *The Death of Industrial Civilization: The Limits to Economic Growth and the Repoliticization of Advanced Industrial Society.* Albany: State University of New York Press.

Kehoe, Colleen M., and James E. Pitkow. 1996. *Surveying the Territory: GVU's Five WWW User Surveys.* Atlanta: Graphics, Visualization, and Usability

Center, Georgia Institute of Technology. http://www.gvu.gatech.edu/
   user_surveys/papers/w3j.html
Leclerc, Michel, and Jean Gagné. 1994. "International Scientific Coopera-
   tion: The Continentalization of Science." *Scientometrics* 31 (3): 261–92.
Letouche, Daniel. 1991. *Science and Technology in Canada: An Essay on the New
   Strategic and International Context.* Ottawa: Science Council of Canada.
Lipsey, Richard C. 1991. "Rapporteur's Comments." In McFetridge (1991,
   361–88).
Litvak, Isaiah. 1990. "U.S. Multinationals: Repositioning the Canadian
   Subsidiary." *Business in the Contemporary World,* Autumn, 111–19.
Lynam, John K., and Robert W. Herdt. 1989. "Sense and Sustainability:
   Sustainability as an Objective in International Agricultural Research."
   Agricultural Economics 3:381–98.
MacEvoy, Bruce. 1992. *Business, the Public, and the Environment: U.S. Environ-
   mental Attitudes and Business Strategies.* SRI International, Business Intelli-
   gence Report no. 812.
McFetridge, Donald G., 1993. "The Canadian System of Industrial Innova-
   tion." In Nelson (1993, 299–323).
–, ed. 1991. *Foreign Investment, Technology and Economic Growth.* Calgary:
   University of Calgary Press.
Martin, Richard. 1992. "Canadian Labour and North American Integration."
   In S. Randall, H. Konrad, and S. Silverman, eds, *North America without
   Borders? Integrating Canada, the United States, and Mexico,* 181–8. Calgary:
   University of Calgary Press.
Nelson, Richard R., ed. 1993. *National Innovation Systems: A Comparative
   Analysis.* New York: Oxford University Press.
Nichols, Rodney W., and Thomas Ratchford. 1996. "North America." In
   World Science Report 1996, 23–44. Paris: UNESCO.
Niosi, Jorge. 1983. *Les multinationales canadiennes.* Montreal: Boréal Express.
Niosi, Jorge, Paolo Saviotti, Bertrand Bellon, and Michael Crow. 1993.
   "National Systems of Innovation: In Search of a Workable Concept."
   Technology in Society 15 (2): 207–27.
OECD (Organization for Economic Cooperation and Development). 1991.
   The State of the Environment. Paris: OECD.
– 1993. *Technologies for Cleaner Production and Products: Towards Technological
   Revolution for Sustainable Development.* Paris: OECD.
– 1997. *National Innovation Systems.* Paris: OECD. http://www.oecd.org/dsti/
   nispub.pdf
Office of Technology Assessment (OTA), 1994. *Industry, Technology, and the
   Environment: Competitive Challenges and Business Opportunities.* Washington,
   D.C.: OTA, U.S. Congress.
Perez, Carlota. 1983. "Structural Change and the Assimilation of New
   Technologies in the Social and Economic System." *Futures* 15 (5): 357–75.

Pestieau, Caroline. 1993. "Globalization and Restructuring: Aspects of the Canadian Experience." Paper presented at the 1993 Canada-India Economic and Business Policy Linkage Program, New Delhi, January.

Philips, Paul. 1991. "New Staples and Mega-Projects: Reaching the Limits to Sustainable Development." In D. Drache and M. Gertler, eds, *The New Era of Global Competition: State Policy and Market Power*, 229–46. Montreal and Kingston: McGill-Queen's University Press.

Porter, Michael E. 1990. *The Competitive Advantage of Nations.* New York: Free Press.

– 1991. *Canada at the Crossroads: The Reality of a New Competitive Environment.* Ottawa: Business Council on National Issues and Ministry of Supply and Services.

Porter, Michael E., and Claus van der Linde. 1995. "Toward a New Conception of the Environment-Competitiveness Relationship." *Journal of Economic Perspectives* 9 (4): 97–118.

Powers, Charles W. 1991. "The Role of NGOs in Improving the Employment of Science and Technology in Environmental Management." Working paper, Carnegie Commission on Science, Technology, and Government, New York.

Prosperity. 1992. *An Overview of Selected Studies on Canada's Prosperity and Competitiveness.* Ottawa: Prosperity Initiative, Industry, Science and Technology Canada.

Rath, Amitav, and Brent Herbert-Copley. 1993. *Green Technologies for Development: Transfer, Trade and Cooperation.* Ottawa: International Development Research Centre.

Rothwell, Roy, and W. Zegvold. 1985. *Reindustrialization and Technology.* London: Longmans.

Rugman, Alan M., 1990. *Multinationals and Canada–United States Free Trade.* Columbia: University of South Carolina Press.

Rugman, Alan M. and Joseph D'Cruz. 1991. Fast Forward: Improving Canada's Competitiveness. Toronto: Kodak Canada.

– 1993. "The 'Double Diamond' Model of International Competitiveness: The Canadian Experience." *Management International Review* 33 (2): 17–39.

SCC (Science Council of Canada). 1992a. *Reaching for Tomorrow.* Ottawa: SCC.

– 1992b. *The Canadian Non-Ferrous Metals Sector.* Sectoral Strategy Series, no. 11. Ottawa: SCC.

– 1992c. *The Canadian Forest Products Sector.* Sectoral Strategy Series, no. 9. Ottawa: SCC.

Shrybman, Steven. 1993. "Trading Away the Environment." In Grinspun and Cameron (1993, 271–94).

Simonis, Udo Ernst. 1990. *Beyond Growth: Elements of Sustainable Development.* Berlin: Wissenschaftszentrum Berlin fur Sozialforschung.

UN (United Nations), 1993. *World Investment Directory, 1992.* Vol. 3, *Developed Countries.* New York: UN, Transnational Corporations and Management Division.

UNCTAD (United Nations Conference on Trade and Development) 1993. *Environmental Management in Transnational Corporations: Report of the Benchmark Corporate Environmental Survey.* New York: UNCTAD. Programme on Transnational Corporations.

UNEP/UNIDO (United Nations Environment Programme Industry and Environment Office/United Nations Industrial Development Organization) 1991. *Audit and Reduction Manual for Industrial Emissions and Wastes.* Technical Report Series, no. 7. Paris and Vienna: UNEP and UNIDO.

UNIDO/UNEP. 1992. "National Cleaner Production Centre Programme: Background Information." UNIDO and UNEP, Vienna and Paris, December.

Wallace, Iain. 1996. "Restructuring the Canadian Mining and Mineral-Processing Industries." In Britton (1996, 123–36).

Weintraub, Sidney. 1992. "North American Free Trade and the European Situation Compared." *International Migration Review* 26:506–24.

Winn, S.F., and N.J. Roome. 1993. "R&D Management Responses to the Environment: Current Theory and Implications to Practice and Research." *R&D Management* 23 (2): 147–60.

Yakowitz, H., and R. Hanmer. 1993. "Policy Options for Clean Production." In Jackson (1993a, 295–322).

Yamashita, Shoichi. 1991. "Japan's Role as a Regional Technological Integrator in the Pacific Rim." Paper presented at the conference on "The Emerging Technological Trajectory of the Pacific Rim Nations," Tufts University, Somerville, Mass.

2 Techno-nationalism and Meso Innovation Systems

GILLES PAQUET

Mon crâne est tellement lourd qu'il m'est impossible de le porter. Je le roule autour de moi lentement ... une fois je me suis dévoré les pattes sans m'en apercevoir.

Gustave Flaubert

INTRODUCTION

The notion of a national system of innovation refers to elusive arrays of national public and private institutions and organizations and public policy thrusts that are purported to shape stable patterns of behaviour and particular incentive systems in the innovation process. Supposedly, the national system of innovation weaves together in a creative way different logics embodied in technical trajectories, production systems, national institutions, and action plans by stakeholders (Niosi et al. 1992; Bes 1993).

In the introductory chapter of his *National Innovation Systems*, Richard Nelson develops a central hypothesis about "a new spirit of what might be called technonationalism ... combining a strong belief that the technological capabilities of a nation's firms are a key source of their competitive prowess, with a belief that these capabilities are in a sense national, and can be built by national action" (Nelson 1993, 3). While Nelson and Nathan Rosenberg are careful to explain that one of the central concerns of their multi-country study is to establish "whether, and if so in what ways, the concept of a 'national' system made any sense today," they also add that *de facto* "national governments act as if it did" (Nelson and Rosenberg 1993, 5). Our objective is to raise some questions about this hypothesis.

We suggest in the first section of this chapter that any meaningful characterization of a modern economy must start with a fair assessment of the paradox inherent in the process of globalization of economic activities and the impact of globalization on national production and governance systems. In the second section, we explore the dynamics of the organization and growth of knowledge that underpin the innovation system and the complex way in which institutions effect cognitive processes and learning and, through this channel, generate the thrust that generates innovations in and pressures on the existing institutional order (Johnson 1992). In the third section, we suggest that the innovation process, even when defined broadly, rarely encompasses the "national" scene, but would appear to be congruent with the meso regional/ sectoral realities that are the genuine source of synergies and social learning (Dahmen 1988; Acs, de la Mothe, and Paquet 1996). In the fourth section, we critically appraise the phenomenon of the *centralized mind* that seems to permeate the study of innovation systems. There would appear to be a strong attachment to "centralized ways of thinking, assuming that every pattern must have a single cause, an ultimate controlling factor" (Resnick 1994, 35). This, in turn, underpins a tendency to bet on means of problem solving that almost inevitably lead to compulsive centralization and misguided approaches. In the fifth section, we examine in a preliminary way the manner in which the three countries of North America are confronting this issue, and we identify, in passing, some key research challenges facing those who are really concerned about catalysing the innovative society.

THE REINVENTION OF GOVERNANCE

Empirical economies are *institutionalized processes*, that is, they are governed by sets of rules and conventions that vest the wealth-creation process with relative unity and stability by harmonizing the geo-technical constraints imposed by the environment with the values and plans of decision makers. The wealth-creation process of the late nineteenth century was mainly instituted as a social armistice between the somewhat rigid constraints imposed by technology, geography, and natural resource endowments, on the one hand, and the less than perfectly coordinated plans of private and public decision makers, on the other. As both constraints and preferences evolved, economies came to be instituted differently because of the degrees of freedom afforded them by the extent to which they were protected from the rest of the world by relatively high transportation costs, transaction costs, and tariff walls.

However, in the recent past, the wealth-creation process has changed dramatically: it has become dematerialized as its mainsprings ceased to be natural resources and material production and became knowledge and information activities. Transportation costs, transaction costs, and tariff walls have tumbled. As a result of important information and communication economies and of growing organizational flexibility, transnational firms have become capable of organizing knowledge and production globally and escaping to a great extent from the constraints that both geography and nation-states might wish to impose on them. Therefore, economic activity has become in many instances truly de-territorialized.

This process of globalization has often been simplistically characterized as a process of liberalization. This is inaccurate. There has been much liberalization, but a mutation of the economic process has also made firms and nations increasingly dependent on intangibles like know-how, synergies, and untraded interdependencies that are at the core of the production of knowledge and of the new wealth-creation process.

This new transnational techno-economic world has triggered important changes in the governance process of socio-economies (Paquet 1990). First, firms and governments have become rather fuzzy concepts: it is often no longer possible to distinguish between the inside and the outside in the complex web of networks and alliances in which they are enmeshed. Second, the knowledge/information fabric of the new economy has led to the development of a large number of non-market institutions, as information and knowledge proved not to be handled well by the market (Paquet 1989). Finally, the traditional and narrow economic notion of *competition* has been replaced by the broader and more socio-politico-economic notion of *competitiveness* as a benchmark for assessing the process of wealth creation and as a guide in designing cooperative links among stakeholders.

As a result, private and public organizations have become more foot-loose and therefore compatible with a variety of locations, technologies, and organizational structures (de la Mothe and Paquet 1994b). They have also become potentially affected to a much greater extent by the synergies, interdependencies, socio-cultural bonds, or trust relationships capable of producing comparative advantages.

The central challenge of the new economy has been to find ways to create an environment in which knowledge workers do as much learning as possible – from their experience, but also from each other, from partners, clients, suppliers, and so on. For learning to occur, however, there must be *conversations* between and among partners, and since working conversations that create new knowledge can only emerge where there is trust, it and confidence prove to be essential inputs (Webber 1993).

Two very significant transformations in our modern political economies in the last decades have been ascribable to a large extent to the challenges posed by the new socio-economy: a fragmentation and balkanization of existing national economies and a concurrent massive devolution in the governance system of both private and public organizations.

Fragmentation

First, global competitiveness has led advanced industrial nations to specialize in the export of products in which they have technological or absolute advantages. Since those export-oriented absolute-advantage industries tend to be found in subnational regions, this has led to the emergence of a mosaic of subnational geographical agglomerations and regional "worlds of production": *product-based technological learning systems* resting in important ways on conventions rooted in the cultures of local economic actors (Storper 1992, 1993).

Second, the pressures of globalization have put so great a strain on the nation-state that subnational regions and communities have strongly felt a need for roots and anchors in local and regional bonds of ethnicity, language, and culture. This budding *tribalism* (Naisbitt 1994) has in turn been reinforced by the fact that it often proved to be the source of a robust entrepreneurial culture as well as a competitive advantage in the new context.

Third, the dysfunctionality of the nation-state has triggered the emergence of a genuine community of shared economic interests at the regional level, and the dynamics of collective action has led to the rise of the *region-state*. Subnational governments or loose alliances among local authorities have become active as partners of foreign investors and providers of the requisite infrastructure to leverage policies capable of making the region an active participant in the global economy (Ohmae 1993).

Fourth, as the region-state emerged, it was often in a position to provide support for development blocs through the nurturing of complementarities, interdependencies, and externalities via infrastructure, networking of economic and business competence, and so forth, and to dynamize the transformation process at the meso-economic level (Dahmen 1988; de la Mothe and Paquet 1994c).

Devolution

First, the search for speed of adjustment, variety, flexibility, and innovation generated by global competitiveness has forced corporations to adapt ever faster, and this has led them to "deconstruct" themselves into networks of quasi-autonomous units capable of taking action as they see fit in the face of local circumstances. Managers ceased to be "drivers of people" and became "drivers of learning." This required a shift from vertical hierarchical structures of governance to more horizontal networking structures conducive to innovative conversations.

Second, the same process has been witnessed in the governance of public organizations, where the need to do more with less, together with the growing pressure for more subnational states to cooperate actively with private organizations to ensure success on the global scene, has led governments to implement massive privatization or to devolve power to lower-order public authorities (Paquet 1994).

Third, this has led to general praise for the flexibility and genuine *souplesse* of the federal system as a system of governance for both private and public organizations and to the general celebration of bottom-up management (Handy 1992).

Fourth, in transforming the governance of economic, social, and political organizations, the growing search for flexibility has not stopped at decentralization and privatization strategies. There has been a growing pressure to dissolve permanent organizations so as to allow maximum use of all the possibilities of networking. This has led to the proposal that virtual enterprises and governments might provide the ultimate flexibility (de la Mothe and Paquet 1994a). This form of dissolution of governance systems has not only proved to be dynamically efficient, but has also led to a reinforcement of community bonds as private and public organizations cease to be the main source of identification.

THE ORGANIZATION OF KNOWLEDGE

Since organizations are basically information or knowledge systems, their capacity to *transform* (which is another way of saying "to learn") has become crucial to their survival, and their co-evolution (with the institutional environment and the other stakeholders) has been the source of value added. While the traditional view is that individual people learn, what is suggested by more recent analyses is that the learning organization does not store its knowledge in separate heads, but in the relationships between and among stakeholders: it co-creates value by a dialogue of equals (Boisot 1987, 1995; Wikstrom and Normann 1994).

The flexibility and adaptability of organizations have become the new gauge of effective performance in lieu of simple allocative efficiency. In a rapidly evolving, surprise-generating context, plagued with uncertainty and ignorance, the challenge is not simply to make the highest and best use of existing resources and knowledge, to better *exploit* the available possibilities, but also to *explore* new possibilities and opportunities. The strategic choice has been to strike a balance or a trade-off between exploitation and exploration. Undue emphasis on the exploitation of available knowledge may trap an organization in suboptimal situations, while undue emphasis on exploration may prevent an organization from gaining much from successful experimentation (March 1991; Marengo 1993; Dosi and Marengo 1994).

This may be a mistaken strategy. One could probably more profitably search for the complementarities, synergies, and intercreation among work, organization, learning, and innovation (Brown and Duguid 1991). That is the strategy we will follow here.

Our reason for adopting this second strategy is that it holds the possibility of prying open the dynamics of the work-organization-learning-innovation nexus. This will be useful as a stratagem to deal in a different way with the central question posed by James March about the balance between coherence and experimentation, between exploitation and exploration, in choosing which learning regime to promote. But this strategy will also help us to discriminate among the alternative strategies that are proposed these days for catalysing the innovation process by allowing us to explore (1) the way in which knowledge organization underpins economic progress and (2) the manner in which communities of practice play a central role in this process. This is likely to sharpen our understanding of the role of partnering in such a context, but it might also suggest ways in which tinkering with organization and organizational innovation may hold the key to a more effective exploration-exploitation arrangement.

Knowledge and Economic Progress

In an information economy, economic progress is mainly generated by the growth of knowledge; thus, the way in which knowledge production is organized determines whether more or less economic progress is achieved. This is a matter already discussed at some length by Alfred Marshall in the early part of the twentieth century, as Brian Loasby (1991, 39) has reminded us. For Marshall, "capital consists in great part of knowledge and organization." Since information and knowledge are becoming the pillars of the new economy and economic organizations themselves are significant parts of knowledge systems, knowledge has become the central engine of economic progress.

Marshall had a rather primitive but effective way of dealing with organizations as knowledge systems. It is a three-step construction. First, business people are expected to use their knowledge to build up the firm's *internal organization,* combining specialization and integration and making use of the diversity of knowledge, abilities, and experience of their employees. Second, when similar businesses, either collected in an industrial district or dispersed over a wide territory, recognize that they have much to learn from one another, they begin to form some sort of invisible college through which they collaborate loosely. This is a *horizontal organization,* external to the firm but internal to the industry. Finally, there are the networks linking firms to customers and suppliers in a third form of organization for the exchange of information and ideas that Marshall calls *external organization* (Loasby 1991, 40–1).

These forms of organization will be the locus of ongoing conversations that will produce new knowledge and value added through networking and partnering. That is the central message of Wikstrom and Normann (1994): the idea that the value-creating process is the result of co-production through interlinkages and conversations among all partners. The main challenge, then, is to determine what is the best organization of knowledge production if the objective is to generate an organization characterized by learning and innovation.

According to Marengo (1993), this will depend greatly on a balance between commonality and diversity of knowledge, between coherence and mutual learning, between exploitation and exploration. But ethnographic work on the daily life of organizations suggests that practices differ significantly from job descriptions or rules and procedures and that the actual practices are the central feature of successful organizations. Thus, the difference between *de jure* and *de facto* work procedures may indeed be of central concern, since the corporate culture embodies a communal interpretation that may have little to do with the documentation available.

Corporate culture embodies generally unwritten principles meant to generate a relatively high level of coordination at low cost by bestowing identity and membership. This corporate culture is nested at the organization level in the central features of work practice: stories of flexible generality about past and current practice that act as repositories of accumulated wisdom, the evolution of these stories constituting not only a collective learning of an evolving way to interpret conflicting and confusing data, but also an ongoing social construction of a community of interpretation.

Communities of Practice

This redefinition of work as conversation, as sharing stories, as becoming a member of a community of practice, may appear somewhat unconventional, but it is at the core of the recent writings of Webber (1993), Peters (1994), and Handy (1995). In the same way that actual practice in the workplace has a communal base, learning also has such a base. It is not about transmission of abstract knowledge from someone's head to another person's head, it is about learning to "function in a community," about the "embodied ability to behave as community members," about "becoming a practitioner." Learning is *legitimate peripheral participation*, and it is fostered by membership in the community of practice and interest (Brown and Duguid 1991).

This learning is not necessarily easy to do, but it is fundamentally a matter of trust. Trust is at the core of both the fabric of the communities of practice and the fabric of shared leadership. Trust is a way to transform "laborers into members," to convert an employment contract into a membership contract: "the concept of membership, when made real, would replace the sense of belonging to a place with a sense of belonging to a community" (Handy 1995, 48). Belonging is one of the most powerful agents of mobilization. Therefore, what is required is a significant moral component to the new employment contract. This new, refurbished *moral contract* is not mainly contractual but mainly moral: "a network of civic engagement ... which can serve as a cultural template for future collaboration ... broaden the participants' sense of self ... enhancing the participants' 'taste' for collective benefits" (Putnam 1995, 67).

However, a situation in which such a membership contract would become hegemonic would correspond to a situation in which a dominant macroculture would prevail. If such were the case, in the long run, it would become homogeneous and coherent, but would cease to be innovative. Innovation requires a certain diversity of knowledge and stems from the interplay between separate communities, from the interplay between the core community and the emergent communities at the periphery (the suppliers and the customers of a firm, for instance) to that between the organization and the environment with which it interacts actively. Exploration calls for diversity, for separate stories to be in good currency. It happens at the interface between the organization and its environment and depends on the capacity for the non-canonical to prevail over the canonical.

It is therefore in the structure of the communities of practice that one must seek the levers likely to foster both learning and innovation, and this involves intervening in the workplace. When the gap between canonical and actual practices widens too much, the only way to promote the growth of knowledge is to legitimize and support a number of enacting activities that may be disruptive, to foster a reconception of the organization as a community of communities, and to promote the view that communities of practice must take some distance from the received wisdom.

The very coherence that makes learning easier is likely to make innovation more difficult. The central challenge for the promotion of the growth of knowledge is to find the requisite degree of dissonance necessary for a system to become innovative, and to identify the most effective schemes for the decomposition of large organizations into quasi-isolated subsystems likely to provoke the emergence of a workable degree of inconsistency and therefore of innovation.

The differences in the way the suborganizations search for knowledge increase the scope of the search. So, as these differences are legitimized and have maximum opportunity to rub against one another (as in industrial districts or more closely interconnected communities of practice), innovation will ensue.

For similar reasons, institutional learning proceeds faster when the institutional infrastructure allows a fair degree of diversity. This is a point that Granovetter (1973) emphasizes when he suggests that a certain degree of heterogeneity, and therefore of social distance, might foster a higher potentiality for innovation because of the fact that the different parties bring to the conversation a more complementary body of knowledge. This is likely to trigger more fruitful synergies.

MESO INNOVATION SYSTEMS

In an economy dynamized by information, knowledge, and competence, and consequently balkanized and decentralized, the new relevant units of analysis have to be those that serve as the basis on which to understand and nurture innovation. Focusing either on the firm or on the national economy would appear to be equally misguided: under the microscope, too much is idiosyncratic and white noise; under the macroscope, much of the innovation and restructuring going on is bound to be missed. One may therefore argue persuasively that the most useful perspective is the Schumpeterian-Dahmenian meso-approach that focuses on development blocks, technology districts, subnational forums, and so on, where the learning is really occurring (de la Mothe and Paquet 1994b, 1996, 28 ff.).

In an evolutionary model, the process of learning and discovery is only one blade of a pair of scissors. The other blade is the interactive mechanism with the context or environment through which selection occurs. Whether the unit of analysis is the technology or the firm, this interactive mechanism is fitness driven, and firms' search processes "both provide the source of differential fitness – firms whose R&D turn up more profitable processes of production or products will grow relative to their competitors – and also tend to bind them together as a community" (Dosi and Nelson 1994, 162).

It is very important to realize that social proximity is bound to play a fundamental role on both sides of the equation. Both on the organization side and on the forum/environment side, proximity breeds interaction and socio-economic learning. Moreover, these interactive mechanisms are fuelled by the dynamic increasing returns owing to agglomeration. In most cases, these agglomeration economies are bounded and therefore do not give rise to monopoly by a single region or location, but they do generate increasing returns (Arthur 1990).

While we do not know much about the innovation process and the process of diffusion of technical and organizational innovations, the research agenda on those issues has been much influenced by Nelson and Winter (1977). At the core of their scheme is the notion of a *selection environment*, which is defined as the context that "determines how relative use of different technologies changes over time" (61). This context is shaped by market and non-market components, conventions, socio-cultural factors, and the broader institutional structure. This selection environment constitutes the relevant *milieu*, which may be more or less important in explaining the innovative capacity of a country and a sector/region.

The notion of *milieu* connotes three sets of forces: (1) the contours of a particular spatial set vested with a certain unity and tonus; (2) the organizational logic of a network of interdependent actors engaged in cooperative innovative activity; and (3) organizational learning based on the dialectics between *adapting actors* and the *adopting milieu*. At the core of the *dynamic milieu* and of the innovation network are a number of intermingled dimensions (economic, historical, cognitive, and normative), but these all depend to a certain degree on trust and confidence and therefore on a host of cultural and sociological factors that tend to be found in localized networks and are more likely to emerge on a background of shared experiences, regional loyalties, and the like. This is social capital in Coleman's sense, and such social and cultural capital plays a central role in meso-systems' dynamics and in their capacity to learn and transform (Coleman 1988; Saxenian 1994).

The innovation process depends a great deal on the central features of a selection environment or milieu.

First, innovation is all about continuous learning, and learning does not occur in a socio-cultural vacuum. The innovation network is more likely to blossom in a restricted localized milieu where all the socio-cultural characteristics of a *dynamic milieu* are likely to be found. Moreover, it is most unlikely that this sort of *milieu* will correspond to the national territory. Therefore, if one is to identify *dynamic milieux or milieux porteurs* as likely systems on which one might work to stimulate innovation, they are likely to be local or regional systems of innovation.

Second, some geo-technical forces would appear to generate meso-level units where learning proceeds faster and better. As Storper argues, "in technologically dynamic production complexes ... there is a strong reason for the existence of regional clusters or agglomerations. Agglomeration appears to be a principal geographical form in which the trade-off between lock-in technological flexibility (and the search for quasi-rents), and cost minimization can be most effectively managed, because it facilitates the efficient operations of a cooperative production network. Agglomeration in these cases is the result not simply of standard localization economies (which are based on the notion of allocative efficiency in minimizing costs), but of Schumpeterian efficiencies" (Storper 1992:84).

Third, the deconstruction of national economies, the dispersive revolution in governance, the rise of region-states, and the growth of the new tribalism would tend to provide a greater potential for dynamism at the meso-level. But Storper has argued that "codes, channels of interaction, and ways of organizing and coordinating behaviors" are what makes learning possible (85). He feels that the confluence of issues (learning, networks, lock-in, conventions, and types of knowledge) must be rooted in political-economic cultures, rules and institutions, and that in many countries these are highly differentiated at the regional level.

Therefore, one region may affect technological learning and innovation networks in one subnational area much faster than in others. Canada, the United States and Mexico are countries where one may reasonably detect a mosaic of political-economic cultures, rules and conventions with differential innovative potential (Maddox and Gee 1994). Consequently, one might say that there is a genuine "territorialization of learning" in such a Schumpeterian world.

THE CENTRALIZED MINDSET

In the face of these strong presumptions in favour of the existence of meso innovation systems, it is surprising to find that so little has been done to escape the mindset of national systems of innovation. The reason for this bias is, however, not very difficult to understand. Since the cost of thinking is not zero, humans adopt paradigms and mindsets to routinize their thinking to some degree. Ideologies are simplification machines of that sort, providing mechanical responses to a battery of difficult questions by first decomplexifying and sanitizing the issue. The attraction of techno-nationalism falls into this category.

Mitchel Resnick has analysed the bizarre intellectual and institutional legacy that explains that, in an era of decentralization in every domain, centralized thinking remains prevalent in our theories of knowledge, in our ways of analysing problems, and in our search for policy responses. "Politicians, managers and scientists are working with blinders on, focusing on centralized solutions even when decentralized approaches might be more appropriate, robust, or reliable" (Resnick 1994, 36).

This mindset is a generalized blockage that has affected Canada, perhaps even more dramatically than other countries, because of our economic culture. Over the last 125 years, circumstances have often endangered Canadian prosperity. Canada has had to learn ways and means to cope with these challenges in a manner that reconciled the geo-technical and socio-political constraints it operated under with the values, plans, and idiosyncrasies that its diverse population had chosen to prioritize at the time. There evolved a system of habitualized dispositions and inclinations to use certain institutional devices or stratagems that appeared to do the job of reconciling all those constraints most effectively.

The *economic culture* that has evolved in this fashion has underpinned the governance of the Canadian economy over the last century and has been based, as Herschel Hardin would put it, on the extensive use of two fundamental elements: *public enterprise* and *interregional redistribution* of the economic surplus (Hardin 1974). These two root stratagems have been used repeatedly from the earliest days of the federation, and one could chronicle their use at most stages in the evolution of the country during its first century.

In the recent past, both these tenets of the Canadian *economic culture* have come under attack: there has been a massive disengagement by the federal government from its public enterprises and from the massive interregional redistribution of resources. There are many reasons for this.

First, there has been some disenchantment with the results of central planning for national/regional development and an ensuing humbling of central planners. Disenchantment with guidance from the centre has led to decentralization in its two forms – privatization and subsidiarity. Many public enterprises have been privatized or have ceased to play a central policy role, and the weakening of the central government's financial capacity has eroded its capacity for massive interregional transfers.

Second, the globalization of markets and the attenuation of national economic borders, together with the greater modesty of federal policymakers, have forced all regions and provinces to consider the desirability of designing their *own* development strategies. Many provinces and regions had been engaged in such activities for quite a long time, but the process has been catalysed in the recent past.

A new economic culture has developed, building on a view of economic growth as emerging from below, through cities, communities, and regions, which are the real loci of networks, of entrepreneurship, and of the untraded interdependencies that are at the true source of economic dynamism. Growth in that sense "cannot be commandeered; it can only be nurtured and encouraged by providing a suitable environment. Growth occurs; it is not made. Within a growth model, all that human intervention can do is to discover the best conditions for growth and then try to meet them. In any given environment, the growing organism develops at its own rate" (Franklin 1990).

This new economic culture calls for upside-down thinking. In the beginning there are *local circumstances*. Each portion of the garden has specific needs and wants; only social interactions at the local level can play a big role in the construction of development networks and in ensuring that the social learning they underpin is effective (Paquet and Roy 1995). Yet even though this alternative cosmology has been suggested, it has had very little impact on the Canadian *gestalt* in good currency. The science and technology policy and corresponding innovation system that are currently discussed remain based on the idea of a centralized national system of innovation to be kickstarted from the centre rather than a fragmented and localized set of systems of innovation that would be nurtured from the periphery and only very lightly and subtly coordinated from the centre if need be (Paquet 1992; de la Mothe and Paquet 1994d).

WAYS OF ADAPTING

In Canada, the United States, and Mexico, the centralized mind syndrome looms large. In each country, however, it has taken different forms, and in each, in different ways, a process of questioning has begun.

The existing legal framework, a common language, a shared culture – these are the facts that underpinned the presumption that national character and national boundaries not only mattered, but were and are playing a determining role in shaping and catalysing the innovation process. Indeed, Nelson and Rosenberg (1993) state, in connection with the post–Second World War period, that "general perceptions about national societies and cultures tend to reify national systems" (16) echoing a strong sense that these national systems have sufficient resilience and robustness to make a significant difference, to influence meaningfully the national innovation system in the face of transnational forces that tend to shape business and technology.

But little attention has been paid to subnational cultures (state or local governments), to the new powers they have acquired as international integration triggered national disintegration, or to the new rules and conventions at that level. These latter may not be of equal importance in every country, but there is already plenty of evidence that these regional/community features, compounded with the joint regional/community-cum-sectoral/industrial effect built on specific synergies in the organization-location-technology nexus, may indeed play a significant role in explaining the dynamics of innovation (de la Mothe and Paquet 1994b).

New regional/local rules and conventions are important features of the Canadian industrial landscape where the industrial structure is sharply differentiated from region to region, where many of the ten provincial governments are powerful stakeholders and policymakers, where certain major metropolitan private and public organizations are actively involved in providing key resources to their innovation system, where national and provincial institutions such as research laboratories and universities and colleges have significant and differential local impacts very much shaped by proximity, and where even legal and cultural backgrounds vary widely. This explains a very diversified industrial landscape, one that would require a thorough subnational analysis to expose the real causes and sources of innovation and competitiveness. It also explains why, more than a decade ago, the Science Council of Canada made metropolitan technology councils a key feature of their proposed strategy (Conseil des sciences du Canada 1984).

The same point can be made about the United States with the extraordinary diversity of its regional/sectoral landscape, its various subcultures, its very different state strategies, its network of state universities, and so on. And the same may also be said of Mexico, where the thirty-two states may not weigh equally in the innovation equation, but where a certain degree of differentiation is already obvious. A recent survey of science in Mexico has revealed to the rest of North America that there is a much greater variety on the innovation system front in Mexico than one might gather from the superficial press coverage in the rest of North America (Maddox and Gee 1994).

We know that much of the progress of the wealth-creation process in the three countries is ascribable to the innovation system and rooted in product-based technology learning *à la* Storper, and we know that these innovativeness/competitiveness capabilities are based to a great extent on what Storper has called "conventions of identity and participation" (1993, 450). This remains, however, an unexplored corner in the new literature on economic development. Indeed, one must suspect that the regional worlds of production have not been sufficiently recognized as the source/cause of innovation and that a better use of the conventions of identity and participation as levers for policymakers might pay handsome dividends. But it is unlikely that this sort of strategy will be pursued with any robustness in Canada, the United States, or Mexico because of the centralized mind syndrome.

In Mexico, the resistance is clearly built into the socio-political system: the centralized governmental institutions underpinning the innovation system are quite reluctant to build on existing and potential regional strengths or even to allow the regional innovation systems to develop (Maddox and Gee 1994).

In the United States, even though there is no sign of an integrated strategy animating the national innovation system, and evidence that the federal policies in the post–Second World War period have "displaced the role of state governments as actors in this innovation system and contributed to some weakening in the informal ties that linked many corporate and academic research institutions" (Mowery and Rosenberg 1993, 61–2), the national innovation system concept appears alive and well. It may be nothing more than an *être de raison*, but it has remained such an icon that even those in positions of authority, arguing for massive devolution of federal powers towards the states, have not dared to suggest that it be altered.

As for Canada, there are three main factors in the equation: (1) the extent of the balkanization of the country and of the power of the regional stakeholders who are demanding more autonomy; (2) the federal determination to maintain a centralist stand even though the federal government lacks the fiscal capacity to inject significant resources; and (3) a powerful set of academic forces that for generations have been pressing to neutralize the emergence of any strong national strategy. These factors are bound to ensure that Canada will remain a stalled omnibus on the innovation system front with neither a meaningful top-down nor a significant bottom-up strategy (de la Mothe and Paquet 1994d).

CONCLUSION

A presumption put forward very cautiously by a few scholars a few years ago suggested that the most effective way to analyse an innovation system, and to intervene in it strategically, is to tackle the problem at the national level. Our contention is that focusing on subnational units of analysis would provide better insights into the workings of the "real worlds of production" and better levers for policy interventions on the innovation front (de la Mothe and Paquet 1998).

One might have expected that observers, researchers, and policy-makers would have focused more of their work and analyses on meso-innovation systems. However, this would be discounting unduly the power of the centralized mindset at work in so many sectors of politics, management, and science. The result is the ongoing pursuit of putative national systems where there are only regional/sectoral systems in fact.

The cost of such strategies is likely to be very high if, as we surmise, what is called for is a bottom-up policy. Consequently, it may not be unimportant to call for a return to the drawing board before it is too late: (1) a return to the cautious and tentative language used by Richard Nelson and a recognition that the hypothesis of national systems of innovation has not been validated yet, and (2) a plea for a more serious and careful examination of the alternative hypothesis suggested by the new paradigms of economic geography.

REFERENCES

Author's Note: The assistance of Anne Burgess, Monica Gattinger, and Dominique St-Arnaud is appreciated.

Acs, Z., J. de la Mothe, and G. Paquet. 1996. "Local Systems of Innovation: Toward an Enabling Strategy." In P. Howitt, ed., *The Implications of Knowledge-Based Growth for Microeconomic Policies*, 339–58. Calgary: University of Calgary Press.

Arthur, W.B. 1990. "'Silicon Valley' Locational Clusters: When Do Increasing Returns Imply Monopoly?" *Mathematical Social Sciences* 19:235–51.

Bes, M.P. 1993. "Partage des informations au sein des systèmes locaux d'innovation." *Revie d'économie régionale et urbaine* 3:565–77.

Boisot, M. 1987. *Information and Organizations*. London: Fontana/ Collins.

– 1995. *Information Space*. London: Routledge.

Brown, J.S., and P. Duguid. 1991. "Organizational Learning and Communities in Practice: Toward a Unified View of Working, Learning and Innovating." *Organization Science* 2 (1): 40–57.

Coleman, J.S. 1988. "Social Capital and the Creation of Human Capital." *American Journal of Sociology* 94 (supplement): 95–120.

Conseil des Sciences du Canada. 1984. *Le développement industriel au Canada – quelques propositions d'action*. Rapport no. 37. Ottawa: Conseil des sciences du Canada.

Dahmen, E. 1988. "Development Blocks in Industrial Economics." *Scandinavian Economic History Review* 36 (1).

de la Mothe, J., and G. Paquet. 1994a. "The Dispersive Revolution." *Optimum* 25 (1): 42–8.

– 1994b. "The Technology-Trade Nexus: Liberalization, Warring Blocs, or Negotiated Access?" *Technology in Society* 16 (1): 97–118.

– 1994c. "The Shock of the New: A Techno-Economic Paradigm for Small Economies." In M. Stevenson, ed., *The Entry into New Economic Communities: Swedish and Canadian Perspectives on the European Economic Community and*

North American Free Trade Accord, 13–27. Toronto: Swedish-Canadian Academic Foundation.

– 1994d. "Circumstantial Evidence: A Note on Science Policy in Canada." *Science and Public Policy* 21 (4): 261–8.

–, eds. 1996. *Evolutionary Economics and the New International Political Economy.* London: Pinter.

– 1998. "National Innovation Systems, Real Economies and Instituted Processes." *Small Business Economics* (forthcoming).

Dosi, G., and L. Marengo. 1994. "Some Elements of an Evolutionary Theory of Organizational Competences." In R.W. England, ed., *Evolutionary Concepts in Contemporary Economics*, 157–78. Ann Arbor: University of Michigan Press.

Dosi, G., and R.R. Nelson. 1994. "An Introduction to Evolutionary Theories in Economics." *Journal of Evolutionary Economics* 4 (3): 153–72.

Franklin, U. 1990. *The Real World of Technology.* Toronto: CBC Enterprises.

Granovetter, M. 1973. "The Strength of Weak Ties." *American Journal of Sociology* 78 (6): 1360–80.

Handy, C. 1992. "Balancing Corporate Power: A New Federalist Paper." *Harvard Business Review* 70 (6): 59–72.

– 1995. "Trust and the Virtual Organization." *Harvard Business Review* 73 (3): 40–50.

Hardin, H. 1974. *A Nation Unaware.* Vancouver: J.J. Douglas.

Johnson, B. 1992. "Institutional Learning." In B.A. Lundvall, ed., *National Systems of Innovation: Towards a Theory of Innovation and Interactive Learning*, 23–44. London: Pinter.

Loasby, B.J. 1991. *Equilibrium and Evolution.* Manchester: Manchester University Press.

Maddox, J., and H. Gee. 1994. "Mexico's Bid to Join the World." *Nature*, 28 April.

March, J.G. 1991. "Exploration and Exploitation in Organizational Learning." *Organization Science* 2 (1): 71–87.

Marengo, L. 1993. "Knowledge Distribution and Coordination in Organizations: On Some Social Aspects of the Exploitation vs Exploration Trade-off." *Revue internationale de systémique* 7 (5): 553–71.

Mowery, D.C., and N. Rosenberg. 1993. "The U.S. National Innovation System." In Nelson (1993).

Naisbitt, J. 1994. *Global Paradox.* New York: William Morrow.

Nelson, R.R., ed. 1993. *National Innovation Systems: A Comparative Analysis.* Oxford: Oxford University Press.

Nelson, R.R., and N. Rosenberg. 1993. "Technical Innovation and National Systems." In Nelson (1993, 3–27).

Nelson, R.R., and S.G. Winter. 1977. "In Search of a Useful Theory of Innovation." *Research Policy* 6 (1): 36–76.

Niosi, J., et al. 1992. "Les systèmes nationaux d'innovation: à la recherche d'un concept utilisable." *Revue française d'économie* 7 (1): 125–44.

Ohmae, K. 1993. "The Rise of the Region State." *Foreign Affairs* 72 (Spring): 78–87.

Paquet, G. 1989. "Science and Technology Policy under Free Trade." *Technology in Society* 11:221–34.

– 1990. "Internationalization of Domestic Firms and Governments: Anamorphosis of a Palaver." *Science and Public Policy* 17 (5): 327–32.

– 1992. "The Strategic State." In J. Chrétien, ed., *Finding Common Ground*, 85–101. Hull: Voyageur Publishing. A much extended and updated version of this paper was published under the same title in *Ciencia Ergo Sum* 3 (3): 257–61 (1996); 4 (1): 28–34 (1997); and 4 (2): 148–54 (1997).

– 1994. "Reinventing Governance." *Opinion Canada* 2 (2): 1–5.

Paquet, G., and J. Roy. 1995 "Prosperity through Networks: The Economic Renewal Strategy That Might Have Been." In S. Phillips, ed., *How Ottawa Spends 1995*, 137–58. Ottawa: Carleton University Press.

Peters, Tom. 1994. *Crazy Times Call for Crazy Organizations*. New York: Vintage.

Putnam, R.D. 1995. "Bowling Alone: America's Declining Social Capital." *Journal of Democracy* 6 (1): 65–78.

Resnick, M. 1994. "Changing the Centralized Mind." *Technology Review* 97 (5): 32–40.

Saxenian, A. 1994. *Regional Advantage*. Cambridge: Harvard University Press.

Storper, M. 1992. "The Limits of Globalization: Technology Districts and International Trade." *Economic Geography* 68 (1): 60–93.

– 1993. "Regional Worlds of Production: Learning and Innovation in the Technology Districts of France, Italy and the USA." *Regional Studies* 27 (5): 433–55.

Webber, A.M. 1993. "What's So New about the New Economy?" *Harvard Business Review* 71 (1): 24–42.

Wikstrom, S., and R. Normann. 1994. *Knowledge and Value – A New Perspective on Corporate Transformation*. London: Routledge.

3 Making the Most of North American Integration: The Challenges

SIDNEY WEINTRAUB

INTRODUCTION

The North American Free Trade Agreement (NAFTA), if it is to provide optimal benefits to the three member countries, must deepen well beyond the removal of border barriers and even the unimpeded flow of direct investment. Deepening refers to such issues as establishing common or compatible industrial standards, especially for inputs into final products; agreeing to non-restrictive standards for the provision of technical and professional services; upward harmonization of environmental and sanitary standards; compatible requirements for trucks and other surface transportation; rapid customs clearance; and the ability of each country to penetrate the regulatory processes of the others to monitor and prevent import restrictions in the guise of regulatory activity. Each of these areas is the subject of trinational negotiation.

Deepening has both positive and negative aspects. Co-production of final products in two or more countries and more efficient inventory controls, such as the use of the Japanese just-in-time techniques, demand this deepening.[1] This positive aspect is particularly germane in the automotive industry, by far the most important industrial sector in North American trade; it is essential in the provision of financial services in view of the large amount of funds and financial instruments that are exchanged daily; and most crucially, it is essential in data transmission.

The negative aspect is one familiar to trade policy: as one barrier declines, another is employed to take its place. As tariffs declined, non-tariff barriers grew in importance. When producers could not keep out foreign goods under the normal escape clause, as it exists in article 19 of the General Agreement on Tariffs and Trade (GATT) and in national legislation, other techniques were used, such as anti-dumping (AD) and countervailing duty (CVD) actions.

Deepening is necessary if NAFTA countries are to make the most of technical and managerial developments, such as basing production location on economic rather than protectionist factors or setting up plants of sufficient scale to service the needs of the North American market and beyond. The latter is particularly true for homogeneous products, such as toiletries, soaps, and detergents, but also for inputs into manufactured goods.

The pages that follow will develop these themes further and point to some necessary elements of the research agenda. The sentiment that pervades this discussion is that deepening is not just an option, it is a necessity: unless NAFTA deepens along the lines indicated, it should not and probably will not survive. A straightforward preferential area, protected by tariffs against outside countries and by regulatory and technical non-tariff barriers against other member countries, has little of a constructive nature to offer the world.

PRODUCTION AND INNOVATION

The conventional wisdom is that, under NAFTA, plant location and production will look more and more to servicing the entire North American market and not just national markets. As Lorraine Eden (1994b, 11) puts it, production is likely to be increasingly segmented, thereby increasing vertical intrafirm trade. At the same time, there will be greater plant specialization for horizontal trade across the entire North American market. Eaton, Lipsey, and Safarian (1994, 73) reach a generally similar conclusion, that a free trade area (FTA) encourages both inward and outward foreign direct investment (FDI) among the member countries. I accept these conclusions. It is precisely because I do that I insist on the importance of deepening to facilitate the outcomes that are posited.

For the purpose of this chapter, however, the more germane question is whether this double spread of production – increasing segmentation of production of inputs and greater concentration of the output of some final products for regional distribution and marketing – will lead to the spread of technology from the United States to the two economically weaker countries, particularly Mexico.

To answer this question requires some sorting out of definitions. There is a familiar distinction in the literature between basic research, little of which would be undertaken without public support, and various degrees of product-specific support of innovation – that is, forms of industrial policy (Scherer and Belous 1994, 35–7). Another familiar division of R&D is between innovation and adaptation. The need to serve local markets may stimulate adaptation of products and thus encourage decentralized innovation (Eaton, Lipsey, and Safarian 1994, 94).

Still another distinction would be between innovation in the form of new products and services, followed by substantial variations in these new products and services, and innovation in terms of managerial technology. An example of the first variety – devising and then significantly altering a product – is the personal computer: since its introduction, there have been rapid changes in computer technology. One would be tempted to call this phenomenon changes in hardware, except that the hardware changes in the computer industry stimulated a rash of software innovations. In the automobile industry, by contrast, the rapid changes in technology are not primarily related to the nature of the product itself, the automobile, but rather to managerial technology – that is, to the method of production and the relationships between suppliers and final assemblers. Lean production techniques deal with the latter. According to the U.S. Department of Commerce, value added per employee in the U.S. auto supplier industry rose from U.S.$48,000 in 1981 to U.S.$68,000 in 1991, and this was essentially the result of managerial and process innovation, not of changes in the underlying products (Klier 1994, 9).

This distinction – between managerial and process changes and product innovation – has special relevance for a relative newcomer to industrial development such as Mexico. Lean production in the U.S. auto industry was adapted from the Japanese example and is now being transferred to Mexico. The speed of diffusion is likely to be relatively rapid, stimulated by the expansion of the industry into Mexico as a result of the promise and now the reality of NAFTA.[2] This is particularly significant in that Mexico is unable to devote the same level of resources to basic R&D as the United States, or even Canada; nor, in general, can its firms invest as much in product innovation as its two integration partners. However, intrafirm process innovation holds much promise for Mexico, as already demonstrated by the new auto plants set up by Ford and General Motors. This transfer of process technology is likely to spread rapidly in the Mexican financial sector now that this market is being opened even sooner than contemplated by the negotiators of NAFTA; many U.S. and other non-Mexican banks have opened branches in Mexico or are showing an interest in establishing operations there.

Vertical integration of production will almost certainly lead to the spread of process innovation in the NAFTA countries. This is at the core of flexible production techniques.[3] Horizontal integration – the alloca-

tion of an entire product line to one location in the three-country area
– already is taking place for relatively homogeneous items, including
rather complex products such as auto engines, for which the Mexican
role is growing, but the innovation consequences of this type of product mandate are less certain. In still other industries, the traditional
separation of functions is likely to prevail, and thus for these the spread
of innovation is apt to be slow. The pharmaceutical industry is of this
nature. Here, the active ingredients for which R&D are most crucial
will most probably continue to be produced in the United States for
assembly into final products in the other NAFTA partner countries.

In sum, the integrative forces of NAFTA will stimulate the spread of
process innovation, particularly in the case of majority-owned subsidiaries.[4] The spread of basic and product R&D is likely to be slower, especially to Mexico. The outcomes will depend heavily on the nature of
the industry or service. This tentative conclusion should be an area for
future research.

DEEPENING AND EFFICIENCY

Technological and process improvements are optimized as economies
are integrated. It is evident that co-production of final products, or vertical integration, requires low border barriers. Without this, unneces-
sary costs are imposed, as tariffs must be paid on intermediate inputs.
Vertical integration does not require zero tariffs; the *maquiladora* system grew up on the Mexican border with the United States even though
the tariff on reimport of the enhanced commodity was levied on the
value added in Mexico. Clearly, however, a more privileged situation
will exist when the limit of zero tariffs is reached. Because the tariff on
value added will continue for this type of vertical trade (i.e., further
processing of inputs shipped from the United States and then reimported
after foreign value is added) between the United States and countries
with which it shares no free trade area, Mexico will have a tariff as well as
a proximity advantage. Most of this trade is intrafirm, but it need not be;
it is not completely intrafirm in the automobile industry.

One significant merit of NAFTA is that it formalizes this process: NAFTA
makes backsliding on tariff elimination most unlikely. This became evident in 1995 when Mexico responded to its economic crisis by imposing higher duties on imports from countries with which it had no free
trade agreement, but maintained the lower duties for other NAFTA countries. However, NAFTA has not assured the elimination of non-tariff barriers. The most important of these in North American trade are anti-
dumping regulations and countervailing duties. Enough has been written on this theme in the context of the Canada-U.S. FTA to obviate the

need to add here to this verbiage.[5] The constant concern of producers over petitions for CVDs and especially ADs adds to uncertainty and prejudices the smooth functioning of flexible production. It has proved politically impossible to complete the logic of an FTA and treat predatory practices as they are dealt with internally in the North American countries. The greatest chance that current AD and CVD practices will be altered lies in the hope that, one day, powerful corporations with great influence and clout in their own countries will seek modification in the interest of increasing their productivity as a consequence of NAFTA.

Just as AD and CVD usage soared as other import barriers declined, so should other less transparent barriers to trade multiply now that NAFTA is being implemented. A number of examples of this have surfaced: Mexico imposed labelling requirements with short notice on imports of consumer electronics; inspections for meat entering Mexico from the United States now take longer than before; the United States has been reluctant to lift the embargo on tuna imports from Mexico despite the dramatic reduction in incidental dolphin kills by Mexican tuna fishermen; and delays have grown on the U.S.-Mexico border because of the complexity of the rules of origin (Meyerson 1994).

Many of these impediments to trade, and consequently to the spread of process innovation, may merely reflect the problems of a new venture. This is apparently the case for customs delays, which are the result of the inexperience of customs inspectors and the complexity of the new rules. These inadvertent barriers can be expected to be overcome as NAFTA procedures become more familiar. Training of customs inspectors in the new rules and greater networking by customs officials in the three countries should alleviate many of these start-up problems.

However, other barriers are likely to be quite deliberate. The restrictiveness of U.S. anti-dumping procedures did not arise by accident. Deepening requires overcoming both types of impediments, the first kind (those involving the need for more experience) by training and the other (the search by domestic producers for non-transparent import barriers) by vigilance. The potential for the second type of barrier is greatest in the regulatory field and in the setting of standards. Mexico's original labelling requirements may or may not have had a protective intent – my view is that they did not – but they disrupted trade. In any event, they were promulgated by Mexico without prior consultation with its free trade partners. Mexico still does not routinely publish draft regulations in a sufficiently timely manner to receive public comments. Private industrial and service associations set their own standards in many fields – for products, legal and accounting services, the provision of insurance, data transmission, the size of trucks – and, unless the practice is monitored closely, it can be abused quite readily.

Deepening, therefore, requires the means whereby such processes in one country can be penetrated by governments, producers, and service providers in the other two countries. NAFTA does not have the elaborate judicial and monitoring institutions that exist in the European Union (EU) for this type of penetration, but even the EU needed a protracted process under Europe '92 to achieve internal free trade among the member countries. The future research agenda should include examination of deliberately obscured as well as inadvertent protection and suggestions on how to overcome these problems.

If NAFTA provides a basis for enhanced transfers of innovation techniques, it makes little sense to dilute these opportunities by impediments to trade in goods and services. This is what I have in mind by deepening – those actions necessary to avoid this dilution.

AREAS OF CONTROVERSY

By far the most controversial issue in the NAFTA debate in the United States was the fact that the U.S. was making a free trade agreement with a low-wage country like Mexico. The issue persists despite all the explanations given by economists that wage rates do not necessarily determine unit costs. My purpose here is not to enter into this debate except as it relates to the transfer of technology and the spread of innovation from the two richer countries to Mexico.

According to the U.S. Bureau of Labor Statistics, hourly compensation costs for production workers in manufacturing in Mexico were 15 per cent of those in the United States in 1992, but there were large variations by industry in Mexico. Setting overall manufacturing industry compensation in Mexico at 100, the index was highest, 186, for motor vehicles and equipment, and lowest, 50, for lumber and wood products (U.S. Department of Labour 1993). Technology gaps do not determine all the differences, either between Mexico and the United States or within Mexico itself, but they do provide a major part of the explanation.

There is need for caution in reaching general conclusions about the relationship between wages and productivity in Mexico. First, the data on productivity are not reliable. Second, because of the high level of unemployment/underemployment, increases in productivity do not translate rapidly into wage increases. Third, the relative youth of the Mexican population, the still low level of female participation in the workforce, and the continuing migration from rural areas to the cities together mean that the supply of labour in Mexico, especially low-skilled labour, will exceed the demand for some years to come and this will surely affect wage levels for the majority of the Mexican workforce.

Nevertheless, following their sharp decline in the mid-1980s, Mexican wages as a proportion of U.S. manufacturing wages rose incrementally but steadily from 1988 to 1994. This was reversed during the economic depression of 1995, but there were signs of recovery in 1996. Wages in Mexico are highest in those manufacturing sectors in which process innovations are most extensive. This reinforces the need to deepen NAFTA – to increase the potential for such innovations – in order to reduce the salience of the wage-gap issue in both Canada and the United States.

Two other issues that dominated the U.S. debate on NAFTA were the relationships between trade and the environment and between trade and working conditions. My purpose is not to enter into the justification for the linkages, but rather to discuss their potential for becoming new trade barriers.[6] There are already proposals for green (environmental) and blue (labour-related) AD measures. There is considerable pressure in the United States for strengthening the labour and environmental provisions of NAFTA for additional countries that might wish to accede to the agreement.[7]

My concern is that the linkages will be pushed too far and will then, either out of sincere motives or cynically, be transformed into additional non-tariff barriers. There is already a growing literature in the United States for the establishment of a new international environmental agency to operate in concert with the World Trade Organization to reconcile the conflicts at the intersection of the two themes.[8] The linkages between the three themes – trade, the environment, and labour conditions – are here to stay, and the research agenda should focus on the content of these linkages and on ways to promote the improvement of all three without placing an undue burden on the world's poorer countries. The target for the environmental and labour linkages in NAFTA was Mexico, not Canada or the United States, and the targets in the future are again likely to be developing and not economically mature countries.

THE RESEARCH AGENDA

I have written this brief essay not to reach conclusions, but primarily to point to areas that need further research if North American economic integration is to accomplish fully the aspirations of its founders.

Technology Transfer

Much more research needs to be done on the relationship between economic integration in North America and the encouragement of technology transfer. I have posited that the transfer of technology is most apt to come in the form of process technology – flexible production in industry and better utilization of information technology in services. If this is an accurate conclusion, what are the conditions for its optimization? How can other forms of R&D be promoted? Our information on the links between FDI and technology is growing but far from complete. These links almost certainly need elaboration in the context of an economic integration agreement such as NAFTA.

The Setting of Standards

A key component of deepening NAFTA is to work out common or compatible standards in a variety of fields – industry, the environment, sanitary and phytosanitary measures, trucking, finance, and many others. Industrial standards are relatively easy to work out in intrafirm trade, but not across firms. Standards are established by governments and private associations, sometimes working together across borders, sometimes confined to a single country. Studies are needed on how to institutionalize the setting of standards in order to facilitate coproduction and trade in goods and services and to prevent use of these standards as protectionist devices.

Regulations

Each country issues thousands of pages of new regulations each year, and many of these will affect production and trade. Regulations can be deliberately written to favour domestic interests, or they can impede trade and investment inadvertently. In either event, an institutional structure is needed so that the public and private sectors in each of the three NAFTA countries can penetrate the regulatory processes of the other two before new regulations are set in concrete. The research agenda should include techniques for accomplishing this.

Customs Inefficiencies

Customs delays can impede flexible production and, hence, the transfer of process innovations. Some of the current delays as goods cross borders are due to the slow learning curve with respect to the new rules involving country of origin and tariff levels. Others are physical, such as the inadequate infrastructure leading to and located at border-crossing points. Still others, particularly for entry into the United States from Mexico, are due to inspections for drugs and undocumented aliens. Some delays are the consequence of the inadequate networking of the computer systems of the customs officials of the exporting and importing countries. There is a broad research agenda for developing techniques to speed up customs and border-crossing procedures.

Other Aspects of Deepening

Many of the foregoing suggestions deal with devising techniques for deepening the operations of NAFTA. To this point, this discussion has focused on just one aspect of deepening. Deepening, however, can mean many other things. It can deal with, among other matters, infrastructure, transportation links, ease and rapidity of communications, common or compatible accounting standards, and compatible tax systems. Each of these areas merits examination.

Consultation and Coordination

The word "coordination" is used loosely by commentators on international affairs. Countries rarely coordinate their fiscal or monetary policies in order to satisfy some foreign concern. These matters are determined largely by domestic concerns. There is, however, scope for substantially closer consultation among key officials of the NAFTA countries. Mexico was not forewarned when the U.S. Immigration and Naturalization Service instituted what it first called a blockade to keep undocumented immigrants from crossing from Ciudad Juárez, Chihuahua, into El Paso, Texas. Advance notice would have helped and might have eased irritation. In some cases, advance notice is problematic. Despite the fact that there was as big an impact on Mexico and Canada as on the U.S. when the U.S. Federal Reserve Board raised interest rates repeatedly in 1994, it would have been difficult to forewarn the other two countries for fear of leaks. Nevertheless, there is room for consultation about monetary and fiscal thinking well before decisions to act are taken. A detailed examination of when and how consultation should take place among the three countries of NAFTA would be most valuable.

Monitoring Productivity Changes

It would be useful to Canada and the United States to have more reliable information on productivity changes, by sector, in Mexico and on how productivity increases are translated into wage increases. This could serve to calm the fears of many individuals and institutions in the two richer countries about the competitive pressures arising from low-wage Mexican labour.

Trade, Environment, and Labour Linkages

Finally, much research is necessary on the proper linkages among trade, the environment, and labour conditions. How far should these linkages go, what types of penalties should be considered, and what institutional arrangements would be desirable? Is the establishment of a new environmental organization for precisely this purpose – to facilitate the linkages and to establish penalties for violation of agreed standards – a good idea?

NAFTA, in my view, can be a valuable stimulus to productivity in North America. Improving productivity, as the above makes clear, requires more than the removal of border barriers; it needs continual innovations in all three countries, particularly in Mexico, the least developed of the three.

RELATIONSHIPS AMONG INNOVATION, COMPETITIVENESS, NAFTA AND SUSTAINABILITY

The following premises help define the nature of these relationships among innovation, competitiveness, and the sustainability of NAFTA.

1 For NAFTA to endure, each of the three member countries must be convinced that the agreement is beneficial to it. Equality of benefit is not essential, and indeed, the degree of benefit is impossible to measure, but a sense of individual overall benefit is necessary.
2 The elements that a country considers in deciding whether it is benefiting from NAFTA require definition. For the politician, these criteria include the number of jobs created from exports as compared to the perceived loss of jobs through imports, the shift in bilateral or trilateral trade balances, and economic impacts in particular districts or regions. For the economist or technician, the criteria are different. They include the growth in two-way trade, since year-by-year bilateral trade balances are largely ephemeral and essentially meaningless in a global trading structure; the growth in vertical and horizontal specialization that one would expect from economic integration; and improvement in technology sophistication, whether in product innovation or in production processes.
3 An important institutional aspect to the success of an integration arrangement concerns the speed with which defects in the operation of the agreement are corrected (e.g., the streamlining of customs procedures and the simplification of rules of origin; and the rapidity with which disputes are resolved).

An underlying assumption of an integration agreement between two highly developed and technologically advanced countries (Canada and the United States) and a low-income and technologically backward country (Mexico) is that the latter will advance more rapidly in income growth and technology development than the former. Failing this, the disparities that existed at the start of the process will grow, and in this case, the benefits to Mexico will be hard to discern. Mexico may not catch up for some time in product innovation, but it should be able to adapt process technology more rapidly with the agreement than without it. The product specialization inherent in vertical integration and the concentration of production stemming from horizontal integration should stimulate these advances in Mexico.

The implication is that over time the more advanced countries must continue to innovate if they wish to retain high incomes. The politicians who define benefits in terms of job loss and job creation, or who use bilateral trade balances as their measuring rod, resort to protectionism to rectify any catching up by Mexico. They are thus prepared to sacrifice the competitive stimulation that comes from vertical and horizontal integration in favour of short-term palliatives.

The division of labour among the three countries in the production of goods and services will inevitably change as integration proceeds. All can benefit only if innovation is stimulated in all three. The comparative advantages that now exist, such as cheaper labour in Mexico and greater innovation in the other two, will alter, but this will take time. The benefits of free trade will be shared by all three countries only if innovation occurs in each one of them.

NOTES

1   Thomas H. Klier (1994, pp. 8–18) notes that the U.S. automobile supplier industry produces thousands of parts which, in 1991, amounted to U.S.$63 billion in shipments and U.S.$25 billion in valued added. Under co-production, parts can also be produced outside the United States.

2   Mansfield (1993) concludes that the rate of intrafirm diffusion of flexible manufacturing systems has been lower in the United States than in Western Europe and Japan.

3   Flexible manufacturing is driven by advances in information technology. An interesting article by Paul B. Carroll (1994) deals with the exploding use of computers in industry, the media, agriculture, and other sectors now that Mexico is part of NAFTA.

4 This circular flow of technological, marketing, and organizational transfers from parent to majority-owned subsidiary and then back again is noted in Encarnation (1994, 310).

5 I will cite only two books here, one by Canadians and the other from the United States: Boddez and Trebilcock (1993) and Boltuck and Litan (1991).

6 As an aside, I supported the linkages in the context of a trade integration agreement such as NAFTA.

7 U.S. congressmen Richard Gephardt and Bill Richardson, both senior in the Democratic leadership of the House of Representatives, have proposed that any FTA with Chile be bilateral, rather than through accession to NAFTA, precisely to strengthen the environmental and labour provisions as well as make them an integral part of the agreement, not supplemental as in NAFTA. My reading of the situation is that whether Chile enters via accession or reaches a bilateral FTA with the United States, there will be intense disagreements on how to deal with the labour and environmental provisions.

8 Two books on this subject are Runge (1994) and Esty (1994).

REFERENCES

Boddez, Thomas M., and Michael J. Trebilcock. 1993. *Unfinished Business.* Toronto: C.D. Howe Institute.

Boltuck, Richard, and Robert E. Litan, eds. 1991. *Down in the Dumps.* Washington, D.C.: Brookings Institute.

Carroll, Paul B. 1994. "Foreign Competition Spurs Mexico to Move into High-Tech World." *Wall Street Journal,* 5 July 1.

Eaton, B. Curtis, Richard G. Lipsey, and A. Edward Safarian. 1994. "The Theory of Multinational Plant Location in a Regional Trading Area." In Eden (1994a).

Eden, Lorraine, ed. 1994a. *Multinationals in North America.* Calgary: University of Calgary Press.

– 1994b. "Multinationals in North America: An Introduction to the Issues." In Eden (1994a).

Encarnation, Dennis J. "Intra-firm Trade in North America and the European Community." In Eden (1994a).

Esty, Daniel C. *Greening the GATT: Trade, Environment and the Future.* Washington, D.C.: Institute for International Economics.

Klier, Thomas H. 1994. "The Impact of Lean Manufacturing on Sourcing Relationships." *Economic Perspectives,* Federal Reserve Bank of Chicago, July/August, 8–18.

Mansfield, Edwin. 1993. "The Diffusion of Flexible Manufacturing Systems in Japan, Europe and the United States." *Management Science* 39 (2): 149–59.

Myerson, Allen R. 1994. "Free Trade with Mexico? Not for All." *New York Times*, 2 June, D1.

Runge, C. Ford. *Freer Trade, Protected Environment: Balancing Trade Liberalization and Environmental Interests.* New York: Council on Foreign Relations Press.

Scherer, F.M., and Richard S. Belous. 1994. *Unfinished Tasks: The New International Trade Theory and the Post-Uruguay Round Challenges.* Washington, D.C.: National Planning Association; Toronto: C.D. Howe Institute.

U.S. Department of Labor, Bureau of Labor Statistics. 1993. "Hourly Compensation Costs for Production Workers in Manufacturing Industries, Mexico, 1975–1992." December.

PART TWO

National Systems of Innovation in North America

4 Canada's National R&D System

JORGE NIOSI

THEORY

Technological innovation is conducted for the most part within business enterprises. However, the institutional environment is key to understanding whether firms will be successful or not in creating new products and processes. In fact, innovation is a nation-specific phenomenon: almost all of it takes place in a limited number of national settings, basically the OECD (Organization for Economic Cooperation and Development) countries in Western Europe, Southeast Asia, and North America. Even among these industrialized countries, national differences are enormous. They differ not only in the share of the gross domestic product (GDP) that they invest in research and development, but also in the industries they have privileged, their areas of comparative advantage and the functioning of their institutions vis-à-vis innovation.

The larger of these industrial nations are better characterized as having an *offensive strategy*: many of their companies excel at launching new and improved products and processes in high-technology areas. These countries (like the U.S., the U.K., France, and Japan) typically spend nearly 3 per cent of their GDP in R&D. Other, smaller nations, like Sweden and Switzerland, are *niche innovators*, with their high R&D spending concentrated in a few industries in which they are leaders. Other countries are more typically *followers*, like Belgium, Canada, and Denmark. Many of their companies follow foreign innovation through some R&D, or buy it in either intangible or tangible form, from more innovative countries. Most less-developed countries have a *traditional strategy*: they do not conduct R&D, and they buy embodied technology from more advanced nations.

Some countries are superior to others in the "upstream" areas of innovation, like the United States and the United Kingdom in basic and applied research. Others, like Japan or South Korea, are more active in the area of development, particularly in improving existing industrial products and processes.

In some countries, like Canada, universities play a major part in the national system of innovation (NSI), with business enterprises having a less pivotal role. In the United States, research universities are closely linked to business enterprises through numerous agreements, research contracts, and cooperative work. In Japan, business enterprise performs the dominant role in the national system of innovation, and government laboratories and universities play a more subordinate part.

Similarly, public funding varies in importance from country to country and in the different missions that governments have favoured. In countries like the U.S., the U.K., and France, military missions have traditionally absorbed the majority of government funds for R&D. Conversely, in Canada, Denmark, and Switzerland, civilian missions (communications, health, or environmental R&D) have been the major preoccupations of public and publicly financed R&D. Since the Second World War, Germany and Japan have also given priority to commercial rather than defence missions, a factor that contributed to their outstanding performance in most markets for civilian products.

The concept of national systems of innovation tries to capture some of these national specificities. In the more strict sense, national systems of innovation are defined as *R&D systems:* sets of organizations (universities, government laboratories, and industrial enterprises with R&D capabilities) that contribute to the creation of new and improved products and processes within national boundaries (Niosi et al. 1993). The environment of these innovating agencies is sustained by financial and government institutions and organizations that fund, regulate, and support innovation. These organizations are linked by flows of personnel, funding, information, and regulations, as well as cooperative agreements and competition. But the relative importance of the three main components (academia, government-run labs, and industry) as well as the type of links between them vary from one country to another. When the public and financial environment is included, one is defining a *national system of innovation.*

The idea that countries differ in the way they conduct technological innovation – that they each have a unique NSI – was first proposed by B.-A. Lundvall (1988, 1992), R.R. Nelson (1988, 1992, 1993), and C. Freeman (1987, 1988, 1995). These authors have produced somewhat different definitions of national innovation systems. Lundvall emphasized the knowledge dimensions and the interactive character of the learning processes taking place between users and producers within the borders of the nation-state. Freeman stressed the role of private institutions in supporting innovation, such as corporate R&D, in-house training, and industry-university cooperation. Nelson put more accent on the public institutions that regulate, finance and keep the innovative process alive. All three make the distinction between the narrow definition of NSI, which encompasses only the R&D-active institutions and the public regulatory agencies, and the broad sense of the concept, which includes the supporting private (i.e., banks) and public (government infrastructure, education systems) institutions. In spite of the emphasis put on one or another of the elements and notwithstanding some theoretical differences (Nelson is a committed evolutionist, while Lundvall and Freeman are not), the three authors are making reference to the same phenomenon and their arguments for advancing the concept are similar.

Historical and geographical factors explain the specific characteristics of the different NSIs. From the seventeenth century, the United Kingdom and France were the largest colonial powers in Europe, and their rivalries and conflicts explain a good part of the world's political geography. The United States became a world hegemonic power only during and after the Second World War, and it has, since then, made the largest military R&D effort of any country on the globe. Conversely, smaller countries like Canada and the Scandinavian and Benelux nations have little or no military vocation, considering their powerful neighbours, and have invested government credits for R&D in civilian missions. Also, countries without colonies, like Germany and Japan, have sought either to develop synthetic materials or to save (reuse) imported materials: their innovation systems have been directed more towards reducing the consumption of natural materials that other countries, like the U.K. and France, could find in their overseas territories. Countries with abundant resources and space, like the United States, conversely, favoured material-intensive innovations. Finally, industrial latecomers have tended to give the state a larger role in their innovation system, either as a direct promoter of innovation, as in France, or as a coordinator and supervisor, as in Japan.

Technological innovation is all about learning, and particularly about interactive learning. Institutions facilitate a society's learning by promoting the flow of ideas both from abroad to national innovative agents and among the latter. Students trained at national universities move scientific and engineering knowledge from academia to industry. Conversely, industrial innovation stimulates university research through new equipment, new ideas, and direct enquiries. The user-producer relationship is also key to industrial innovation (Lundvall 1988; von Hippel 1988), and most user-producer interaction takes place within national boundaries.

The issue of the relative importance of *national* as opposed to *international* flows of ideas and personnel is increasingly debated (Niosi and Bellon 1994). The internationalization of corporate R&D is a growing phenomenon, one that accompanies the growing multinationalization of industrial firms. International technological alliances are moving ideas and people from one country to another. The international transfer of technology is a key factor in the Southeast Asian industrial miracles. International productivity has converged, at least within regions (Abramovitz and David 1996; Maddison 1994). And institutional innovations can also be copied: after the First World War the Japanese and the West European corporations adopted American manufacturing techniques, like Fordism and Toyotism; conversely, U.S. corporations copied just-in-time and total quality management from the Japanese. What, then, remains "national" in national systems of innovation?

National systems of innovation remain different, in spite of some elements of convergence, for three reasons. First, national differences in resource endowments still exist, as do market sizes. Small industrial countries, like the Scandinavian nations, will develop much more specialized areas of innovation, while countries like the United States may be the host of a very diversified innovation system.

Second, the general trend towards decreased state intervention means less control over market forces. These forces increase divergence among industrial countries, not convergence. Krugman (1993) shows that the geographical spread of the auto industry in Europe, compared to its geographic concentration in North America, is due to national barriers. In the absence of these barriers, the European auto industry would probably be concentrated to a much greater degree in only a few locations.

Finally, even though institutional and technological imitation and transfer are universal, both technical and managerial knowledge is altered when it crosses borders. Nippon industrial products, even those that imitate Western products, tend to be smaller, owing to the lack of physical space in Japan. Quality control, an American management innovation, experienced a qualitative change when it was adopted in Japan, to become a major competitive weapon in international business. In addition, organizational innovation cannot be thoroughly imitated: it flows with perpetual adjustments and changes. This is also true with respect to public institutions that support innovation: they can only be partially copied in other countries, as they must be adapted to existing public institutions that reflect other social forces and national cultures.

Technological and institutional convergence, therefore, does not come close to erasing national differences in innovation systems.

CANADA'S NATIONAL SYSTEM OF INNOVATION

Canada as a Technological Follower

Canada was a latecomer to industrialization, contemporary with Japan, Sweden, and Italy. Unlike Japan and Sweden, Canada did not make any major policy effort to accelerate its catching up with early industrializers. Its slow start in, and low level of, industrial R&D is generally explained by the combination of two factors: "[while] many Canadian subsidiaries had free access to the research of large parent companies, most Canadian companies were too small to embark on original research" (Eggleston 1978, 379).

Few Canadian firms were conducting R&D before the Second World War. Government laboratories were among the most visible R&D performers. In the nineteenth century, the first public laboratories to appear conducted agricultural and fisheries R&D in order to support the small and medium-sized enterprises active in these areas. Ontario Hydro's research division was, and remains, one of the most important, having started its research activities in 1912. Several provinces started R&D programs in the 1920s. Such initiatives included the Alberta Research Council, created in 1921, which later produced the basic methods for extracting oil from tar sands, and the Ontario Research Foundation, founded in 1928 and credited with, among other early achievements, important studies for the textile industry (Brown 1967, 215). In 1916 the National Research Council (NRC) was founded by the federal government as an advisory organization. It became the largest and most diversified government laboratory in Canada. The NRC built its first laboratories in 1932; its personnel increased from 300 in 1939 to 700 in 1945, 2,400 in 1959, and 3,400 in 1987. The NRC now represents nearly 15 per cent of Canadian federal laboratories expenditures. In 1947 the NRC created a crown corporation, Canadian Patents and Development Limited, in order to make available to industry, through licensing agreements, the intellectual property resulting from publicly funded R&D. By 1990, when it was disbanded, this corporation had become one of the largest patent holders in the country. In 1947 the Department of National Defence took responsibility for all military R&D conducted in the NRC. In 1952 Atomic Energy of Canada Limited (AECL) was created as a federal crown corporation in order to develop Canada's electro-nuclear system, the Candu, on the basis of the research conducted in NRC labs.

Up to the mid-1960s, however, the links between industrial and government research were less pronounced in Canada than in the United States. In 1965, for instance, 53 per cent of U.S. federal government intramural R&D expenditures were allocated to development in contrast to 16 per cent in Canada. This inward orientation of Canadian government laboratories was attributable to the smaller size of Canada's industrial base, to its smaller defence effort, and to the lack of university research facilities. Canadian government laboratories, up to this point, filled in for an underdeveloped university research system. In 1963 the ratio of U.S. to Canadian university research expenditures was 40:1 (Lithwick 1969).

In Canadian private industry, R&D was unusual before the Second World War. In 1924 Imperial Oil, the Canadian subsidiary of the Standard Oil Company of New Jersey (today's Exxon), formally started R&D in Canada, building its first lab in 1930. In 1925 a group of pulp and paper companies teamed together with McGill University to start what has become the oldest and most active industrial research consortium in Canada: Paprican, the Pulp and Paper Research Institute of Canada.

During and immediately after the Second World War, several large government R&D centres were created, including those of the federally owned Polymer Corporation and the provincial B.C. Research (both in 1944), Ottawa's Defence Research Board (1947), and the already mentioned AECL.

In this period, the private sector also increased its involvement in R&D, but at a slower pace. Canada's economy was enjoying high rates of growth in these years because of foreign direct investment and massive development of natural resources. The first official government survey of industrial R&D, conducted in 1955, showed that 377 corporations had a research program; their aggregate expenditures that year were Can$66 million. Prominent among them was Alcan, which had started its R&D program in Canada in 1946. By 1961, when the second survey took place, Canadian industrial R&D expenditures were close to Can$100 million. New companies were undertaking R&D in this period. Many of the largest industrial labs of today were formed then, among them Northern Telecom (starting in 1957). However, by comparison with the American R&D effort (U.S.$11 billion or 110 times the Canadian expenditure), Canada's R&D was still at the infant stage.

In 1968 another federal survey found that 580 private companies had R&D facilities. Of these new research facilities, that of IBM Canada in Toronto, founded in 1967, was the most important. The 1960s and 1970s witnessed expanded R&D efforts by both federal and provincial governments. Quebec was a latecomer that embraced the new trend with particular devotion. In 1969 the Quebec government, almost half a century after Alberta's first commitment to R&D, founded the Centre de recherche industrielle du Québec, which became Canada's second-largest provincial research organization. In 1970, following Ontario Hydro by more than fifty years, Hydro-Québec founded the Institut de recherche en électricité du Québec (IREQ), which became one of Canada's largest research organizations.

CANADA'S PRESENT R&D SYSTEM

This impressive growth notwithstanding, Canada's effort was and remains small by international standards. A first and often cited macro-indicator of the country's weak technological and scientific effort is the expression of its R&D expenditures as a percentage of GDP. Canada ranks sixth among the world's seven largest industrial countries (G-7), well behind the United States, West Germany, Japan, the United Kingdom, and France, and almost on a parity with Italy. Smaller industrial economies, like those of Sweden, Switzerland, or the Netherlands, also spend more than Canada on R&D (Table 4.1). Canada's effort, compared to that of the United States, is only 6.7 per cent, and 11 per cent to that of Japan. This is due both to Canada's smaller economy and to its lower R&D effort.

A second indicator of Canada's weakness is patents. Japan took the world leadership in patents in the late 1970s, followed by the United States, West Germany, France, and Korea (see Table 4.2). Canada ranks low among industrial countries, following even smaller competitors like Sweden, Switzerland, Austria, Australia, and Finland. On a per capita basis, Canada's position looks still more fragile: in 1994 Canada's residents obtained only 30 patents per million population, against 216 for the United States, 582 for Japan, and 355 for Switzerland. On that ranking, Canada stood only higher than Spain.

Table 4.1
R&D Expenditures in the G-7 Countries, 1993

	U.S.	Japan	Germany	France	U.K.	Italy	Canada
Total $billions	123.1	74.8	37.3	26.0	21.6	13.2	8.3
% of GDP	2.72	2.93	2.48	2.41	2.19	1.3	1.5

Source: OECD, *Main Science and Technology Indicators* (Paris, 1995).

Table 4.2
Patents Granted to Own Residents as a Percentage of Total World Patents: Industrialized Market Economies, 1994

Country	Share of World Total Patents	Patents per Million Patents (%)	Population
1. Japan	72,757	29.4	582
2. United States	56,067	22.7	216
3. West Germany	20,766	8.4	260
4. France	13,575	5.5	234
5. Korea	5,774	2.3	131
6. Italy	5,393	2.2	93
7. United Kingdom	5,222	2.1	90
8. Switzerland	2,485	1.0	355
9. Sweden	2,068	0.8	230
10. Austria	1,465	0.6	183
11. Australia	1,259	0.5	70
12. Netherlands	1,182	0.5	79
13. Finland	935	0.4	187
14. Canada	852	0.3	30
15. Belgium	760	0.3	76
16. Spain	704	0.3	18
17. Ireland	494	0.2	124
18. Denmark	439	0.2	88
19. Israel	392	0.2	78
20. Norway	316	0.1	79
World total	247,363	100	

Source: World Intellectual Property Organization.

Owing to the smaller size of Canada's markets and its scarce human resources, its NSI is specialized, its R&D efforts concentrated in only a few industries. These areas are telecommunications equipment, aerospace, engineering, and scientific services, including biotechnology. When three other industries are added (finance, other electronic equipment, and pharmaceutical products), the six together represent over 50 per cent of Canadian firms' R&D, as measured by their spending intentions in 1995 (Table 4.3).

Within these industries, the concentration of R&D is also fairly high. The ten largest spenders account for a full one-third of Canada's business expenditure on R&D (BERD), and the twenty-five largest represent nearly 50 per cent of this amount (Tables 4.4 and 4.5).

Among the largest performers there are a significant number of foreign-owned corporations, including IBM Canada (computer software), Pratt & Whitney Canada (aircraft engines), and Ericsson Telecommunications (communications software). In fact, Canada's percentage of domestic R&D under foreign control is one of the highest in the world.

In 1993 some 449 foreign firms performed R&D in Canada (nearly 10 per cent of the country's business performers), and their total expenditures represented Can$2,017 million – that is, 19 per cent of the Can$11 billion of Canada's total intramural expenditures (TIE) on R&D or 31.7 per cent of the Can$6,374 million of business expenditures on R&D. Because of its good education system, affluent market, and political stability, Canada is one of the most attractive countries for expatriate industrial R&D. Its business sector, however, has not been the most active among industrial countries in R&D (Table 4.6). This explains Canada's overall underinvestment in R&D as evidenced in previous tables.

Table 4.3
Percentage of GERD by Industry Intentions, 1995

Industry	% of GERD
Telecommunications equipment	15
Aircrafts and parts	11
Engineering and scientific services*	9
Finance, insurance, and real estate	6
Other electronic equipment	6
Pharmaceutical products and medicine	6
Business machines	5
All other industries	42
Total, all industries (%)	100
Total amount spent on R&D, all industries (Can$millions)	6999
* Includes dedicated biotechnology firms.	

Source: Statistics Canada, *Industrial Research & Development 1995 Intentions* (Ottawa 1995), Cat. No. 88-202.

Table 4.4
Concentration of Industrial R&D among Canadian Companies, 1995
(percentage of total BERD)

Rank	Percentage of Total BERD
Top 10	33
Top 25	45
Top 50	55
Top 75	61
Top 100	65

Source: Statistics Canada, *Industrial Research & Development* (Ottawa 1995), Cat. No. 88-202.

Table 4.5
Top Twenty-five Industrial Performers in R&D in Canada, 1994

Name	1994 (Can $ millions)	Control	R&D as a % of Revenue	Industrial Sector
1. Northern Telecom Ltd.	1491	Canada	12.3	Telecomm. equipment
2. IBM Canada Ltd.	257	U.S.	3.0	Computers, software
3. Pratt & Whitney Canada	221	U.S.	14.4	Aircraft engines
4. CAE Inc.	181	Canada	17.6	Electronics
5. Atomic Energy of Canada	176	Can. govt	53.8	Nuclear energy
6. Ontario Hydro	165	Ont. govt	1.9	Electric utility
7. Hydro-Québec	134	Que. govt	1.9	Electric utility
8. Merck Frosst Canada	104	U.S.	24.2	Pharmaceuticals
9. Bell Canada	103	Canada	1.3	Telecomm. services
10. Alcan Aluminum Ltd.	98	Canada	0.9	Mines and metals
11. Ericsson Communications	93	Sweden	37.2	Telecomm. equipment
12. Bombardier	89	Canada	1.9	Transp. equipment
13. Connaught Laboratories	79	France	19.4	Pharmaceuticals
14. Imperial Oil Ltd.	89	U.S.	1.0	Oil and gas
15. Noranda	62	Canada	0.9	Metals and forest products
16. Newbridge Networks	60	Canada	10.9	Telecomm. equipment
17. Nova Corp.	53	Canada	1.4	Oil, gas, chemicals
18. Telus Corp.	51	Canada	4.1	Telecomm. services
19. Apotex Inc.	47	Canada	16.2	Pharmaceuticals
20. Inco	45	Canada	1.3	Non-ferrous metals
21. Mitel Corp.	37	Canada	7.5	Telecomm. equipment
22. Magna International	36	Canada	1.0	Automotive parts
23. Allied Signal Canada	36	U.S.	9.7	Avionics
24. Wyeth-Ayerst Canada	35	U.S.	n.a.	Pharmaceuticals
25. Spar Aerospace	34	Canada	6.0	Satellites, electronics

Source: Globe & Mail, Report on Business Magazine (Toronto), July 1995, 91.

Table 4.6
Percentage of GERD Financed by Each Sector in the G-7 Countries, 1993

	Business Enterprises	Government Sector	Other National Sources	Abroad	Total
Canada	42.3	42.4	5.3	10.0	100
France*	45.7	44.3	1.3	8.7	100
Germany	60.1	37.1	0.5	2.3	100
Italy	49.9	45.9	n.d.	4.2	100
Japan	68.2	21.4	10.3	0.1	100
United Kingdom	52.1	32.3	3.9	11.7	100
United States	58.9	39.0	2.1	n.d.	100

Source: OECD, Main Science and Technology Indicators (Paris, 1995).
*French data are for 1992.

The issue of Canada's industrial underinvestment in technological development has been much debated. Today, it seems evident that several independent factors have been at work. First, because of its abundant natural resources, Canada's industrial structure exhibits an overrepresentation of resource-based, non-technology-intensive industries, such as pulp and paper and other forest industries, metal transformation, oil and gas refining, and basic petrochemicals. Conversely, high-technology industries requiring large markets, such as consumer electronics, semiconductor fabrication, and pharmaceuticals, are underrepresented.

Second, nearly 50 per cent of Canada's manufacturing industry is under foreign control. Foreign-owned subsidiaries in some key industries, like automobiles, tend to perform little R&D in Canada.

Third, many Canadian corporations are too small in size to perform any R&D or to be captured by official statistics. This is true in some high-technology industries like software development, biotechnology, and advanced materials (Lipsett and Lipsey 1994). Larger firms display a greater propensity to perform R&D than smaller ones, and when they do so their efforts are generally visible.

Finally, Canadian-owned and -controlled multinational corporations tend to perform an important and increasing share of their R&D abroad, close to larger markets. This point will be developed later.

THE THREE MAIN COMPONENTS OF CANADA'S NSI

Industry

Some 5,000 enterprises are now conducting R&D in Canada. Some of their characteristics were described in the previous section. Most of these performers are small and medium-sized enterprises; a majority operate in areas like engineering and scientific services (including biotechnology), software development for computer services, machinery, electrical and electronic equipment, and fabricated metal products.

Canada's industrial innovators are linked together through a dense set of cooperative research networks. These collaborative networks are concentrated in four areas: electronics (including the production of electronic parts and components, telecommunication equipment, computers and other electronic equipment), biotechnology, advanced materials, and transportation equipment. The Canadian R&D activity in these four areas includes hundreds of cooperative agreements among private firms, and between these and government laboratories and universities (Niosi 1995). Most of these agreements are company-to-company alliances – that is, collaborative research contracts between independent firms for the purpose of creating new and improved processes and products. These include a majority of national alliances (close to 80 per cent of the technological alliances of Canadian firms occur within Canadian borders) and a minority of international alliances (the remaining 20 per cent). Among the former, we should mention the numerous technological agreements that both Ontario Hydro and Hydro-Québec have with their respective equipment suppliers in order to improve the performance and reliability of the electrical equipment that the utilities purchase; these are cases of user-producer interaction. A major case among the latter has been the long-term alliance between Bio-Chem Pharma, a leading Montreal biotechnology company, and the British multinational Glaxo Plc for the purpose of developing and manufacturing 3TC, a drug that has become the most successful pharmaceutical in the treatment of AIDS.

Some of these alliances, however, are long-term standing agreements creating non-profit collaborative research centres. One such collaborative non-profit venture is the Computer Research Institute of Montreal (CRIM), created in 1985; the institute has mixed public and private funding and close to 100 private computer and telecommunications software members.

Universities

With some seventy-seven higher-education institutions, Canada's university sector has become the second most important institutional actor in the country's national innovation system, relegating government laboratories to third place. In the last twenty-five years, the number of Canadian universities has grown and the numbers of advanced-studies programs, research centres, university laboratories, and graduate students have grown at an even faster pace. By 1994, fifty-six Canadian universities had graduate programs (Statistics Canada 1996). In 1993–94, university enrolment reached 574,000 full-time students and 285,000 part-time students, with almost 37,000 full-time teachers. At the end of the 1980s, Canada had the world's highest proportion of university-educated adults, the highest university enrolment rate, and the highest public expenditure on education (Statistics Canada 1993). However, Canada falls to eighth place when only the proportion of university graduates with engineering and applied sciences degrees is considered.

In the last decade, from the mid-1980s to the mid-1990s, the links between Canadian industry and the university system have become much more dense and more similar to the close industry-university relationship in the United States (Doutriaux and Barker 1995). The universities of Toronto, McGill, Montreal, British Columbia, Laval, Alberta,

McMaster, Queen's, Waterloo, and Calgary were the most active in terms of industry-sponsored research, patents, royalties, licences, industrial spin-offs, and other indicators of technology transfer activities.

Linkages between industry and universities also include research contracts awarded to university researchers by business enterprises, collaborative industry-university research projects, permanent industry-university research centres, the provision of highly qualified personnel to industry by universities, co-organized university-industry training programs, and technology transfer *stricto sensu* (licences awarded by universities and university researchers to industrial firms).

By 1993 Canadian universities were spending some U.S.$2,100 billion (11 per cent of which was funded by industrial firms) as compared to the U.S.$20,550 billion spent by American universities, a ratio of 1:10 (OECD 1995). In financial terms, and with respect to Canada's population and GDP, the Canadian university system had succeeded in catching up with the American university system.

In addition, Canada ranked sixth in the world in terms of scientific publications in refereed journals. Its performance was comparable to that of any advanced industrial nation, both in terms of the number of publications and in terms of the impact (as measured by citations) of those publications (National Science Board 1993).

Government Laboratories

In 1995 the laboratories reporting to Environment Canada, the National Research Council (NRC), Natural Resources Canada, and Agriculture Canada were the most important elements of federal research and development. The nearly 200 federal laboratories represented some 17 per cent of Canada's gross expenditure on R&D.

The provincial governments showed a smaller commitment. Their efforts were mostly concentrated on the development of local natural resources and the support of small and medium-sized enterprises. In 1995 provincial research organizations (PROs) represented only 1 per cent of Canada's GERD, but they played an important role in the support of local enterprises and in the development of some natural resources, like hydroelectricity and oil sands.

The general trend in the 1980s and 1990s, in Canada as in most other developed countries, including the U.S. and the U.K., was a relative decline of the state's direct research activities and stagnant direct funding of innovation activities. In the 1990s this meant reduced or frozen budgets for Canadian government laboratories and the privatization of a few of them. This observation is also valid for provincial research organizations.

THE INTERNATIONALIZATION OF CANADA'S INDUSTRIAL R&D

Like most multinational corporations (MNCs) based in other countries, Canada's largest industrial enterprises are delocalizing their R&D activities. This trend started after the Second World War when some large primary metal producers, pulp and paper companies, and other industrial firms with headquarters in Canada acquired – and in a few cases created – industrial laboratories abroad.

Market considerations seem essential in the decision to create or acquire R&D capabilities abroad. Multinational corporations based in the smaller industrial countries invest closer to the larger markets (primarily the United States and Western Europe, and secondarily Japan and Australia) and maintain R&D capabilities in order to support foreign manufacturing, interact with foreign customers, and learn from users and innovative milieus (Granstrand et al. 1992). Another motivation for creating foreign laboratories was to support technology transfer from the parent company (Ronstadt 1984).

By 1994, Canada's MNCs had founded or taken over R&D laboratories in the United States, the United Kingdom, France, Germany, Italy, Switzerland, Spain, Japan, Australia, and Austria. They had also created laboratories in a few of the largest developing countries, including Brazil, China, India, Mexico, and Turkey.

Most Canadian firms with foreign R&D capabilities were large MNCs, among them Alcan, Bombardier, Inco, McCain Foods, Moore, Molson, Noranda, Northern Telecom, Seagram, and George Weston. Others were large corporations with substantial foreign direct investments, including CAE Inc., John Labatt, Magna International, Mitel, Nova, Spar Aerospace, and Unican. A few were small and medium-sized firms with some industrial activities abroad, such as BioChem Pharma, Davstar Industries, Deprenyl Research, SBN Systems, and TecSyn International.

Between 1983 and 1986, Canada's largest firms conducted over one-third of their R&D abroad and obtained from foreign locations over 35 per cent of their total patents (Cantwell 1992). This compares with 31 per cent of patents obtained by Swedish multinationals abroad, 43 per cent by Swiss, 45 per cent by British, and 70 per cent by Dutch firms.

These figures pinpoint the significant, but by no means overwhelming, degree of internationalization of Canada's national R&D system. By 1993, of R&D expenditures of foreign subsidiaries in the United States, those by Canadian subsidiaries, at U.S.$2.1 billion, were fourth in importance after those by Swiss (U.S.$2.5 billion), German (U.S.$2.3 billion), and British firms (U.S.$2.3 billion).

CONCLUSION

Canada has pursued the technological strategy of a follower, mostly imitative and defensive. Contrary to other late industrializers, like Sweden, Japan, or even Korea, Canada has not developed a technology-intensive industry of any significance. Its privileged links to the successive industrial leaders of the world economy (first Britain, then the United States) have permitted Canada to adopt foreign technologies rapidly, sometimes through foreign direct investment.

Canadian governments have fostered technologies that promote national unity, such as transportation in the nineteenth Century and telecommunications in the twentieth. Another sector worth mentioning is energy. Both the federal government and the provinces have implemented policies for the development of the huge hydroelectric, nuclear, and hydrocarbon potential of the country. Technological development has followed. Canada has made some major innovations in this area (such as the Candu nuclear reactor, long-distance high-tension electrical transportation technology, and the Canmet heavy oil refining technology) and attracted both foreign and domestic investments into energy-intensive industries. Aircraft and aerospace are other areas of Canadian expertise that have government support.

In the future, this strategy may be self-defeating as mineral and hydrocarbon deposits and easy-access forests are depleted and feasible hydroelectric sites are developed. Furthermore, the toll on the environment is proving increasingly heavy, and the population's resistance to industrial polluters has become more widespread. However, it is difficult to imagine how Canada can adopt a more centralized or *dirigiste* policy. Provincial governments have increased their political power, and Ottawa appears incapable of imposing discipline on them or of obtaining their cooperation. Besides, the Anglo-Saxon tradition is one of individual liberalism, of being opposed to strong governments. A Japanese or even a European kind of technology policy would be difficult to implement in Canada.

The free trade agreement between the United States and Canada, signed in January 1989 and later extended to include Mexico, does not seem to have altered the slow pace of Canadian innovative activities. Preliminary figures show that neither Canada's private firms nor its government laboratories have massively increased or decreased their R&D efforts. The new context is one of deficit reduction, and science and technology policies and government laboratories have been curtailed accordingly. The private sector has taken over some of the financing of innovation that was previously funded by the federal government, and has also become somewhat more committed to R&D on its own.

REFERENCES

Abramovitz, Moses, and P. David. 1996. "Convergence and Deferred Catch-up." In Ralph Landau et al., eds, *The Mosaic of Economic Growth*, 21–62. Stanford, Calif: Stanford University Press.

Brown, John J. 1967. *Ideas in Exile: A History of Canadian Invention*. Toronto: McClelland and Stewart.

Cantwell, John. 1992. "The Internationalization of Technological Activity and Its Implications for Competitiveness." In Granstrand (1992, 75–95).

Dalton, Donald H., and Manuel Serapio, Jr. 1995. *Globalizing Industrial R&D*. Washington, D.C.: U.S. Department of Commerce, Office of Technology Policy.

Doutriaux, Jérôme, and M. Barker. 1995. *The University-Industry Relationship in Science and Technology*. Ottawa: Industry Canada. Occasional Paper No. 11.

Eggleston, Wilfrid. 1978. *National Research in Canada: The NRC 1916–1966*. Toronto: Clarke Irwin.

Freeman, Christopher. 1987. *Technology Policy and Economic Performance: Lessons from Japan*. London: Pinter.

– 1988. "Japan: A New National System of Innovation?" In G. Dosi et al., eds, *Technical Change and Economic Theory*. London: Pinter.

– 1995. "The National System of Innovation in Historical Perspective." *Cambridge Journal of Economics* 19 (1): 5–24.

Granstrand, O., et al., eds. 1992. *Technology Management and International Business*. Chichester: Wiley.

Krugman, Paul. 1993. *Geography and Trade*. Cambridge, Mass.: MIT Press.

Lipsett, M.S., and R. Lipsey. 1994. *Benchmarks, Yardsticks and New Places to Look for Industrial Innovation and Growth*. Vancouver: Centre for Policy Research on Science and Technology, Report 94–7.

Lithwick, N.H. 1969. *Canada's Science Policy and the Economy*. Toronto: Methuen.

Lundvall, Bengt-A. 1988. "Innovation as an Interactive Process: From User-Producer Interaction to the National System of Innovation." In G. Dosi et al., eds, *Technical Change and Economic Theory*. London: Pinter.

–, ed. 1992. *National Systems of Innovation*. London: Pinter.

Maddison, Angus. 1994. "Explaining the Economic Performance of Nations, 1820–1989." In R.R. Nelson et al., eds, *Convergence of Productivity*, 20–61. New York: Oxford University Press.

National Science Board. 1993. *Science and Engineering Indicators*. Washington, D.C.: Government Printing Office.

Nelson, Richard R. 1988. "Institutions Supporting Technical Change in the United States." In G. Dosi et al., eds, *Technical Change and Economic Theory*. London: Pinter.

– 1992. "National Innovation Systems: A Retrospective on a Study." *Industrial and Corporate Change* 1 (2) 347–74.

–, ed. 1993. *National Innovation Systems.* Oxford: Oxford University Press.

– 1994. "The Coevolution of Technology and Institutions." In Richard England, ed, *Evolutionary Concepts in Contemporary Economics*, 139–56. Ann Arbor: University of Michigan Press.

Niosi, Jorge, P.P. Saviotti, B. Bellon, and M. Crow. 1993. "National Systems of Innovation: In Search of a Workable Concept." *Technology in Society* 15:207–27.

Niosi, Jorge. 1995. *Flexible Innovation: Technological Alliances in Canadian Industry.* Montreal and Kingston: McGill-Queen's University Press.

Niosi, Jorge, and B. Bellon. 1994. "The Global Interdependence of National Innovation Systems." *Technology in Society* 16:173–97.

OECD (Organization for Economic Cooperation and Development). 1995. *Science and Technology Indicators.* Paris: OECD.

Ronstadt, R. 1984. "R&D Abroad by U.S. Multinationals." In R. Stobaugh and L.T. Wells, Jr, eds, 241–64. *Technology Crossing Borders: The Choice, Transfer, and Management of International Technology Flows.* Boston: Harvard Business School Press.

Statistics Canada. 1993. "Educational Achievement: An International Comparison." *Canadian Social Trends.* Ottawa. Cat. No. 11–008.

– 1996. *Education in Canada 1995.* Ottawa. Cat. No. 81–229.

von Hippel, Eric. 1988. *The Sources of Innovation.* New York: Oxford University Press.

World Intellectual Property Organization (WIPO). 1996. *World Intellectual Property Report.* Geneva.

5 Mexico's National Innovation System in the 1990s: Overview and Sectoral Effects

J. CARLOS RAMÍREZ AND KURT UNGER

INTRODUCTION

The adoption of the North American Free Trade Agreement (NAFTA), which took effect in January 1994, represented the formal culmination of the process of opening the Mexican economy that had been initiated a decade earlier. Mexico's initiative to join the General Agreement on Tariffs and Trade (GATT) in 1986 was probably the most important measure taken to open its economy and increase its competitiveness globally.

Both of these trading arrangements introduced important changes in the Mexican business environment. Domestic industry was abruptly exposed to competition from abroad, and technology policy also became more liberal. The response of Mexico's innovation and technology transfer systems to these changes remains moderate to date, as we will show. Funding for science and technology continues to be insufficient and highly dependent on public funds, there is limited utilization of the public technological infrastructure by private enterprises, and the nurturing of learning between domestic users and producers of technology and other innovative activities is understandably weak given the limited scope of their relations.

This chapter is divided into three sections. First, we offer an updated overview of science and technology (S&T) efforts to show how limited they are and the extent of their reliance on public funds. The second section introduces some qualitative estimates of the weakness of the system, stressing in particular how the weak technological linkages impinge negatively on the learning potential of the country. A final section produces detailed evidence on the types of adjustments experienced in some of the leading industries during the initial restructuring and opening period. For a few industries the response seems positive, but for most of the nationally controlled industrial sectors technological adjustment has been stifled. Indeed, the overall result of change to date brought about by the modernization agenda seems far less promising than anyone anticipated.

THE R&D SYSTEM IN THE EARLY 1990S[1]

The review of science and technology policy undertaken by the Organization for Economic Cooperation and Development (OECD)[2] in 1993 clearly identified the ineffective nature of the Mexican research and development system. This situation remains essentially unchanged today. Below we summarize the OECD review. Although the information has been updated, the basic OECD conclusions remain the same.

Insufficient Funding of S&T

All through the 1980s and 1990s, R&D expenditures in Mexico were insufficient and the participation of the private sector remained extremely modest. Total national spending on science and technology for 1991 was estimated at U.S.$1,351 million, or 0.48 per cent of gross domestic product (GDP)[3] (Table 5.1). Spending on experimental or applied R&D for 1993 was estimated to be a larger monetary figure of about U.S.$1,959 million, although the level of this effort remained at a modest 0.32 per cent of GDP.[4]

S&T spending deteriorated during most of the 1980s. From 1980 to 1989, the federal government expenditures on S&T declined at an average annual rate of 3.1 per cent. More recently, between 1989 and 1993, spending in this area grew at an average yearly rate of 27.8 per cent (current prices). The net effect, however, is that federal government expenditure on science and technology (FES&T) as a percentage of GDP has declined from 0.46 per cent in 1981 to 0.41 per cent in 1993 (Table 5.2).

Human resources devoted to science and technology activities are also insufficient in Mexico. The proportion of engineers and scientists is 9.4 per 10,000 of the labour force. This ratio compares unfavourably with, for instance, 35.9 engineers and scientists per 10,000 of the labour force in the United Kingdom and 68.8 per 10,000 in Japan. In 1991 a total of 57,016 individuals were engaged in R&D activities in Mexico. Only 40 per cent of these were scientists or engineers, the other 60 per cent being technicians and support personnel (Table 5.3).

Table 5.1
Mexican National Expenditures on Science and Technology, 1991

Sector Financing	Sector Performance	Millions U.S.$	Ratio/Total %	Ratio/Sector %	Ratio/GDP %
Federal government		1,050	78	100	0.36
	Government agencies	722	54	69	
	Higher education	328	24	31	
Private sector		301	22	100	0.12
	Business enterprise	291	21	97	
	Higher education	10	1	3	
Total		1,351	100		0.48

Sources: Public sector data were obtained from SHCP (Secretariá de Hacienda y Crédito Público), *Federal Treasury Account, 1991*; private sector data were obtained from CONACyT (Consejo Nacional de Ciencia y Tecnología), estimates based on INEGI (Instituto Nacional de Estadística, Geografía e Informática) Surveys.

Table 5.2
Mexican Federal Expenditures on Science and Technology, 1980–1993 (millions of dollars)

Year	FES&T[1]	GDP	FES&T as % of GDP	Govt Expenditures[2]	FES&T as % of Govt Exp.
1980	836	194,775	0.43	50,528	1.66
1981	1,145	250,005	0.46	73,571	1.56
1982	715	170,574	0.42	46,274	1.54
1983	472	148,779	0.32	35,334	1.33
1984	646	175,667	0.37	42,566	1.52
1985	653	184,432	0.35	41,145	1.59
1986	454	129,535	0.35	28,129	1.62
1987	395	141,442	0.28	28,698	1.38
1988	467	173,512	0.27	32,983	1.42
1989	569	206,923	0.27	35,983	1.58
1990	725	244,508	0.30	41,073	1.77
1991	1,050	287,737	0.36	49,514	2.12
1992	1,143	329,076	0.35	55,912	2.04
1993	1,454	355,931	0.41	67,218	2.16

1 Federal spending on science and technology.
2 Total public sector (not including debt service).

Sources: SPP (Secretaría de Planeación y Presupuesto), *Federal Treasury Accounts, 1980–1990*; SHCP, *Federal Treasury Accounts, 1991–1992*; SHCP, *1993 Federal Budget BANXICO, 1992 Annual Report.*

Table 5.3
Mexican Scientific and Technological Personnel, 1991

Sector	Scientists and Engineers	Technicians	Support Personnel	Total
Federal government	11,304	9,043	8,139	28,486
SEP-CONACyT centres	1,059	847	762	2,668
IMP (petroleum institute)	816	343	144	1,303
ININ (nuclear research)	378	302	272	952
IIE (electrical research)	795	636	572	2,003
INIFAP (agricultural research)	1,528	1,222	1,100	3,850
LANFI (industrial research)	80	64	58	202
IMSS (social security)	1,081	865	778	2,724
ISSSTE (government security)	297	238	214	749
Health Secretary	1,254	1,003	903	3,160
Others	4,016	3,523	3,336	10,875
Higher education	11,125	8,900	8,010	28,035
Public universities	10,756	8,605	7,744	27,105
UNAM (national university)	2,641	2,113	1,109	5,863
UAM (metropolitan university)	1,609	1,287	1,158	4,054
IPN (polytechnic)	1,233	986	888	3,107
Autonomous University of Chapingo	555	444	400	1,399
Regional technical institutes	248	198	179	625
Others	4,470	3,577	4,010	12,057
Private universities	369	295	266	930
ITESM (Monterrey Tech)	213	170	153	536
Others	156	125	113	394
Business enterprises	155	124	112	391
Peñoles Industries	109	87	78	274
HYLSA	15	12	11	38
Petrocel S.A.	10	8	7	25
Others	21	17	16	54
Private non-profit	41	33	30	104
Sonora College, A.C.	18	14	13	45
Alfa Cultural Centre	12	10	9	31
Research Centre for Development	9	7	6	22
Others	2	2	2	6
Total	22,625	18,100	16,291	57,016

Source: CONACyT-OIKOS, "Preliminary Results Inventory of Institutions and Resources Devoted to Scientific and Technological Activities, 1990–1991." In CONACyT, *Indicadores de Actividades Cientifcas y Tecnológicas.* Mexico, 1994.

The recent Program for Industrial Modernization (1996) recognized the importance of engineers in developing the technological system of the country. It called for a new approach that would put them at the centre of industrial policy, but the time it may take to redress social inertia in favour of engineering and the hard sciences may prove substantial. It is likely that more radical initiatives should be tried.

THE DEPENDENCY OF S&T ON PUBLIC FUNDS

The private sector plays a limited role in Mexico's R&D system. In 1984 the private sector's contribution to national S&T was 15 per cent, although this increased to 23 per cent in 1989. In 1991 the federal government contributed 77 per cent of S&T expenditures and the private sector 22.3 per cent (Table 5.4). The latest estimate, for 1993, decreased the value of S&T financed by business enterprises to 10 per cent (U.S.$358.2/$3,566.2 million nuevos pesos [CONACyT 1996, 38]).

Clearly, Mexican R&D funding not only has been limited, but has also been narrowly concentrated in those very few industrial sectors and scientific areas that have been able, through the benefits of tradition, to accumulate some scientific capabilities. The bulk of basic research infrastructure, both equipment and human capital, is concentrated in a handful of the large state public universities and several government research centres. This is reflected in the human resources engaged in R&D. In 1991, 50 per cent of the total scientific and technical personnel engaged in R&D were working in government S&T institutions, 49 per cent in higher-education institutions, and of the latter 47.5 per cent were employed in state-financed universities. Only 1 per cent were working in industry and private non-profit institutions (Table 5.5).

Table 5.4
Mexican National Expenditures on Science and Technology, 1984–1991

Sector	1984	1989	1991	1984	1989	1991
	(Millions of Dollars)			(Percentages)		
Federal government	646	569	1,050	85.0	76.9	77.7
Private sector*	114	171	301	15.0	23.1	22.3
Total	760	740	1,351	100.0	100.0	100.0

*Estimated figures.

Sources: Inter-American Development Bank; INEGI, Mexico; SPP, Mexico.

Table 5.5
Mexican Scientific and Technological Personnel, 1991 (percentages)

Sector	Scientists and Engineers	Technicians	Support Personnel	Total
Federal Government	50.0	50.0	50.0	50.0
SEP-CONACyT system	4.7	4.7	4.7	4.7
IMP	3.6	1.9	0.9	2.3
ININ	1.7	1.7	1.7	1.7
IIE	3.5	3.5	3.5	3.5
INIFAP	6.8	6.8	6.8	6.8
LANFI	0.4	0.4	0.4	0.4
IMSS	4.8	4.8	4.8	4.8
ISSSTE	1.3	1.3	1.3	1.3
Health Secretary	5.5	5.5	5.5	5.5
Others	17.8	19.5	20.5	19.1
Higher education	49.2	49.2	49.2	49.2
Public universities	47.5	47.5	47.5	47.5
UNAM	11.7	11.7	6.8	10.3
UAM	7.1	7.1	7.1	7.1
IPN	5.5	5.5	5.5	5.5
Autonomous University of Chapingo	2.5	2.5	2.5	2.5
Technical institutes system	1.1	1.1	1.1	1.1
Others (including state universities)	19.8	19.8	24.6	21.2
Private universities	1.6	1.6	1.6	1.6
ITESM	0.9	0.9	0.9	0.9
Others	0.7	0.7	0.7	0.7
Business enterprise	0.7	0.7	0.7	0.7
Peñoles Industries	0.5	0.5	0.5	0.5
HYLSA	0.1	0.1	0.1	0.1
Petrocel S.A.	0.0	0.0	0.0	0.0
Others	0.1	0.1	0.1	0.1
Private non-profit	0.2	0.2	0.2	0.2
Sonora College, A.C.	0.1	0.1	0.1	0.1
Alfa Cultural Centre	0.1	0.1	0.1	0.1
Research Centre for Development	0.0	0.0	0.0	0.0
Others	0.0	0.0	0.0	0.0
Total	100.0	100.0	100.0	100.0

Source: CONACyT-OIKOS. "Preliminary Results Inventory of Institutions and Resources Devoted to Scientific and Technological Activities, 1990–1991." In CONACyT, *Indicadores de Actividades Científicas y Tecnológicas.* Mexico, 1994.

The concentration of R&D efforts, of course, is not a bad thing per se. What is troublesome, however, is that the sectors and scientific areas of concentration do not pertain to a purposeful targeting of priority activities. Rather, they reveal an earlier inertia, when scientists identified a broad spectrum of sciences to foster without having a clear sense of the specialization that would be needed; nor did Mexican scientists focus on the emerging global pressures that subsequently challenged Mexico's productive industrial sectors.[5]

As a counterpart to public-funding deficiencies, there is also little private capacity to perform R&D, as shown above. While this is most acute in small and medium-sized firms, which comprise 98 per cent of all manufacturing establishments, it also applies to large ones (see INEGI 1992): R&D constituted 0.7 per cent of expenditures in large establishments, barely above the average 0.6 per cent for the entire sample, which included firms of all sizes (CONACyT 1996, 72). Even this measure of R&D is probably inflated, since only a few larger enterprises, about a dozen or so industrial firms belonging for the most part to national conglomerates, gave evidence of developing the technological capability to compete internationally. Likewise, only a small proportion of these types of firms created their own R&D divisions or technology centres (Table 5.6). On the contrary, for many of them, survival in the face of international competition has meant having to apply drastic "downgrading" measures, as has been shown elsewhere (Unger 1994; see OECD 1994).

Mexican firms face a variety of constraints. The firms and foreign observers alike point to the inadequacy of R&D funding. Commercial banks have neither the experience nor the will to evaluate risky projects involving technological components. Clearly, some kind of consistent government involvement is required, although even the Program for Industrial Modernization of 1996 has largely ignored the specifics of financing.

USERS AND PRODUCERS OF TECHNOLOGY: THE WEAKNESS OF THE SYSTEM

The need for a stronger relationship between the users and the producers of science and technology has been recognized since the early writings of the "dependency" school. Regardless of the wide spectrum of radicalism associated with many writers of that school, those who addressed the issue of the development of science and technology all saw the need to foster links between users and producers.[6] These topics remain of importance today, whether they be technology transfer, property rights, or the supply of capital goods. At the same time, there has been a revival of the user-producer approach, albeit more evident in

Table 5.6
Mexican Companies and Their R&D Activities, 1993

Company	Sector	Sales (millions of new pesos)	Assets (millions of new pesos)	Personnel	R&D Unit	R&D Activity
Industriales Peñoles S.A. de C.V.	Mining	2,285	3,629	10,382	Centre for Research and Technological Development	Metals, minerals, and chemicals
Vitro Corporativo	Glass	n.a.	n.a.	n.a.	six R&D divisions	Glass and bottle Manufacture
						Non-metallic new materials, metallurgy, machinery, industrial equipment
Grupo Industrial Resistol	Petrochemistry	646	651	2,244	Grupo IRSA, Centre for Research and Technology Development	Polymers (rubber, plastics, additives)
Celanese Mexicana S.A.	Petrochemistry	2,903	4,275	8,278	Technology Research and Development Centre	Chemical products
Hylsa	Iron and steel	2,505	4,104	4,997	*	Steel
Grupo Condumex S.A. de C.V.	Electronics and manufacturing	2,409	2,599	12,028	Condumex Research and Development Centre	R&D on materials, metallurgy, electric testing, machinery and tools
Richold Quimica	Chemistry	n.a.	n.a.	n.a.	Research and Development Department	Polymers
CYDSA	Chemistry	2,559,509	4,470,113	12,381	Different research units	Chemicals
Commercial Mexicana de Pinturas	Chemistry	n.a.	n.a.	n.a.	Polymers Research Centre	Polymers

Sources: Expansion, 18 August and 1 September 1993; data gathered from the various companies by phone.

studies of European industrial economies.[7] Here, however, we will argue that most Mexican industries reveal a poor system of domestic user-producer relations because of their excessive dependence on imported technologies.

TECHNOLOGICAL INFRASTRUCTURE AND PRIVATE ENTERPRISES

Technology transfer has commonly been a subtle code for technology importation.[8] Only recently has the development of local institutions' ability to meet the local demand for technology appeared as a crucial priority for research and policymaking. Previously, technological institutions (TIs) – mainly the government-funded institutions mentioned above – were created and developed largely in isolation from industry, without much connection to specific market demands for technology. As a result, there are few TIs in Mexico, and almost no linkages between TIs and industry, as evidence collected for several industrial sectors will show.[9]

First, to understand the wide variety of technological needs, it is necessary to differentiate among industrial sectors with respect to their sensitivity to various types of technical change. Some sectors are subject to changes in process technology, others more to product redesign and innovations; others are controlled by production complexity, and there are still others where R&D/best practices are at the heart of technical change.

Second, the access to technological innovation (or the ability to keep pace with technical changes, if preferred) is a consequence of the type of technical change and of the structure and ownership characteristics of an industry. These determine the potential role for independent TIs. At the risk of an oversimplification, we can say that the access of R&D sensitive and product-innovating industries to technical changes is limited by their own R&D capabilities, including their need to attract foreign participation. TIs are not a major source of the kind of innovations that have to be under the close control of firms. Most process technology, on the contrary, can be obtained through licences and patent rights, which offer a certain scope for the screening services of TIs, mainly services for small and medium-sized firms that may not have substantial technical in-house capacities. Other TI services for these industries may involve standards and quality tests, training schemes, and organizational systems, although we found much fewer such cases in Mexico than originally anticipated.

Finally, the acquisition of machinery and specialized plant designs involves specialized suppliers; usually foreign producers supply imported technology already incorporated into machines and equipment.

In summary, Mexican technological institutions which ought to facilitate the private sector's use of the country's predominantly public infrastructure, are for the most part cut off from industry and operate largely in isolation of real demand conditions. Their potential role is limited. Given that these demand-side limitations are also aggravated by major inefficiencies in the way they develop,[10] the result is a poor system of technological linkages within the country.

THE USER-PRODUCER LEARNING NETWORK

The changes in relation to technology policy, which liberalized imports and foreign investment, played a decisive role in maintaining the weakness in, and probably further weakening, links between Mexican users and producers of technology and technology-intensive products. Those policy changes reflected the liberalizing goals of the 1990s, calling for less restrictions in those areas, as we have documented elsewhere (see Unger 1995, chap. 2).

The most direct results can be seen in the poor development of local sources of technology, as argued above with respect to technology institutions. The ratio of technology receipts to technology payments has remained around 1:5 all through the 1990s, while the deficit of the technology balance of payments increases every year (see CONACyT 1996, 73). According to the OECD, this ratio is useful in evaluating the extent of learning that developing economies achieve from imported technology; a ratio of 1:0 would express an end of technology payments.

Another expression of the limited technological development of Mexico is found in the specialization of industry in mature segments that rely on imports of technology-related products. The latter effect is suggested by an analysis of trade flows that follows Pavitt's typology of industries according to the sources and importance of technological innovations. On the whole, the recent restructuring and specialization of Mexican industry has had serious drawbacks for the technological development of the country.[11] Industrial specialization has led to a duality of competitive conditions: while a few scale-intensive and mature industries, many of which exploit natural resource advantages, have become highly competitive in export markets, the majority of other industries remain separate from this small group and below internationally competitive standards.

The result is that Mexican industrial dynamism now depends on the exports of a few mature industrial sectors. For the most part, and in spite of a few notable exceptions to be further noted below, these sectors are of only moderate interest in the longer term from an innovation-led perspective. Furthermore, many of these mature activities are also devoid of substantial linkages to other activities. In fact, these same sectors also depend on comparatively large proportions of imports, which grow in tandem with the sectors' exports. Indeed, increasing the import content of Mexican industry has in some instances been taken to the extreme of turning industrial firms into mere commercializing ventures. The associated loss of industrial and technological capabilities in that process may prove substantial in the immediate future.

In summary, we also note that the state of depressed investment in Mexican S&T was further aggravated by the largely conservative reaction of the vast majority of the firms to the driving measures of public adjustment, privatization, and competition from imports. Rather than investing in technological upgrading efforts, most shifted their attention to their basic sources of comparative advantage. As might be expected, such an atmosphere is hardly conducive for industrial firms to engage in major technology development or acquisitions. In turn, this general policy limited the development and use of technological institutions in Mexico. Concrete evidence of this is offered below for a few specific industrial sectors.

TECHNOLOGICAL EFFECTS OF RESTRUCTURING AT THE FIRM LEVEL

In general, the exposure of Mexican industry to international competition has consolidated its mature segments. In spite of this general trend, some changes have taken place.

First of all, the firms are affected in different ways depending on the sector, type of firm, and the business environment they face. The findings of previous studies, such as the one we conducted for petrochemicals and machine tools (Unger 1994), suggest substantial differences between sectors and also some differences between firms within each sector, particularly in the way that technology issues relate to the liberalizing measures adopted in recent years. This is also evident among the motor firms, as we found in another study (Ramírez 1995).

For firms in the petrochemical industry, the main technological issues derive from changes in international markets for chemical products. Basic petrochemicals, intermediate chemicals, and finished specialty products face different and changing market conditions. To be competitive internationally, new projects must adopt international economies of scale, which in turn requires large gestation and construction periods for each plant. Feasibility studies for such projects are based on long term projections of international supply and demand. These world market projections may change dramatically within a few years, as some of Mexico's industrial players have attested.

By the end of the 1980s, most firms considered the markets for finished, specialty products more promising than that for intermediates. This led to the conclusion that the production of traditional commodities should be abandoned in favour of R&D and new plants in order to capture the more profitable specialty markets. During the last five years (1991–96), the results have been very different than earlier assumptions. Because the rapid opening of the Mexican market has exposed national firms to immediate competition from abroad, their development of complex specialties has been precluded. At the same time, some traditional plastics and fibres firms have regained major international market shares to the advantage of the more traditional producers of mature products.

As a result of these international and domestic trends, Mexico's technological leaders are now in difficulty – specifically those firms that followed the specialties upgrading route, investing in R&D and committing themselves firmly to technological development. This is especially true of those firms that did not have a foreign partner to share the risk.[12]

Recently successful firms, on the other hand, see their future in consolidating the basic and intermediate petrochemical chains, which are both less technologically demanding and more profitable in the near term. These firms invest in R&D, but much less than the other sectors, both in terms of quantity and quality.[13] The rules of international competition are anticipated to apply in the domestic market of the future as well. These rules are dictated by large vertically integrated chemical conglomerates that may use transfer pricing in order to obtain a profitable return for their integrated operations.

Some of the most promising related areas involve intensifying vertical upstream integration. This process can extend as far as final consumer goods, which may be less subject to cost competition and more to product differentiation. This is illustrated by a firm with a long tradition in the fibre business that only recently decided to enter the clothing line. Other more promising new ventures relate not so much to the development of new products as to the commercial exploitation of down-to-earth environmental concerns: recycling of plastics, sewage and other forms of water treatment, biotechnology applications to chemical pollution, and the like. In all these cases, the result is not the upgrading of their industrial capabilities, but the contrary.

The effects of international competition on machine tools producers are less evident than on petrochemicals producers. Domestic demand is the driving force of machine tools producers, and although such demand is highly dependent on new fixed investment, the rhythm of activity that we observed in this industry showed some lags with respect to the trends of total investment. This meant that some machine tools firms did not experience reduced production until several years after the collapse of most other domestic markets in 1982.

The machine tools producers that have survived in the 1990s are of two kinds: (a) small firms that produce simple standard machinery, where keeping close contact with a diverse variety of consumers becomes a competitive determinant; and (b) subsidiaries of large transnational corporations (TNCs) that act as suppliers of specialized machinery and components for the replacement market and thus may have more to sell when users decide to extend the life of older machinery rather than replace it with new equipment.

Some producers initially suffered from the penetration of low-cost imported machine tools after the trade liberalization of 1985. The main competitors were from Taiwan, Singapore, and China. After a few years, however, imported machines were on the whole discredited as of lower quality and less reliability with respect to repair and maintenance. For all but a few competing Mexican producers, the results of that experience were reassuring. They now feel confident in their ability to remain competitive provided they stick firmly to their traditional domestic consumers.

Perhaps the most serious technological development in this sector is that local producers see the scope of their production confined to the standard mature markets for machine tools. They neither see a need to upgrade the profile of their product-mix nor believe they could close the technology gap that exists between foreign producers of more advanced equipment and themselves. In so far as machine tools and other capital goods are considered important vehicles of technological development, and a source of beneficial externalities for other parts of the Mexican economy, the quality of the capital goods that a country chooses to produce is not a value-free decision (Krugman 1986; Harris 1991).

Other technological effects are of minor importance. Imports of technology by the machine tools producers themselves have never been substantial in either technology transfers or equipment. Training, R&D, new organizational technologies, and the like are not of importance and have not been directly affected in any substantial degree by the new environment of the early 1990s.

The motor industry experience can be seen in a different perspective. Nowadays, this industry exhibits a dual pattern of specialization in which northern plants produce for export, while those in the south concentrate on supplying the domestic market. Transactions between these two types of plants are minimal. A critical aspect of this spatial pattern is the way firms are linked to their parent companies. Plants in the north rely much more on imports than those in the south because of the more integrated nature of their activities vis-à-vis the parent conglomerates, including intensive intrafirm trade. All but 10 per cent of the total value of northern plants' transactions take place along the supplier-assembler circuit and with parent companies. This explains why motor firms have increased their exports while raising the ratio of imports to local manufacturing production in recent years.[14]

With the exception of some producers of principal components in the south, the largest northern plants have become the main beneficiaries of this spatial division.[15] Their incomparable productive success is particularly due to the implementation of radical organizational changes. These plants have led the way in upgrading automation levels and in adopting new managerial approaches, transforming the traditional relations between capital and labour.

These changes, which are roughly in accord with the industrial goals pursued by the government since 1982, have allowed the motor industry to become the core of Mexico's exports-led program. The motor industry along with the *maquiladoras*, is the largest exporter and value-added generator in manufacturing. It contributes 60 per cent of the country's total exports. But in contrast to the petrochemical and machine tools cases, the motor industry's export projects are led by a handful of subsidiaries of foreign-based multinationals. In particular, the six U.S. Big Three (Ford, General Motors, and Chrysler) facilities, which located in the north after 1981, account for the majority of motor industry exports.[16] Organized around flexible complexes, they effectively apply the most advanced just-in-time (JIT) manufacturing methods in Mexico. In fact, the Big Three assembly plants have lately recorded the highest levels of productivity and quality in manufacturing, due mainly to their efficient JIT networks of suppliers.[17]

The placement of six plants in northern Mexico is a result of the headquarters' strategy to make Mexico the most important "consolidation centre" in Latin America. The development of prototypes in northern plants, to be implemented later around the world, and the production in Mexico of models that were usually made in the U.S. and Canada exemplify the effectiveness of this strategy.

This new role of the six facilities was tempered by the headquarter's decision to enter into technological agreements with Mexican partners only if the Mexicans agreed to practise "simultaneous engineering." This strategy has involved assemblers and a handful of Mexican innovative suppliers in certain experiments of product design and development since 1990. The most relevant example is a joint venture between Chrysler and six Mexican firms to design an engine. This association has been very successful.[18]

Unfortunately, this strategy has been limited to suppliers that have agreed to joint ventures with TNCs or that have acquired licences to upgrade their technological and organizational levels (Table 5.7). We found that twelve first-tier suppliers concentrate nearly 40 per cent of total sales and 85 per cent of exports in the auto parts industry, excluding engines. Eight of these are located in northeastern Mexico and are single producers of engine blocks, iron and aluminium heads, windscreens, plastic parts, suspensions, and so on (Ramírez 1995).

The opportunities to supply export-oriented plants are limited for minor producers to the extent that they depend on establishing links with first-tier suppliers. In practice, major suppliers decide how many other suppliers will be incorporated into their network. National suppliers contracted by export-oriented plants may not have affiliates elsewhere and are therefore disadvantaged when in competition with transnational suppliers, which can more easily provide parts for motor companies in different countries. Indeed, only a few Mexican companies can survive as independent suppliers, based on their monopolistic position in the domestic market.

By all accounts we can conclude that the opening of the motor industry has partially upgraded the technological levels of a few suppliers, even if the technological sophistication of the Big Three factories has not produced substantial spillovers. In fact, the location of the six assemblers has concentrated, to an even greater degree, the production and technological resources in the hands of the biggest suppliers, both national and international. Thus, it would be venturesome to predict that motor industry exports can act as a solid base for the national export sector or serve to counterbalance imports in other sectors. Nevertheless, the industry may make a major contribution to the development of a national system of innovation in Mexico.

Perhaps the most damaging effect of industrial adjustment policies in these Mexican export sectors, as much as in most other parts of the economy, has been the reduction in concern with long-term opportunities and the extended development of long-term technological capabilities. Short-term opportunities appear more profitable, even when they demand some upgrading adjustments on the part of suppliers in the network. Other profitable areas include commercial options, rather than fabrication, and especially financial ventures. However, success in the long run is a long shot for the short-sighted private sector in countries that have just passed through trade adjustment experiences.

Table 5.7
The Auto Parts Firms: A Sample of Upgrading Exporters, 1993

Firm	Ranking (Sales)	Owner-ship	Production (Q) (U.S.$Millions)	Export (X) (U.S.$Millions)	X/Q	Technology Source	Purpose
Renault auto parts industries	1	French	120	120	1.00	Renault HQ	Components for own makes
Vitroflex	2	Mexican 90% American 10%	95	85	0.89	Ford Glass Division	JV engineering support for sales of windscreens in Mexico AND U.S.
Carplastic	3	American	85	80	0.94	Ford PTDP Division	Licence to produce dashboards
Cifunsa	4	Mexican	69	56	0.81	a) Italian Company b) Ford Affiliate	Process reorganization Licence to automate the premachining and smelting
Tremec	5	Mexican/ American	65	15	0.23	Autoparts American Co.	Licence to produce automatic transmissions
Metalsa	6	Mexican 88% American 12%	54	24	0.44	A.O. Smith	JV assistance for production of chasses and side rails (sales in Mexico and U.S.)
Rassini	7	Mexican	51.5	43	0.83	American Autoparts Co.	Licence to produce spring suspensions
Nemak	8	Mexican 85% Italian 15%	36	19	0.53	Teksid	JV to enhance quality and productivity of aluminium heads
Total			575.5	442*	0.77		

*This figure accounted for 65 per cent of the auto parts industry exports, excluding engines, in 1993.

Source: Ramirez (1995).

NOTES

1 Most of this section is based on chapter 2.A in Unger (1995).
2 OECD-DSTI/STP "Review of National Science and Technology Policy:
   México II: Examiners' Report," vol. 11, 1994.
3 An earlier OECD estimate identified a lower R&D effort of only 0.33 per
   cent of GDP in 1991. See OECD (1994, 142). The figures on science and
   technology usually overestimate the measure of innovative efforts
   because they include most higher-education spending, but they are
   useful for international comparisons.
4 This applies to R&D expenditures, which are not the same as S&T
   expenditures, as pointed out in note 3 (Gasto en Investigacion y
   Desarrollo Experimental – GIDE). See CONACyT (1996, 98). A change in
   emphasis from one to the other as reporting criteria is common when a
   new administration takes office, and this latest time has not been the
   exception.
5 Earlier threads of this debate can be traced back to 1970 when CONACyT
   was created. See *Ciencia y Desarrollo* 1982.
6 See, for instance, papers in the special issue on science and technology
   of the *Journal of Development Studies*, October 1972.
7 The most direct reference is Lundvall (1988). In the Mexican context, see
   the special issue of *Comercio Exterior* compiled by G. Dutrénit (Dutrénit 1994).
8 As a rough indication of the importance of technology transfer, a survey
   of manufacturing firms estimated that 2.5 per cent of the firms' income
   was spent on technology transfer. The same survey estimated R&D
   spending at 0.6 per cent (see CONACyT 1996, 72).
9 The study was sponsored by the World Bank and the IDRC-Canada
   (Industrial Development Research Council, Canada) and is reported at
   length in Unger (1995).
10 TI characteristics are described extensively in chapter 5 of the report to
   the World Bank. There are few highly inefficient bodies to resolve industrial needs, and they generally define their activities independently of the
   markets.
11 The overall effect of industrial restructuring is probably best shown in
   the composition of exports and imports grouped according to Pavitt's
   typology: economy-of-scale and supplier-dominated industries accounted
   for 86 per cent of exports and 60 per cent of imports in 1994. Estimates
   are from Unger (1996).
12 One of the clearest examples of firms that faced difficulties because of
   their previously more aggressive industrial and technological strategy is
   Resistol, one of the companies listed in Table 5.6. It later adopted a more
   moderate approach, one we could refer to as downgrading at the firm
   level, even if not in accordance with others in the industry. The survival

strategy of this firm included sacrificing the search for breakthrough specialties.

13   In such firms, Idesa and Primex in particular, R&D accounts for less than 1 per cent of sales, while their main R&D efforts are devoted to improving efficiency in known processes.

14   For the entire manufacturing sector, this ratio grew from 7.3 per cent in the period 1982–86 to 13.2 per cent in 1990. The leading export firms were responsible for this boom; for instance, the autoparts industry increased its imports to output ratio from 49.2 per cent in 1982 to 120.7 per cent in 1990 (Arjona and Unger 1996).

15   In contrast , southern plants are the net losers of this division. After the opening of the economy, many small producers went out of business, mainly because of the increasing integration of their main client, the largest first-tier suppliers. This integration reduced the small producers' chances to survive, since the first-tier suppliers tended to concentrate their purchases on their affiliates with the purpose of increasing economies of scale, thereby reducing costs.

16   On average, the Big Three exports accounted for two-thirds of the motor industry's total revenue (U.S.$7billion) between 1993 and 1995. This means that these subsidiaries contribute over 20 per cent of the foreign exchange generated by the manufacturing sector, the largest foreign-exchange providers in Mexico after Pemex.

17   According to Shaiken (1994), Ford-Hermosillo and Ford-Chihuahua have recorded the highest productivity and quality standards in the North American auto market. The former, for instance, was acknowledged by the Ford Motor Company as the plant with the highest levels of quality within the Ford global network in 1988. More recently, this plant registered 1,406/TGW (things gone wrong) defective points per auto, against an average 1,520 points for the rest of the corporation's plants.

18   The success story is quoted by an observer: "[Chrysler] expects that Mexican firms will take the lead in the product design of engines in the future" (Morales 1994, 10).

REFERENCES

Arjona, L., and Unger, K. 1996. "Competitividad internacional y tecnológico: la industria manufacturea Mexicana frente a la apertura commercial." *Economía Mexicana* 5 (2).

Ciencia y Desarrollo. 1982). "El Desarrollo de la Ciencia y la Tecnología en México." 45:27–43 (July–August).

CONACyT (Consejo Nacional de Ciencia y Tecnología). 1996. *México – Indicadores de Actividades Científicas y Tecnológicas – 1995.* SEP and CONACyT.

Cooper, C. ed. 1972. "Special Issue on Science and Technology." *Journal of Development Studies* 9 (1).

Dutrénit, G., coord. 1994. "Sistema Nacional de Innovación." *Comercio Exterior* 44 (8).

Harris, R. 1991. "Strategic Trade Policy, Technology Spillover, and Foreign Investment." In D. McFetridge, ed., *Foreign Investment, Technology and Economic Growth.* Investment Canada Research series. Calgary: University of Calgary Press.

INEGI (Instituto Nacional de Estadística, Geografia e Informática). 1992. "Encuesta Nacional de Empleo, Salarios, Tecnología y Capacitación en el Sector Manufacturero." STPS/INEGI/OIT.

Johnson, C. 1988. "Japanese Style Management in America." *Management Review* 30 (4).

Krugman, P. 1986. "Introduction: New Thinking about Trade Policy." In P. Krugman, ed., *Strategic Trade Policy and the New International Economics.* Boston: MIT Press.

Lundvall, B. 1988. "Innovation as an Interactive Process: From User-Producer Interaction to the National System of Innovation." In G. Dosi et al., eds, *Technical Change and Economic Theory.* London: Pinter; New York: Columbia University Press.

Morales, R. 1994. *Flexible Production: Restructuring of the International Automobile Industry.* Oxford: Polity Press.

OECD (Organization for Economic Cooperation and Development). 1994. *Reviews of National Science and Technology Policy: México.* Paris: OECD.

Pavitt, K. 1984. "Sectoral Patterns of Technical Change: Towards a Taxonomy and a Theory." *Research Policy* 13.

Ramírez, J.C. 1995. "The New Location and Interaction Patterns of the Mexican Motor Industry." Unpublished Ph.D. Thesis, University of Sussex, England.

SECOFI (Secretaría de Comercio y Fomento Industrial). 1996. *Programa de Política Industrial y Comercio Exterior,* May.

Shaiken, H. 1994. "Industrial Restructuring, Flexible Production and Mexico." Paper prepared for the conference "Confronting Free Trade: Policies for Technological Development," Mexico, CIDE, February.

Unger, K. 1994. *Ajuste Estructural y Estrategias Empresariales en México: Las Industrias Petroquímica y de Máquinas Herramienta.* Mexico, D.F.: Centro de Investigación y Docencia Económicas.

– 1995. "International Study on Policy and Institutional Priorities for Industrial Technology Development: Mexico." Report to the World Bank and IDRC-Canada.

– 1996. "El Desempeño de los Conglomerados Industriales en México: 'Downgrading' en la Perspectiva Evolutiva." Document for the meeting of Carnegie and ColMex, México, 3 June.

6 The Triple Helix of Academia-Industry-Government: The U.S. National Innovation System

HENRY ETZKOWITZ

INTRODUCTION

We are moving into a new environment for innovation in which universities and other knowledge-producing organizations play a much stronger role. Local, regional, and national governments are more actively engaged in formulating industrial policy. International and multinational authorities are also involved. Even the older, larger firms are revising the way that they develop technology, entering into horizontal and vertical strategic alliances to develop and market new products. Product and process innovation within industry (Mowery 1983) is complemented by techno-scientific innovation (Hilpert 1991). Originating in academia and encouraged by government policies, new technological fields such as biotechnology and alternative energy have become sources of innovation. Industrial and university-based innovations represent stages in economic growth rather than mutually exclusive strategies: current high-tech sectors replicate the emergence of the chemical and electrical industries from scientific research, much of it conducted in German and British universities, in the late nineteenth century (Mowery 1993). Science-based technologies have long since been incorporated into large firms, but their current form of development, rather than their boundary-spanning origins, requires fresh attention. The emergence of a new group of science-based technologies, together with the need to renew older technologies, has revived issues relating to the source and diffusion of innovation in the late twentieth century.

Institutional and national boundaries are transcended in the course of the creation of a new innovation environment. Three institutional sectors (public, private, and academic) that formerly operated at arm's length in liberal capitalist societies are increasingly working together. Start-up firms are a common outgrowth of the three sectors, arising from academic research groups, national laboratories, and the laboratories of large corporations. National systems of innovation (NSIs) are regionalized and internationalized as innovation processes take place across national boundaries, through cooperative arrangements among regions and firms (Kohler-Koch 1993). Three nations (Canada, Mexico, and the United States), with close but often opposing economic interests until quite recently, are contemplating joint innovation initiatives even as firms across two and even three countries enter into an increasingly complex pattern of mergers and joint ventures. Labatt, the Canadian brewer, has acquired a stake in Femsa, a Mexican beverage, packaging, and retail firm; both companies will distribute each other's beer, forming a new operation to distribute their products jointly in the United States (Farnsworth 1994). Few in the U.S. are aware that Corning is closely related to Vitro, a Mexican glass firm. Resistol, Monsanto's Mexican affiliate, sponsors a U.S. start-up firm to develop a new product, based on research at an Ohio university, that it will manufacture and distribute across Latin America.

Innovation systems, a traditional characteristic of the nation-state (Nelson 1993), are being complemented by regional and multinational innovation systems within the European Union (EU) and elsewhere (Kohler-Koch 1993). At the regional level, this is not a new development. The New England regional innovation system, named after a postwar ring-road, "Route 128," originated in the mid-nineteenth century with the founding of the Massachusetts Institute of Technology (MIT), a new type of technological university designed to infuse industry with the results of what is now known as "strategic research" (Etzkowitz 1993). What is new is the spread of technology policy to virtually all regions, irrespective of whether they are research or industrially intensive. At the international and multinational levels, the United Nations (UN), the Organization for Economic Cooperation and Development (OECD), the World Bank, and the European Union have all launched programs to assist economic development; many of these efforts rely on academic-industry-government relations to achieve their goals (Nelson 1993). The North American Free Trade Agreement (NAFTA) originated in the movement to reduce intracontinental trade barriers as a strategy for economic development. Can this contract among nations grow into an institutional environment to encourage innovation in North America its countries, regions, industries, and firms?

THE TRIPLE HELIX MODEL

In working together, the three institutional spheres – public, private, and academic – describe a spiral pattern, forming a "triple helix," with linkages emerging at various stages of the innovation process. There are four dimensions to the development of this triple helix. The first is an internal transformation in each of the helices, such as the development of lateral ties among companies through strategic alliances or an assumption of an economic development mission by universities. The second is the influence of one helix upon another: for example, the role of the U.S. federal government in instituting an indirect industrial policy in the Bayh-Dole Act of 1980 or of state governments in formulating policies and programs to encourage universities to establish industrial ties. The third dimension is the creation of a new overlay of trilateral networks and organizations from the interaction among the three helices, established to generate new ideas and formats for high-tech development. This phenomenon is especially salient at the level of regional industrial clusters that formerly lacked a common organizational structure. These new arrangements are typically born under crisis conditions such as those induced by general economic depression or increased international competition. The fourth dimension of the triple helix model is a recursive effect of these institutional spheres (typically representing academia, industry, and government in contrast to traditional European corporatist models representing government, industry and labour), both on the spirals from which they emerged and on the larger society. One such effect is on science itself as a result of internal changes within academia, strengthened and diffused by government policy.

THE PRIVATE SECTOR

A new mode of production is emerging based on linkages among academia, industry, and government. Not too many years ago, the linear model of innovation was taken for granted. New discoveries made in the industrial laboratories of large companies would pass through various stages of development and eventually be produced in the manufacturing plants of those companies. Large corporations that could afford to maintain research laboratories were expected to be the prime source of technological innovation, industrial expansion, and economic growth. The linear model depicted how innovation took place, or at least how it was supposed and expected to work until the 1970s, exemplified by Dupont's motto of "Better Living through Chemistry." The premise of employment growth and a higher material standard of living emanating from the technological engine of the large corporation was widely accepted even if fault was found with some consumer products and environmental by-products.

Mowery has noted the importance to innovation of a technological trajectory based on improvement in manufacturing processes, apart from market demand or an underlying scientific knowledge base. "While large firm size may not be critical to successful innovation the history and recent development of the semiconductor industry suggests that contractual arrangements among small single product firms will not support a high level of innovation" (1983). This analysis suggests a continuing role for large firms with an ability to commit significant resources to innovation. Even as new elements from academia and government appear, the traditional role of the large national and multinational firm as an organizer of innovation and vehicle for technology transfer continues. The significance of such firms has especially been noted in Canada, where they integrate locally produced elements of innovation into broader transnational systems (McFetridge 1993).

Despite some continuity, large corporations are changing their role in the new innovation environment. Some of these corporations, such as IBM and General Motors, have maintained large basic research laboratories as contributions to their national innovation system, with only long-term benefits expected. IBM, for example, achieved significant advances in superconductivity and reduced instruction set computing (RISC). Advances in superconductivity led to the formation of new firms and possibly a new industry; RISC was exploited by other firms for years before IBM decided to develop its own technology. With the economic downturn of the early 1990s, many of these large companies have downsized their laboratories and required them either to contribute directly to the company or to find income elsewhere.

In response to changing conditions, large companies are revising their individualistic approach to developing and marketing technology, entering into consortia with other firms and national laboratories. Laboratories of large companies, such as Grumman, which used to be officially devoted just to that company, are now setting up technology transfer offices, following the research agendas of universities and the national laboratories, and selling technology to other companies. Closer ties are arranged through strategic alliances or partnerships between two firms (or units of large entities) to bring the special capabilities of each together to carry out a task jointly that neither could do as effectively, cheaply, or quickly on its own. Such alliances were originally organized to carry out a discrete task such as development of a particular product; now they are increasingly thought of as arrangements to develop a series of related products, open to expansion into other corporate tasks such as marketing, finance, and procurement. On a continuum, an alliance lies in between a merger or acquisition and a discrete transaction such as licensing a piece of intellectual property.

There is a felt need for a broad multifaceted relationship between organizations to carry innovation forward and bring new products to market in the stringent internationally competitive climate of the 1990s. The director of research and development in the U.S. for Henkel, the German chemical firm, has concluded that "technology transfer is dead ... The old 1950s model doesn't work anymore; the old way of hoping R&D came up with something brilliant only works if you are the only game in town" (Giorden 1994). The new paradigm is based on meshing the disciplines of marketing, development, and research, creating teams within and across internal and external organizational -boundaries.

For IBM and other firms like it, the issue is not so much the amount spent on R&D as it is the disconnection that often exists between R&D and product development and marketing in these companies. In their growth period, during the early postwar era, such firms typically expanded by separating R&D, organizationally and geographically, from more mundane corporate functions. It is not yet clear whether by just subsidizing R&D the Clinton administration or the companies themselves are sufficiently addressing the need for developing technology transfer and commercialization capabilities for their research campuses, within and among firms.

In this regard, various European Union programs provide some partial models (Malerba 1993, 254–5). In addition to traditional industrial technologies, such as chemicals, in which Europe has maintained great strength, the EU's fourth framework program proposes to emphasize the life sciences, especially biotechnology, medicine, and health as well as agricultural reform and rural development. Environmental concerns, including lowering the pollution levels of transport systems, are also driving the direction of fourth framework R&D programs. These initiatives run parallel to proposals for "green" technology development in North America.

THE PUBLIC SECTOR

It has been more than a century since the U.S. government took its last great initiative to advance civil technology by giving the states federal land for universities that would be devoted to agricultural and mechanical arts and sciences. However, the United States, beginning with a rationale for a patent system in its constitution, has always encouraged technically oriented economic development. The construction of the Erie Canal, the coastal mapping survey, and expeditions to determine the resources of the hinterlands – such as those of Lewis and Clark – nurtured the growth of civil engineering, oceanography, and geology early in the nineteenth century. Since the Second World War, the U.S. government has indirectly supported technological innovation through military spin-offs. The United States has also been fortunate enough to have the National Institute of Health, which through its program of fundamental research has inadvertently cultured a thriving and lucrative biotechnology industry.

In response to the decline of manufacturing industries from the 1970s, state governments have also established science and technology agencies to spur science-based economic development. State programs targeted at a range of industrial and research conditions include research centres at universities to focus on local technological niches, technology extension services for older firms, and venture capital funds to assist new firms. Thus, the U.S. has had a *de facto*, if intermittent, technology policy in the form of programs at the state level, federal initiatives such as grants to support R&D in small businesses, and the beginnings, in a few agencies, of a framework for national laboratories and companies to collaborate on R&D.

In this innovation picture, the state governments undertook to play a greater role in the 1980s by supporting both the universities and business through various measures. In Pennsylvania, for example, the Ben Franklin program encouraged linkages between universities and industry by supporting cooperative research projects. Ben Franklin also made available "seed venture capital" funding for start-up firms. At the federal level, it was ideologically impermissible to encourage these linkages directly, but at the state level such encouragement was relatively common because it was done to promote job creation and that was an accepted role of state governments.

At the federal level, the problems of the older industrial regions came to the fore in President Jimmy Carter's 1978 domestic policy review, with loss of jobs already apparent in automotive and heavy manufacturing industries. Carter's domestic policy advisors suggested that government address this problem by fostering innovation in industry. But when the administration proposed programs that would give it a more activist role in support of industrial innovation, there was strong congressional opposition. Many in Congress believed that government could not play an effective role, that governmental action would likely make the situation worse, not better. Carter's initiative was viewed as interference with the market and called an attempt to "pick winners"; it was not acceptable at that time for government to play an open role. But the issue of innovation or reindustrialization, as the Carter administration called it, was too important to be dropped entirely.

In the face of widespread opposition to a direct approach, advocates of an innovation policy took an indirect approach, focusing on the ancillary issue of the build-up in the universities of discoveries with potential industrial relevance that were made by academic researchers in the course of their investigations. This relatively untapped resource was a by-product of federally funded research, whose patent rights were controlled by the federal government. Intellectual property, potentially available to all interested takers, in practice was utilized by few, since it was expected that successful developers would attract "free riders" who could not be fended off given the uncertain legal status of federally funded academic research.

To address this intellectual property issue and the broader problem of stagnation in industrial innovation, a change in the laws governing intellectual property based on federally funded academic research was proposed. The ownership of the rights to discoveries made with funds provided by the federal government would be shifted to the research site. The Bayh-Dole Act of 1980 turned the intellectual property rights to these discoveries over to the universities, saying it was theirs to commercialize. Undertaking the responsibility to see that the results of research were put to use became a condition of accepting research grants from the federal government.

In addition to the requirement to transfer technology, there was also an incentive: if the university was successful in its technology transfer effort, it could retain the funds that accrue from the sale and licensing of discoveries. Nevertheless, the purpose of the Bayh-Dole Act was not to fund the universities; it was to restructure the relationship of academia to industry, making academic laboratories into a source of technological innovation for industrial firms. The metric of success for Bayh-Dole is university-originated industrial innovation: monies earned by universities from their technology transfer activities are, at best, an indirect indicator of a contribution to innovation.

The Bayh-Dole Act is the "land grant" act of the twentieth century. The Morill Act of 1862 provided federal resources, land, to make it possible for universities to create a system of innovation that would make the U.S. the world leader in agriculture. Carter's 1978 domestic policy review, which focused on the need to renew American industrial technology, led the federal government to give the universities federal intellectual property, the virtual equivalent of land, to encourage them to play a similar role in industrial innovation.

From 1980, universities never before involved in technology transfer established offices, hiring a scientist from industry or giving a university attorney the new task of marketing the technology that professors were producing as part of their research. Until the passage of Bayh-

Dole, only a very few universities, such as MIT and Stanford, had been actively involved in technology transfer. In the past decade and a half, technology transfer activities have spread throughout the university research system. The change induced by Bayh-Dole is part of the new role of the university in the innovation system, both in providing to existing firms the technology produced from the research activities at the universities and in facilitating the establishment of new firms by faculty members and students. Technology transfer offices, often initially set up to show best efforts in meeting federal requirements to put technology to use, typically begin to produce income for their universities in seven years. They are soon accompanied by incubator facilities and research parks as campuses broaden their participation in regional economic development either at their own initiative or as a result of encouragement by local governments.

This new role in promoting economic development has become an academic mission along with research and teaching. Just as it was recently considered unusual for universities to be involved in technology transfer, in the late nineteenth century it was considered unusual for universities to conduct research, something entirely accepted today. A number of U.S. and Canadian universities transformed themselves in the late nineteenth century to become research institutions, much as they are currently expanding their mission to incorporate technology transfer.

THE KNOWLEDGE SECTOR

Economist John Maynard Keynes's post–First World War volume *The Economic Consequences of Peace* provides a framework for understanding the changing role of the research university during the current era of constricted financial support for academic institutions. From the era of the Second World War, many U.S. research universities have been extensively tied to the military, conducting research for future weapons systems such as those based on robotics and computer software. Support also came as a reward from a grateful nation for past contributions to the military, such as the proximity fuse and the atomic bomb.

Despite serious conflicts in Bosnia and Somalia, not since the close of the First World War (the Cold War loomed too soon after the second) has the United States had to face the issues of peace for a sustained period. Can a role in regional economic development and in reviving the technology of U.S. industry take the place of the Cold War as the economic underpinning of research universities let loose from some of their traditional moorings?

The academic model of technology transfer has evolved from the research corporation of the early twentieth century, which was an intermediary organization serving as a buffer between industry and academia, to the decentralized and differentiated models common today. Campus-based licensing offices select from a variety of options for the transfer of technology or formation of firms; indeed, they may be part of a broader administrative unit that also operates an incubator facility or research park. The research corporation, as research corporation technologies, has reinvented itself, identifying a new niche as venture capitalist to the universities.

Whether as handmaiden to industry or as independent entrepreneur, the research university has taken a new role in an emerging civilian innovation environment in which the research laboratories of major firms are only some of a number of players, along with government laboratories and start-up firms. There is no single linear approach to innovation. Instead, we can expect the continuous renegotiation of alliances among university, industry, and government entities (Senker 1994). The economic context for the universities had been irrevocably changed by the end of the Cold War, just as the rules of the game for intellectual property were earlier transformed by the Bayh-Dole Act, Congress's "natural experiment" in industrial policy.

There are special problems in each country. In Canada, researchers with common interests are often widely scattered. To encourage cooperation rather than competition among universities, the Natural Sciences and Engineering Research Council established a program of strategic grants and networks to encourage the formation of centres spanning different universities as well as disciplinary and sectoral boundaries. The goal was to bring together investigators with common interests in fields with long-term industrial relevance (Walden 1993).

The next challenge is to transfer the resulting commercializable knowledge to industry. There are several approaches to achieving this objective, including taking no special steps. Proponents of this approach argue that the most effective technology transfer mechanism is the moving van that transports a newly minted Ph.D.'s personal effects to his or her first industrial post. This laissez-faire approach is based upon the assumption that a large corporation with research facilities is capable of effecting its own transfer of technology through the rest of the firm. A start-up firm strategy of technology transfer has become attractive, moving technology from academia to the marketplace by involving the originator of the knowledge directly in its transfer through the incentive of sharing the financial rewards of its commercial success.

A potential contradiction between regional development and cross-national transfer of technology has arisen in all the NAFTA countries. For example, the Technology Transfer Office at the University of British Columbia reports that it is subject to cross-pressures from the university administration and provincial authorities in making deals. On the one hand, pressed for funds in an era of academic constriction, the president of the university wants the tech-transfer office to license university-originated intellectual property to the highest bidder, which may not be a local or even a Canadian firm. On the other hand, regional authorities, having contributed to the support of the office, wish it to pursue a licensing strategy in accordance with their development policy of encouraging the formation of start-ups locally (Livingstone 1994).

Favouring start-ups, of course, means that immediate revenues will be low, although the long-term economic and social benefits for the university and region can be considerable. A similar contradiction appeared in Mexico where the Center for Technological Innovation (CIT), which was started to promote Mexican economic development, sometimes found that its best, or even only, licensing opportunity was to a firm abroad. Once the mechanisms for technology transfer are in place, deals can be made locally, nationally, and internationally, and it is a matter of conflicting university, regional and national government, and multinational authority interests as to which policy is to be favoured and under what conditions. Such concerns are, of course, not unknown in the United States, where MIT and the Scripps Institute have been attacked in Congress (fairly or not) for transferring technology abroad (Etzkowitz 1994b).

THE NEW POLITICS OF INNOVATION

An innovation environment consists of all the resources in a region, actual and potential, that can be brought to bear to stimulate high-tech economic activity (Gebhardt and Etzkowitz 1996). It consists of linkages among companies, universities, and government agencies as well as of the internal activities of the individual organizations themselves. Oftentimes, stimulating an innovation environment to operate at a higher level of activity involves creating new linkages among actors in the same sphere (e.g., consortia among firms) as well as across spheres (e.g., a contract between a university centre and a company's R&D lab) and encouraging existing institutions, such as universities, to play new roles (e.g., in technology transfer and regional economic development); it also involves creating new entities such as science parks and manufacturing extension services to reconfigure or even create an innovation environment from disparate elements.

The Digital Equipment Corporation grew out of a research project at MIT and was followed by a series of spin-offs, establishing the mini-computer industry in the 1950s and 1960s, assisted by the institutions created through a science-based strategy of economic development that was initiated in New England during the 1930s Depression. The biotechnology industry grew out of those universities that in the 1970s and 1980s had made the decision to shift their focus to the molecular paradigm. Biotechnology is currently an $8 billion industry in the U.S, directly producing 100,000 jobs apart from multiplier effects. This growth is contrary to the expectation that biotechnology would be subsumed into the chemical and pharmaceutical industries (although many firms, of course, have been) as an ancillary technique. Nevertheless, new firms have emerged in other application sectors, such as food and research supplies, as well. Biotechnology represents the growth of a robust industrial sector in its own right, similar to the automobile industry in 1910. It is an industry with broad implications (much like computers) for other parts of the economy, including older manufacturing industries, rather than a subsidiary field that will be incorporated into existing industrial structures.

As science is seen to be salient to economic development, science policy is too important to be left solely to scientists. With knowledge assuming increased importance as a factor of production, the traditional elements of land, labour, and capital are reduced in importance, with various political consequences, including the displacement of labour unions in regional growth coalitions by knowledge-producing institutions such as universities. Moreover, government adopts a much more entrepreneurial orientation. It does not just try to create a general political economic climate favourable to business investment but also actively intervenes at all points in the product development cycle: basic research, applied research, product development, and marketing (Fosler 1988). Such interventions presage the emergence of a new form of corporatism based upon academic-industry-government relations – the triple helix (Etzkowitz and Leydesdorff 1997).

The emergence of a triple helix dynamic can perhaps be most clearly seen in declining and newly emerging industrial regions. In these circumstances, where industry has weakened or has not yet developed sufficient scale to be viewed as an autonomous sector, the role of other spheres in encouraging economic growth has become especially salient. Silicon Valley, an icon of high-tech economic growth, originated in strong bilateral university-industry relations, but more recently has become characterized by an entrepreneurial high-tech sector, dismissive of government. However, the affinity with laissez-faire ideologies had its limits. Buffeted by strong competitive pressures from Japan in the 1980s, the semi-conductor industry called upon the federal government to help finance the creation of new laboratories, drawing together researchers from individual companies and academic scientists and engineers, to become part of an innovation complex based upon university-industry-government relations.

The changing relationship among government, industry, and academia in Mexico over recent years augurs the emergence of a new development paradigm with increasing emphasis on science-based technology (Castenada 1993; Carroll 1994). Prior to the currency shock of 1982, Mexico relied on an import substitution policy in which industries were encouraged to expand behind a protective tariff wall. Counter-intuitively, rather than encouraging local R&D and academic-industry connections, this policy left Mexico dependent on imported technology, largely funnelled through multinational firms. Local industry tended to be low tech and labour intensive. Academic research was oriented to contributing to world science, not to local industry (Blum 1994).

This protectionist orientation to economic development shifted drastically after the 1982 currency shock, leading eventually to the Mexican government's push for the NAFTA treaty, encouraging free trade. Mexico's expanding commitment to academic research and its utility to economic development is expressed through increased funding provided by CONACyT (Consejo Nacional de Ciencia y Tecnología) from the 1970s. Research and technology transfer policies are a fairly recent innovation, prompted by a reconsideration of traditional economic development strategy (Martuscelli 1994).

Having expanded university research in the sciences and engineering, Mexico also faces the problem of how well academic research is accepted by its industry. Only a relatively few firms maintain R&D laboratories that operate on a comparable level to the national university's relatively well-developed system of research institutes. Moreover, academic researchers are typically more attuned to developments in world science than to the needs of local industry. The Center for Technological Innovation of the National Autonomous University of Mexico (UNAM) was established in 1983, supported by the United Nations Industrial Development Organization (UNIDO), to match academic capabilities with local industrial needs. A flow of agreements with firms in Mexico's narrow stream of science-based industry followed. Three hundred and fifty contracts were negotiated, ranging from consultation arrangements to transfer of products and processes.

Given the imbalance between national academic science and industry, the existence of a technology transfer capability unintentionally encouraged the international transfer of technology. For example, in one instance UNAM researchers were assisted in making arrangements to have their research carried forward in Italy where the necessary sophisticated research equipment was available. The imbalance between the university's high-tech potential and the lower technical level of much of Mexican industry, despite the existence of biotechnology and electronics firms, has encouraged the university's interest in creating its own industrial sector by developing an incubator program. Such a strategy has historical resonance with Stanford University's involvement in creating an electronics industry adjacent to its campus in order to provide a context for its engineering school.

The Clinton administration, elected to revive the U.S. economy, has put ideological blinders aside in adopting an activist stance towards science and technology policy. It views all areas of domestic, if not foreign, policy as part of the broader agenda for renewing the role of government in national life. Science policymakers such as John Gibbons, head of the U.S. Office of Science and Technology Policy, and Mary Good, under-secretary for technology in the Department of Commerce, are focusing on improving industry's access to government science resources, coordinating the science programs of federal agencies, and developing an economic rationale for government support of science. The principles of this technology policy include a major role for industry in priority setting, government procurement to stimulate early markets for new civilian technology, industrial extension services and other improved means for distributing information, and a shift of the national laboratories from military research to cost-shared industrial research.

These initiatives are typical of an administration that is trying to reform American life on a scale not seen since the New Deal era of the 1930s, although with far less political support than President Roosevelt had. Although change is expected to take place through administrative actions rather than new laws, the administration's goals are still far-reaching. The Clinton administration is intent on making U.S. science policy a subset of industrial policy in order to foster innovation in industry. This is in striking contrast to the policies of the previous two administrations. The Reagan and Bush administrations viewed support for basic research as a legitimate government activity on the grounds that the market could not be expected to fund it, but by the same rationale they did not consider themselves responsible for industrial and near-market research. The Democrats now in power have a new role in mind for science and are taking steps to translate government-supported research directly into economic goods.

This is part of the restructuring of the military sector of the economy that has been taking place since the end of the Cold War. The U.S. has had a dual economy since the Second World War: a civilian economy, which could, more or less (given the competition-suppressing activities of large oligopolistic corporations), be called a market economy, and a military economy, which has been essentially government controlled. The broader factors driving current U.S. science policy are (1) the contraction of the military economy and (2) the need to make government-supported research contribute more fully to the civilian economy in the context of increased international economic competition. Some Democrats in Congress are pushing even farther along these lines, attempting to transform the National Science Foundation (NSF) from a basic research to an innovation agency.

Ideological prohibitions against breaching laissez-faire walls between government and industry have required elaborate subterfuges to make direct intervention possible. During the Cold War, "national security" was invoked to gain support for measures in such diverse areas as human resources and transportation policy, and state governments maintained their industrial policies on the grounds of their traditional responsibilities for supporting local economies. The federal government, however, was expected to desist from such activities save for the exemptions granted them by all-out war. It was only military and space competition with the former Soviet Union that provided exceptions to this ideology.

The driving forces behind science and technology policy that held sway from the end of the Second World War to the end of the Cold War have been superseded. These forces included the following:

- an expanding military economy led by government R&D agencies;
- government support for basic research legitimated by wartime technological accomplishments; and
- scientific and technological competition between the United States and the Soviet Union.

In this context, government support for science flowed primarily through military agencies such as the Office of Naval Research (ONR) and the Advanced Research Projects Agency (ARPA), supplemented on the civilian side by the National Science Foundation. As economic competition displaces military competition, government science policy and funding mechanisms are being transformed to address a new set of industrial policy issues.

The U.S. science and technology policy agenda has become a subset of industrial policy, driven by

- the transition to a mixed economy;
- the civilianization of military R&D; and
- increased international economic competition.

A redistribution of scientific resources and a reorientation of research funding agencies is under way as the "endless frontier" of science is closed. From now on, a social and economic rationale rather than a military or "knowledge for its own sake" justification will be necessary to open the public purse.

The emergence of industrial policy is part of the transition from a dual (military and civilian) to a single mixed economy. Changes in the mission of the university and in the role of government in the economy are assisting this movement out of a military economy. The civilianization of R&D is driven by increased international economic competition, the loss of a military rationale, and the need to move research resources closer to industrial users in order to have them contribute to the civilian economy.

These forces are the impetus to a shift in the role of the national laboratories from military to civilian purposes. Some of these labs were established as part of the Manhattan Project and other programs for weapons development during the Second World War and were primarily devoted to military purposes until the end of the Cold War. Even before the end of the Cold War, Congress decided that the kind of changes it had undertaken in the universities, by encouraging the transfer of intellectual property to industry, should be made applicable to the national laboratories as well.

In the Stevenson Wydler Act of 1986, Congress mandated the national laboratories to play a technology transfer and cooperative research role with industry. Laboratories typically had one customer, a particular department of the government (e.g., Los Alamos performed nuclear weapons research for the Department of Energy, or Livermore did similar kinds of nuclear and Star Wars research for Defense). National laboratories were instructed that, in addition to what they normally did, if things came up in the course of their research that would be useful to civilian industry, some of their engineers and scientists should transfer that work to industry. Thus, the national laboratories soon began to establish technology transfer offices, often modelled on those existing in the universities, and to conduct joint research with companies through Cooperative Research and Development Agreements (CRADAs).

This role in technology transfer has increased greatly with the end of the Cold War, as some government laboratories have entirely lost their previous mission. In order to stay in existence, they are eagerly taking up the tasks of technology transfer; one of their main missions has become to provide research services to industry. Until recently, it was assumed that most of the money that the federal government gave to universities for research, except that earmarked for health and agriculture, was tied to military purposes.

Much of the funds provided to national laboratories was also tied to military purposes. Now those purposes have lessened or even disappeared; new purposes for those funds must be found or we can expect the research universities and the national laboratories to shrink greatly, reflecting the extent that their research activities were tied to defence-related projects. As a result of the Clinton administration's willingness to engage directly with industry in fostering innovation, various programs that had been in existence for several years, operating on a very small scale and funded at $10 or $20 million (which in federal government terms is virtually nothing), have been expanded to a half billion dollars or more. They go by various names – the Advanced Technology Program or the Technology Reinvestment Program or Defense Conversion – and all are targeted at encouraging industrial innovation.

Consortia of companies, large and small, and universities can apply to these programs to do research that will advance product development. The formation of linkages among sectors, drawing together organizations that work at different stages of the innovation process, constitutes the next step in bringing about a new innovation environment comprising universities, national laboratories, laboratories of large corporations, and start-up firms. These organizations act, not separately as in the old linear model, but through various alliances and consortia, creating ties across the triad of helixes (representing the academic, industrial, and government sectors) whose interconnections we have only begun to model and map. These links are not only among firms in an industry but also between firms and universities, among state governments and universities and firms, and now among elements of the federal government, state governments, firms, and universities.

CONCLUSION

There are still gaps in the innovation environment that cause isolated initiatives to achieve less than their expected success. Too often a particular organizational innovation is perceived by observers as the motor of development. For example, the Stanford Research Park originated as a university real estate venture intended to utilize surplus land to make money for the university as an ordinary industrial park, following the success of the Stanford shopping centre. The park somewhat unexpectedly became the locational embodiment of a critical mass of linkages among technical personnel and firms when companies that had grown up around, and from, Stanford University chose to locate there (Saxenian 1994). The high-tech cast of Stanford Park's tenants was an unintended outcome of a well-thought-out university development strategy, originated by Stanford provost and engineering dean Frederick Terman. The park's success represented decades of informal interaction among academic research groups, centres, and firms. When such a model is chosen for replication elsewhere without sufficient attention paid to the context within which the original initiative flourished or to the local region's strengths and weaknesses, unbalanced development or the failure to achieve viability in a "global milieu" is the result (Gordon 1994).

The U.S. venture capital industry originated to fill an economic development gap identified in an analysis of regional strengths and weaknesses undertaken by a group of business, academic, and political leaders in New England during the 1930s Depression. One of the participants, Karl Compton, the president of MIT, envisioned a strategy of creating new technical industries that would build on the region's research strengths and on existing examples of spin-offs from academia, such as the Raytheon company. He persuaded other members of the New England Council to move beyond traditional development strategies, such as attempting to attract branch plants. An analysis of the lack of viability of traditional development approaches in New England, given its unfavourable locational and natural resource characteristics, also identified the unavailability of venture capital, despite the region's great financial strength built upon its earlier industrial and merchant economies. Just after the Second World War, Compton and his associates founded the American Research and Development Corporation (ARD). The corporation assisted the founding of a number of high-tech firms in the region, often based on research from MIT and its laboratories, and spawned a venture capital industry as its employees went off to found their own firms (Etzkowitz 1993).

The U.S. venture capital industry has expanded greatly since ARD's founding in 1946 as a public corporation. Newer firms were organized as partnerships to allow their principals to have a greater share in earnings than they could receive as employees. The closer connection between investment decision and personal reward may have also had a conservative influence on the industry. In recent years, most venture capital firms have invested in the so-called mezzanine or intermediate stage of firm growth, eschewing walking the corridors of MIT and other universities to scout out leads for investment opportunities with faculty and students who would not seriously contemplate starting a business without the encouragement of a venture capitalist. A "seed venture capital" gap exists – that is, there are insufficient funds available to support the early stages of firm formation.

Government programs extrapolated from the early successes of the venture capital industry have only partially filled this early-stage funding gap. The Small Business Innovation Research (SBIR) program, based upon a small percentage of set-aside funds (currently 2 per cent) from federal research programs above a certain size, claims credit for helping to start Intel and many other firms. Although the SBIR program is a great success in terms of providing funds to test new ideas for companies, and even to create prototypes, there is still a venture capital gap in the U.S. for start-ups, a gap that the Clinton administration, despite its industrial policy emphasis, has not seriously addressed. In 1992 a National Academy of Sciences report, authored by Harold Brown, had called for a publicly funded investment bank, suggesting that $5 billion was needed. The scale of the proposal had put off policymakers, drawing attention away from the principle espoused and making it appear unattainable. In the interim, universities, drawing upon their endowments, and state governments, utilizing a small percentage of employee pension funds, have become venture capitalists on a small scale, focusing on opportunities on their campuses and in their local regions.

Many regions have some elements of the new innovation environment, of academic, industry, and government cooperation, in place. In Pittsburgh and the surrounding western Pennsylvania region, a new innovation environment has been developing as separate streams of activity. There has been a wave of formation of new high-tech firms. There is also an older industrial sector that is consolidated now at a much smaller size but still largely exists as a separate area of technology. Recently, the federal government allocated funds to support the Manufacturing Extension Service program in western Pennsylvania, a program to assist existing firms that had been started by the state government and will now be greatly expanded with federal monies. This directly active role of the federal government in supporting industrial development, already in place in Mexico, is the new element in the innovation environment in the United States. There is potential in the Pittsburgh region to establish linkages between the older and newer technology sectors. An opportunity exists for the local universities (Pittsburgh and Carnegie-Mellon) to play a role in bringing these different industrial sectors, as well as government units, together to create new economic activity. Such interaction among sectors is the defining hallmark of the new era of innovation that we are moving into, both nationally and internationally.

Parallel processes are under way in all three NAFTA countries. Bilateral and even trilateral arrangements among firms and universities in the three countries are likely to be accelerated, not so much by reductions in tariffs as by the social mechanisms for increased interaction and interchange that have been encouraged by the treaty.

Critical technologies span boundaries, not only within NAFTA but across the rest of the world. What might be defined as "critical technologies for North America" are likely be on some agency list in the European Union and Japan. One result of prioritizing research expenditures ("technology foresight"), not to mention budgetary stringencies, is a move towards the internationalization of R&D collaboration.

There is a growing convergence among North America, Japan, and Europe in science, technology, and industrial policy. The Europeans, having concentrated on assisting larger firms through pre-competitive research initiatives, are moving towards greater emphasis on start-ups, a U.S. specialty until recently. The Japanese, having brought the art of targeting critical technologies representing future industrial growth to a high level, are developing their academic basic research and graduate training capacities. The United States, with an overcapacity of basic research supply and undercapitalized intellectual property resources, is acting to assist larger, as well as smaller, companies to take technologies off the shelf and into the factory for production, both as defence conversion and as economic development policy. For its part, Europe plans to spend 13.1 billion ECU (European currency units) (U.S.$1=1.25–1.33 ECU) on its fourth framework program (1994–98) to become more competitive with North America. A triple helix of academia-industry-government relations is likely to be a key component of any multinational innovation strategy in the late twentieth century.

REFERENCES

Blum, Elsa. 1994. "Beyond Autarchy: The Transformation of Mexican Science, Technology and Development Policy in the 1980s." Paper presented at the seminar on "The Second Academic Revolution: Academic-Industry Relations in Canada, Mexico and the U.S.," sponsored by the University of British Columbia's Center for Educational Policy Research, Vancouver, B.C., and North American Network, International Study Group on Academic-Industry Relations, Science Policy Support Group, London, February.
– Ph.D. dissertation in progress, Department of Sociology, New School for Social Research, New York City.
Carroll, Paul. 1994. "Foreign Competition Spurs Mexico to Move into High-Tech World." *Wall Street Journal*, 5 July, 1, 9.
Castenada, Jorge Amigo. 1993. "Proposal of Policy for the Promotion of the Modernization of Technology of the Industrial Sector within the 1990's." Prepared for the Ministry of Commerce and Industrial Development, Directorate General of Technological Development, Mexico.
Etzkowitz, Henry. 1993. "Enterprises from Science: The Origins of Science-Based Regional Economic Development," *Minerva*, Fall.
– 1994a. "Technology Centers and Industrial Policy: The Emergence of the Interventionist State in the USA." *Science and Public Policy* 21 (2): 79–87.

– 1994b. "After NAFTA: Technology Transfer in Mexico, United States and Canada." *Technology Access Report* 7 (6).

Etzkowitz, Henry, and Loet Leydesdorff, eds. 1997. *Universities in the Global Knowledge Economy: A Triple Helix of Academic-Industry-Government Relations.* London: Cassell.

Farnsworth, Clyde. 1994 "Labatt to Buy Part of Mexican Brewer." *New York Times*, 7 July, D3.

Fosler, Scott. 1988. *The New Economic Role of American States.* New York: Oxford.

Gebhardt, Christiane, and Henry Etzkowitz. 1996. "The Regional Innovation Organizer (RIO): A New Quasi-Public Role of Transnational Firms and Universities." Paper presented at the Madrid COSTA3 Conference, June.

Giorden, Judy. 1994. "Managing Strategic Alliances." Paper presented at a conference at Rutgers University, Center for Technology Research Management, Newark, N.J., 30 June.

Good, Mary. 1993. Luncheon address at the "Managing across Boundaries" conference, Conference Board, New York City, 16 November.

Gordon, Richard. 1994. "Industrial Districts and the Globalization of Innovation: Regions and Networks in the New Economic Space." Paper prepared at the Center for the Study of Global Transformations, University of California, Santa Cruz, March.

Hilpert, Ulrich. 1991. *State Policies and Techno-industrial Innovation.* London: Routledge.

Kohler-Koch, Beate. 1993. "Regions as Political Actors in the Process of European Integration." Research paper, Mannheim Centre for European Social Research, University of Mannheim, Germany.

Livingstone, Angus. 1994. "Technology Transfer at the University of British Columbia." Paper presented at the seminar on "The Second Academic Revolution: Academic-Industry Relations in Canada, Mexico and the U.S.," University of British Columbia's Center for Educational Policy Research, Vancouver, B.C., and North American Network, International Study Group on Academic-Industry Relations, Science Policy Support Group, London, February.

Malerba, Franco. 1993. "The National System of Innovation: Italy." In Nelson (1993, 230–60).

McFetridge, Donald. 1993. "The Canadian System of Industrial Innovation." In Nelson (1993): 299–323.

Martuscelli, Jaime. 1994. "Government Policy and the Rise of Academic Research in Mexico." Paper presented at the seminar on "The Second Academic Revolution: Academic-Industry Relations in Canada, Mexico and the U.S.," University of British Columbia's Center for Educational Policy Research, Vancouver, B.C., and North American Network, International Study Group on Academic-Industry Relations, Science Policy Support Group, London, February.

Mowery, David. 1983. "Innovation, Market Structure, and Government Policy in the American Semiconductor Electronics Industry: A Survey." *Research Policy* 12 (August): 183–97.

– 1993. "The Boundaries of the U.S. Firm in R&D." Research paper, Haas School of Business, University of California, Berkeley.

Nelson, Richard, ed. 1993. *National Innovation Systems: A Comparative Analysis.* Oxford: Oxford University Press.

Saxenian, AnnaLee. 1994. *Regional Advantage: Culture and Competition in Silicon Valley and Route 128.* Cambridge, Mass.: Harvard University Press.

Senker, Jacqueline. 1994. "A Transnational Investigation of University/Industry Linkage in Advanced Engineering Ceramics." Research paper, Science Policy Research Unit, University of Sussex, U.K., March.

Walden, Janet. 1993. "The Networks of Centres of Excellence." Paper prepared for ISG/CIT Workshop on Academic Industry-Relations, Mexico City, January.

PART THREE

Regional Systems of Innovation

7 The North American System of Innovation in the Global Context

JOHN ALIC

This chapter seeks (1) to clarify the meaning of innovation systems, stressing the extent to which they are systems for generating and applying knowledge; (2) to outline the North American system of innovation and explore the usefulness of this construct given a world economy in which national boundaries are porous to flows of knowledge; and (3) to speculate concerning the future place of the Americas in the international economy. The focus is primarily on the United States and Mexico. The U.S. national system of innovation, largely a creation of the Cold War and as yet changed relatively little, dominates not only the North American system of innovation but also the world system. Mexico offers a stark contrast with the United States, as well as with developing economies in East Asia.

SYSTEMS OF INNOVATION

Given length limitations, it is impossible for this chapter to provide a review of the various interpretations of the relatively new and somewhat fuzzy notion of national systems of innovation (NSIs).[1] Most of what follows reflects my own opinions, which differ at various points from those of others who have written on the subject.

THE NATURE OF THE SYSTEM

Let us begin with the simple observation that an innovation system is not like a physical system (say a telephone network); rather it is a construct intended to help us think about some problem or answer some question. To get anywhere, we must define the system in a way that contributes to analytical insight. The problem here is that it is no easy matter to understand the nature of technical change and its role in productivity and competitiveness at the national level, including the respective roles of public science, private technology, and government policies. This requires looking inside country borders and highlighting the most significant features of the national system at the expense of much else that might be going on at the same time – in other words, abstracting, for the purposes of analysis, what is "in the system" from what can be left out because it is of secondary importance or incidental.

Technological innovation, especially in the later stages often called "commercialization," is an activity pursued by business firms. Ideas for new products or processes, along with the knowledge needed for reduction to practice, may originate in university research, in government laboratories, or with independent inventors, suppliers, customers, or competing firms – but the innovating firm is rightly the centre of attention. The most common exceptions arise in military systems and in medicine, exceptions that in fact point to central features of the U.S. system of innovation.

Developing a systemic view of innovation means deciding, first, where to place the system boundary. Around the innovating firm? The firm plus its suppliers and customers? Should the schools and universities that train its employees and create new knowledge be included? Perhaps it is the sector that is central (Mexico's auto parts industry) or an industrial cluster or subnational region (Silicon Valley), a nation, or a group of nations (the European Union). Any one of these choices is possible, depending on the analytical questions to be asked.[2]

Private industry is the locus of innovation, the setting where knowledge becomes artifact – for example, a marketed product or the processes used to produce some innovative output. Still, each firm is different, as is each industrial sector and each technology (whatever might be meant by a "technology" or family of technologies). Unless our interest lies specifically with a particular sector or technology, the proper approach to take in analysing national systems of innovation is to examine the institutional settings within which private firms innovate. This shifts the focus from firms themselves, their similarities and differences, to the contextual setting for firm-level behaviour and to government policies.

Before looking at how the subsystems in the North American system of innovation interact, we need to understand each one – the U.S., Mexican, and Canadian systems – individually. But first there is more to say about how technology and technological innovation should be construed and what this implies for the structure and functioning of national technology bases, for the world technology base, and for innovation as a process.

TECHNICAL KNOWLEDGE

I believe the most useful way to think about technology is in terms of knowledge. Taking technology to mean purposeful human artifacts and the knowledge used in creating them, we can then understand technological innovation as a process involving the application of knowledge, together with other inputs, to design, develop, create, and market some product.[3] The artifactual product should be regarded as derivative, the consequence of research, design, development, production, and marketing activities – of what people and organizations know (declarative knowledge) and can do (procedural knowledge).

In this view, the world technology base consists of the global stock of technical knowledge. It includes scientific theory and empirical results; methods for engineering design (synthesis) and for analysis; and tacit knowledge, including that derived from the practice of engineering and from shop-floor manufacturing experience (Alic et al. 1992, 29–43). Most of this knowledge is old. Some is publicly available, some proprietary. Much is unwritten, or tacit – experientially learned by managers, engineers, scientists, and blue- and grey-collar workers during the course of their working and non-working lives.

Acquisition of tacit knowledge takes place not only on the job, but in school and in other settings where people develop the skills to which we apply such murky terms as intuition, insight, creativity, and judgment. Tacit know-how comes in individual and collective varieties, the latter reflecting group learning, history and tradition, organizational style and habit. No one person, for example, can hope to comprehend a large-scale technical system (e.g., a central-office telephone switch), much less supervise its design, construction, and testing; these tasks require groups of experienced professionals. Organizational competence, further, represents something more – something different – than the sum of the know-how of a firm's employees: for the organization, competence is an emergent attribute, not reducible to individual skill endowments. By extension, this is also true for national economies and national systems of innovation.

COMMON FEATURES

Leaving aside the few remaining planned economies, the innovation systems of all countries resemble one another in the following ways:

- Innovation takes place almost entirely in the private sector.
- Innovating firms depend to a considerable degree on a publicly funded, publicly available technology base that, in principle if not in practice, is global in extent; firms may be considered as hunters and gatherers of technical knowledge, conducting internal R&D in part simply to maintain the ability to absorb technology from external sources.
- Innovating firms complement the knowledge they draw in from elsewhere with proprietary know-how, some of it formalized (and perhaps protected through intellectual property rights [IPR]), but much of it residing in the heads and hands of the firm's employees, in organizational practices and routines.
- The core activity of commercialization, the culminating stage of innovation, is engineering design and development – an activity sufficiently different from R&D that we might call it D&D.

The last point deserves elaboration.

THE IMPORTANCE OF DESIGN

For many years, motor vehicles (cars, pick-up trucks, jeep-like utility vehicles) and electronics (e.g., TVs, VCRs, small computers and peripherals, chips and other components) accounted for the bulk of the U.S. trade deficit in manufactured goods. Japanese firms shipped many of these products to the United States, from Japan or from manufacturing plants elsewhere in Asia. Americans bought them because they liked their functional attributes and performance, quality, and price. Behind the product features and value for money of goods from Honda and Toyota, Sony and Matsushita, stood thousands of engineers and technicians, industrial designers and stylists, product planners and market researchers, factory managers, foremen, blue- and grey-collar workers.

This section of the chapter asks the question: What, if anything, do products like pick-up trucks and VCRs have to do with national innovation systems, in particular the U.S. innovation system?[4] The answer requires that we distinguish technology from science, research from development, and R&D from D&D (design and development). The latter term comes closer than R&D to characterizing the processes by which most companies most of the time arrive at the bundles of attributes that characterize particular products. These are the attributes – including, for a pick-up truck or passenger car, cost, carrying capacity, reliability, fuel economy, safety, styling, resale value – that customers evaluate and compare when they make their purchases. Most of the technology on which these product attributes depend is well removed from science and the laboratory. Yet research does play a part, as illustrated by the ability of automakers to simultaneously increase fuel economy and reduce exhaust emissions – two fundamentally conflicting objectives – over the past two decades. Managing the trade-offs between fuel economy and emissions has, in large part, been a matter of steady improvements in electronic engine controls, depending in turn on cheaper, more powerful integrated circuits and on better understanding of the thermodynamics and chemical kinetics of combustion and post-combustion reactions.

FROM SCIENCE TO TECHNOLOGY

It has been common in policy circles, at least since Vannevar Bush's *Science – The Endless Frontier* appeared in 1945, to view science and technology as a seamless web. After all, physics helped win the war (radar, the atomic bomb), Bush's report set the stage for decisions in the 1950s that continue to shape U.S. science and technology policies, and it is scientific research that underlies high-technology industries ranging from microelectronics and computers to biotechnology and satellite communications. As a result, the perception has grown that research and the policies affecting it form a kind of core activity that more or less automatically determines downstream processes of technology development and commercialization. This perception is wrong. The linear or "pipeline" view, in which research leads naturally to development and then to the introduction of new products and processes, gives an incomplete and distorted impression of the technological enterprise.

Since the 1960s, the simple pipeline model has been repeatedly discredited.[5] It fits neither past nor present and has led to mistaken policies. Nevertheless, with the ever-accelerating pace of change in science and technology, many people have assumed that the two activities have, in some sense, converged. In fundamental ways, they have not. Technology is broader than science, especially in its tacit dimensions, and in many respects more complex and difficult (scientists can often simplify where technologists must find some means for dealing with nature's stubborn realities). Scientists and technologists define and approach problems in contrasting ways. They belong to separate though overlapping professional communities and fill rather different kinds of positions in the labour market. Scientists are trained to do research; their job is to analyse – to break things down and understand them. Engineers are trained to undertake product and process design and development; their job is to synthesize – to put things together. Even though some scientists find themselves working as engineers and some engineers engage in research, most people bear the imprint of their educational background throughout their working lives. Analysis and synthesis, moreover, are fundamentally different skills; few people are good at both. At the same time, of course, technology depends on science, and more so than in the past, just as science depends on technology (with instruments such as microscopes, telescopes, and now missions into space the obvious examples). But the two activities have grown in parallel as much as they have grown together.

THE TWO MEANINGS OF DEVELOPMENT

One reason science and technology are so often confused is that we give "development" rather different meanings depending on whether it is coupled with research or with design. As an extension of research, as in R&D, development implies reducing new knowledge to practice – verifying and validating experimental results and theoretical predictions, exploring specific cases, and determining the accuracy and limits of mathematical models and the methods and techniques based on them. One example would be the development of practical methods for predicting the growth of fatigue cracks in aircraft structures (Alic et al. 1992, 38–40). But when coupled with design, development implies the steady refinement of quite concretely conceived products, processes, and systems through an iterative sequence of conceptualization, preliminary design, analysis, testing, and redesign. This is the everyday technical work of industrial firms, often called product development or product engineering (or process development, software development, and so on).[6] The example here could be the application of methods for predicting fatigue crack growth to determine the spacing of "crack stoppers" in an aircraft fuselage, followed by testing to verify the results.

It might be better to think of design and development as D&D, in contrast to R&D, separating activities in which *knowledge is applied* through D&D from activities that *generate knowledge* through R&D. Instead, the latter term has come to stand for either or both. Engineers and scientists, understanding the distinctions, do not have much trouble communicating among themselves. But the jargon sometimes leads to confusion among those outside the community of practitioners – including policymakers, many economists, and not a few non-technical managers in business and industry.

Let us, then, continue to distinguish R&D from D&D. The former is rightly associated with science (including "engineering science") but should be viewed as loosely linked with product/process design and development and sometimes as quite independent of these activities. D&D draws eclectically on the results of R&D. It is R&D that leads to high-temperature superconductors that may someday have practical applications. It is D&D that gives rise to today's electric motors and generators, minivans and motorcycles. There are few if any secrets in D&D, but a great deal of know-how, much of it unwritten and some of it proprietary.

A pipeline view that sees new technologies as moving progressively and predictably from R&D to D&D is false. Only in rare cases does new science lead simply and directly to major technological innovations. Far more often, new products and processes are pieced together from a crazy quilt of old and new science and technology, liberally supplemented with tacit know-how, good and bad guesses, intuitions and heuristics. The technological enterprise remains in substantial part an art and a craft, drawing on science and depending on it, but also, and not infrequently, going beyond hard scientific understanding. New technology sometimes builds on new science. It always builds on old science and on existing technology. The invention of the transistor followed upon the theoretical understanding of electrical conduction in crystal lattices developed during the 1930s, science preceding technology by perhaps two decades. No one could know that the original research would be put to this use. Today, the design of large-scale integrated circuits proceeds at a rapid pace despite theoretical foundations that are surprisingly weak.[7] Interest has recently been high in using x-rays to fabricate very dense integrated circuits; such applications could hardly be anticipated early in the century when x-rays were new tools for studying atomic structure. Today, too, innovations continue to emerge quite independently of scientific research.[8] For example, the just-in-time or *kanban* production systems pioneered by Toyota, which have had impacts reaching far beyond the auto industry, evolved over more than two decades of shop-floor experience and trial-and-error development.

If the distinctions between technology and science are not as sharp today as they once were, they still exist. Scientists explore nature to understand it. Technologists design and develop tools, products, and systems with purposeful ends in view. And it is technology, more than science, that drives economic growth and determines competitive outcomes internationally, especially in the short and medium term. There are more than 350,000 manufacturing firms in the United States. Fewer than 10 per cent report that they conduct R&D, while all except those that function purely as make-to-order subcontractors necessarily engage in D&D. Consider that the U.S. auto industry spends about $10 billion each year on R&D. Almost all of this money goes towards the design and development of new vehicles. Cars and trucks are complex assemblies, but most of the R&D conducted by automakers differs little in its day-to-day character from the R&D/D&D conducted by a firm that makes, say, windshield wiper assemblies sold to auto firms. Yet the windshield wiper manufacturer would probably not claim (except perhaps in advertising) to be conducting R&D.[9]

DESIGN, DEVELOPMENT, AND INDUSTRIAL COMPETITION

During the 1970s, many U.S. manufacturers, large and small, fell behind their overseas competitors in process know-how. Their costs were too high, their quality not high enough. During the 1980s, even as attention swung to manufacturing, many fell behind in product development. Not only did American manufacturers have trouble providing the features customers wanted at a cost they were willing to pay, they found it sometimes took them twice as long as their rivals abroad to design, develop, and introduce new products. (Many of the gaps began to close during the second half of the 1980s, as U.S. firms took steps to benchmark their competitors and improve their own skills.)

When it comes to the manufacture of internationally competitive products, whether consumer goods like cars and VCRs or capital goods like 777s, the single most critical set of design decisions are those made during the early stages, when overall parameters are set, performance criteria and cost/price targets established, and product attributes defined in at least a preliminary way (Alic 1993a). This set of decisions will, in the normal course of events, have little to do with science (except as physical reality constrains what is possible and practical), but everything to do with perceptions of market demand, business risk, and the anticipated cost and difficulty of downstream D&D.

Both ultimate customer appeal and total life-cycle costs depend in large measure on decisions made before the time-consuming, iterative process of design and analysis, redesign and refinement, testing and modification even begins. Early and largely irreversible choices – whether a new car will have front-wheel drive, a transverse or longitudinal engine with four cylinders or six – come first. Often these follow from marketing decisions (or, in the case of military systems, from requirements set by defence planners). Subsequent decisions involve fundamental trade-offs between conflicting goals – acceleration versus fuel economy versus exhaust emissions, weight versus crash safety. Already, design choices have become heavily constrained. Although a great deal of fluidity may remain at the level of detail design, early choices largely determine the course of downstream development.

The story of the video-cassette recorder, finally, illustrates in concrete fashion the significance of design and development for competitiveness Rosenbloom and Cusumano 1987). Often portrayed as a case of pioneering U.S. innovation followed by imitative Japanese commercialization, it was nothing of the sort. RCA began its R&D on video recording in 1951. In 1956 Ampex, another U.S. firm, introduced a recorder intended for use by TV stations; the machine was the size of a closet and cost $50,000. By this time, Japanese companies had started their own projects. Indeed, helical scanning, one of the key steps along the road to a compact recorder, had already been invented – in Japan. During the 1960s and 1970s, some fifteen companies – American, Japanese, European – demonstrated at least nine different technical approaches to home video. Matsushita was the first to enter pilot production, in 1973, but soon decided its design was not good enough and pulled its products from the shelves. Two years later, Sony's Betamax opened the consumer market. Including Sony's pioneering industrial models, the Betamax represented the seventh generation of the company's engineering development. Sony, of course, eventually lost out to a resurgent Matsushita, whose VHS standard found greater acceptance in the marketplace.

The basic technology of recording electromagnetic signals on flexible tape covered with ferric oxide depends on scientific understanding. But commercialization meant solving a long chain of tough engineering problems so that VCRs with features consumers wanted could be produced cheaply and would function reliably. This is where Japanese companies succeeded, through persistence and creative design, while American and European firms failed. Once the VCR became a commercial reality, competition centred on cost reduction, image quality, and longer recording times. The competitive race – those many generations of product development and testing – turned on engineering skills and management commitment, not on scientific expertise. Similar stories could be told in many other product categories and industrial sectors. In most companies most of the time, design has been the principal factor in determining market outcomes. This is true for big companies and small, high-technology industries (aircraft, electronics) and low (furniture, apparel). Few people would argue that the relative success of Boeing compared to McDonnell Douglas, or of General Motors compared to Toyota, has had much to do with research; on the other hand, outcomes have plainly had a great deal to do with product attributes, hence with design and development.

The answer to the question posed at the beginning of this section, then, goes something like the following. Pick-up trucks, VCRs, and other mass-produced goods, traded internationally and sold primarily to household consumers, may embody research results or "high technology," but only occasionally do the product attributes that *differentiate* them depend on R&D. It is D&D that differentiates them. D&D depends heavily on intangibles, tacit skills, know-how, organizational competencies. Models of national innovation systems accommodate these aspects of technological development and competition, but the label itself, because innovation connotes the commercialization of invention, of new knowledge, tends to exaggerate the importance of high technology and research as opposed to the everyday practice of engineering design and development.

FROM RESEARCH TO COMMERCIALIZATION

When innovation occurs, it generally reflects the artful combination of new knowledge with, typically, a great deal of existing knowledge. If new knowledge originating in R&D is critical, then a successful innovation, leaving aside exceptions such as defence systems, is also, by definition, one that meets the test of the marketplace. As discussed above and as Figure 7.1 suggests, the underlying R&D may be far removed in time and place from the design and development that precedes marketplace success. Central to the national innovation system of any advanced economy, then, will be mechanisms both for generating new knowledge through R&D and for applying knowledge, new and existing.

Governments support innovation directly, by conducting and paying for R&D that increases the stock of publicly available, non proprietary knowledge, and indirectly, through measures that encourage R&D, D&D, and commercialization by private firms. The indirect measures range from public education to protection for intellectual property rights to production subsidies. Said another way, government technology or innovation policies have three primary elements:

1. funding for the creation of new knowledge through R&D;
2. support for the diffusion and application of both new and existing knowledge (e.g., through education and training, industrial extension, as a side effect of government procurement); and
3. measures intended to stimulate commercialization and entrepreneurial activity in the private sector by reducing risks (trade protection for infant industries) or raising rewards (IPR) or both (tax preferences).

National systems of innovation are distinguished in part by the mix of policies at a given point in time, in part by persisting patterns of industrial and institutional structure (e.g., government-business relations, university-industry linkages) that form the backdrop for particular cases of innovation and set limits to the policies governments can pursue in the short and medium term. Over the postwar period, some

Figure 7.1
From Research to Commercialization

Old and New Knowledge Originating in Publicly Funded R&D	Old and New Knowledge Originating in Industry R&D
1 Publicly available technical knowledge	3 Product process specific
2 Marketing information insights	4 Product/Process Development (D&D)
	5 Commercialization

have emphasized R&D (the United States), others diffusion and applications (Japan). Nonetheless, governments in all industrialized countries pursue all three sets of policies.

Of course, less-developed economies with fewer needs for new knowledge may benefit from research specialized to their situation. Mexico depends heavily on agricultural technologies developed for U.S. growing conditions; R&D on hybrid seeds, agrochemicals (fertilizers, herbicides, pesticides), and cultivation practices tailored to the varying microclimates of this arid and mountainous country would improve its agricultural productivity (OTA 1992). Still, we would expect to find innovation systems in developing countries that emphasize diffusion of existing knowledge, education and training of technicians, technologists, and managers, and inward flows of know-how from abroad. Many do show these features (a number of rapidly growing economies in Southeast Asia), but others for many years seemed intent on trying to emulate the research-oriented systems of the West (India, much of Latin America).

THE THREE COUNTRIES

U.S. national expenditures on R&D, currently running around $170 billion per year, exceed those of Canada by 20 times (twice on a per capita basis) and those of Mexico by well over 100 times. Canada and Mexico come closer to the United States in the number of engineers they graduate – in recent years, about 65,000 in the United States, 30,000 in Mexico, and 8,000 in Canada.[10] Statistics on R&D spending and the technical workforce give information on inputs to innovation. There are no very useful indicators of outputs, although insight can sometimes be gleaned from patent statistics, bibliometric data, and expert evaluations.

The United States

Continuing the shorthand treatment of innovation systems, we first focus on the United States:[11]

- Given that the U.S. government spent vastly more than other Western governments on R&D during the Cold War, much of the newer knowledge in the world technology base originated in the United States. (In 1960 the U.S. Department of Defense, alone, paid for one-third of all R&D conducted in the West.)
- U.S. government spending on R&D, little changed since the late 1980s in current dollars at about $60 billion annually (thus declining in real terms), has traditionally reflected government missions, notably defence, space, and health care. (Federal agencies, which paid for about 36 per cent of U.S. R&D in 1995, accounted for two-thirds of the national total in 1960 and more than half until the end of the 1970s.)
- In 1995 the U.S. government paid for about 17 per cent of R&D carried out in U.S. industry, a figure that has been declining steadily; in 1960 more than half of R&D funds spent by U.S. industry came from federal agencies, mostly for defence.

Spending by U.S. industry from internally generated funds, currently more than about $100 billion annually (about half of the reported total accounted for by the fifty largest R&D spending firms), although impressive in absolute terms, represents a smaller fraction of business revenues than in Japan or Germany. A half-century of mission-driven government spending has led to an innovation system that, if not distorted, has been very much focused on electronics, aerospace, and the biomedical sciences (where spending has grown especially rapidly since the early 1980s). During the Cold War, defence agencies pursued new knowledge in a multitude of fields, many of them far-removed from immediate military needs, seeking to ensure that discoveries would occur first in the United States. Research was a hedge against technological surprise, high-technology weapons a counterweight to the numerical superiority of the Soviet Union. In the case of health care, U.S. policies have stressed science rather than its applications.

Competitive difficulties in a number of U.S. industries since the 1960s suggest that the portfolio of government-funded R&D has been too narrow to support a vast and diverse economy. Private firms, accustomed to munificent federal funding of the underlying technology base, looked for breakthroughs while neglecting incremental innovation and shop-floor production. With quick and easy access to new technical knowledge, U.S.-based firms often gained early leads in emerging technologies, but in recent years they have rarely been able to use the resulting capabilities to establish substantial competitive advantages. A rather miscellaneous array of measures intended to stimulate commercialization and entrepreneurial activity – R&D tax credits, in place since the early 1980s; the 1984 National Cooperative Research Act, signalling that government would take a tolerant view of collaborative R&D; the Small Business Innovation Development Act, which established R&D set-asides for small firms; a long list of policies intended to create closer links between federal laboratories and private industry – have not been enough to compensate for an innovation system that, as a whole, continues to reflect Cold War priorities.

The U.S. system of innovation will change over the next two decades, because it must. The needs seem plain (Alic et al. 1992):

- new forms of support for *pathbreaking* technologies (long term/high risk), of the sort that defence agencies frequently sponsored in the past, but which firms rarely fund on their own because the paybacks are too uncertain and/or too far in the future;
- greater support for *infrastructural* (generic) technologies, where industry tends to underinvest because no single company can appropriate the full economic benefits, even though widespread if incremental social returns can be expected;
- support for *strategic* R&D, where business risks and financial constraints combine to slow the development of technologies having substantial importance for industrial competitiveness, national security, or both (Sematech has been the prime example); and
- greatly strengthened mechanisms for the *diffusion* of both new and existing technologies.

With such undertakings as the Technology Reinvestment Project (TRP), authorized in the Defense Conversion, Reinvestment, and Transition Act of 1992, and the Commerce Department's Advanced Technology Program (ATP), authorized in 1988 and first funded in 1990, the U.S. government in effect began to seek a new set of mechanisms for supporting commercially relevant industrial technologies. At the same time, in emphasizing environmental protection, energy conservation, and sustainability, the Clinton administration has returned, with updated rationales and rhetoric, to policy priorities much like those under President Jimmy Carter. Other than the dual-use thrust of the TRP and the explicit intent of the ATP to support pathbreaking technology development, there is little in the current mix without ample precedent in postwar U.S. technology policy. Like other recent administrations, that of President Clinton has talked a great deal about education, training, and related investments in human resources without much meaningful action.

MEXICO AND CANADA[12]

The North American Free Trade Agreement (NAFTA) links three very different countries – two rich, the other poor; two with political and legal traditions rooted in England and France, the third a blend of Spanish and ancient Amerindian civilizations. While per capita incomes in Canada approach those in the United States, and not a few people would say the quality of life in Canada is superior, Mexico is semi-industrialized, struggling with rapid population growth and the legacy of a deep economic downturn in the 1980s and a more recent crisis earlier in the current decade – all this as the country negotiates the transition from a highly regulated and protected economy to one open to the forces of international competition. During the 1980s, as prices for Mexico's oil exports fell and interest rates on its foreign debt rose, the peso lost 99 per cent of its value against the dollar and the real wages of Mexican workers dropped by some 40 per cent. Into the next century, as it seeks to attract foreign investment and to educate, train, and create jobs for a workforce in which unemployment and underemployment have been endemic, Mexico will have to cope with a continuing exodus of labour from an overlarge and underproductive agricultural sector. Immersion in the international economy is relatively new for all three countries, although it represents the sharpest break with the past for Mexico, which pursued a policy of import-substitution industrialization from roughly 1950 until joining the General Agreement on Tariffs and Trade (GATT) in 1986. Canada, for its part, rich in natural resources but viewing itself as a branch-plant economy, has long worried over its dependence on U.S. investment. Canadian auto plants, for instance, turn out large numbers of cars and trucks (nearly 2.4 million in 1995), but Canada conducts very little automotive R&D or D&D: the plants are foreign owned, their products designed in the United States or the Far East.

The strengths of Canada's innovation system include first-rate universities and research laboratories, along with a considerable range of niches in sectors such as telecommunications hardware, aerospace, mining equipment, pulp, paper, and printing machinery, and biotechnology. But no one would expect Canada, with one-tenth the population of the United States, to be a leader on the broad front of technology. Policy debates have tended to oscillate between two poles. One pole reflects a desire to encourage independent technology development as a means of breaking with Canada's branch-plant heritage. Others, seeing the country's greatest strengths in its natural resource base, argue for policies that would complement Canada's existing niches primarily through development of new technologies linked with that resource base.

Canada's problem is one of allocation: Canadian technology has been excellent in fields such as nuclear power where the country has focused its resources. Mexico's problem is much more fundamental. For reasons explored in the rest of this section, the country has very limited technological resources. In part for that reason, it is harder to discern a national system of innovation in Mexico than in Canada.

Mexico's economy, like its society, is highly segmented. A relatively small number of export-oriented firms, many of them foreign owned, operate world-class factories. Like Canada's auto plants, they import technical knowledge and managerial practices. Some multinational enterprises (MNEs) undertake modest amounts of R&D or D&D in Mexico, but the scale is small – a few dozen, perhaps a few hundred, engineers and scientists per establishment. Although a number of large Mexican-owned firms pursue technology-intensive lines of business (steelmaking, petroleum and petrochemicals), these are the exceptions, and they too tend to rely on imported technology. Most domestically oriented manufacturers are small, use labour-intensive production practices, and have had trouble competing with the imports flooding into Mexico following deregulation and the post-GATT opening of the economy.

To move into more complex production and more demanding markets, both indigenous firms and the Mexican subsidiaries of MNEs need capable engineers and managers. Like other Latin American countries, Mexico traditionally provided good educational opportunities for upper-class élites on a European model, emphasizing the arts and humanities, rather than technology and the sciences (a model that European countries themselves have largely discarded). This pattern has been changing; during the past decade, enrolments in Mexican colleges and universities grew faster in engineering than in any other field. Mexico's high graduation rate of engineers has already been noted; by the beginning of this decade, the country had 4.3 engineers per 1,000 people, compared with 11.6 in the United States (*El Estado* 1991). But many of the country's engineering graduates seem to be underemployed.

Academic coursework is only a starting point in the development of competence: expertise depends on experience. This is especially true in design and development, where problems are fluid and open-ended and cannot be solved with textbook methods. Engineers learn calculus and the principles of electronic circuit design in school. They learn to apply these tools on the job. In recent years, there have been few entry-level jobs in which newly graduated Mexican engineers (and scientists) could begin to build their stores of tacit knowledge and skill. Many, unable to find technical work, have left engineering, taking jobs as production workers or entering non-technical fields. Mexico currently has a surplus of academically trained engineers and a shortage of those tested and tempered by experience; effective deployment of the country's engineers must seemingly await demand. The point can be extended in modified form to business in general. Although demand for managerial expertise is high, time for learning has been scarce; import competition overwhelmed many small Mexican firms before they could adapt and improve.

Comparisons with newly industrializing economies (NIEs) in Asia suggest the difficulties facing Mexico. Singapore spends 0.9 per cent of its gross domestic product (GDP) on R&D, more than twice Mexico's level; Taiwan and South Korea invest at still higher rates (1.7 per cent and 1.9 per cent, respectively) (NSA 1995). Government pays for more than two-thirds of Mexico's R&D. Much of the money goes to public institutions that have little contact with industry; business-funded R&D does not reach $500 million annually. Mexico's government has no active technology policy. Current industrial and tax policies provide little incentive for MNEs to conduct R&D or D&D locally. There are few channels for diffusing technical knowledge and methods, managerial expertise, and other aspects of organizational competence. Dense networks of small subcontractors have helped Taiwan and Hong Kong move rapidly into higher-value-added production. Mexico has nothing resembling these networks. So far, the country has not been able to generate a self-sustaining technological infrastructure.

Nor has Mexico laid the human capital foundation needed for balanced development. The labour force averages six-plus years of schooling. While officials frequently voice their commitment to education, the government has repeatedly cut educational expenditures to steer scarce funds to managing its recurrent debt crises. When family incomes fall, children leave school and enter the labour market. For Mexico to grow economically and develop, large numbers of people will have to improve their knowledge and skills – not only engineers and managers, but bankers and farmers, teachers and technicians. Although Mexico's rate of population growth has begun to decline, fundamental change in the existing patterns will take decades. It is hard to see how Mexico can hope to match the rates of economic growth of the Asian NIEs that began implementing comprehensive policies for human capital development during the 1950s and 1960s.

NORTH AMERICA AND THE GLOBAL ECONOMY

Since the end of the Second World War, notwithstanding efforts to block transfers of technology to the Soviet Union and negotiate stronger IPR protections with many countries, the United States has sought not only to reduce trade barriers but to maintain free flows of technical information, especially the results of scientific research. Nonetheless, a substantial portion of the world stock of technical knowledge remains inaccessible – proprietary or tacit. It would be quite wrong to claim that innovation takes place in a "borderless world."

NATIONAL INNOVATION SYSTEMS AND GLOBAL KNOWLEDGE FLOWS

National systems of innovation are embedded within the international economy, linked with one another through flows of capital and labour, goods and services (including scientific equipment and consulting), information and knowledge. By definition, technological innovation requires inputs of technical knowledge. An analysis of any national system would therefore include two key considerations: (1) the extent to which the country is more or less self-sufficient in knowledge; and (2) its capacity to absorb and utilize knowledge from outside. Obviously, the United States is more nearly self-sufficient than Canada, and Canada more so than Mexico. At the same time, the United States cannot be viewed in isolation. Not only do major discoveries like high-temperature superconductivity originate elsewhere and at rates that are probably increasing, but U.S. firms import or emulate innovations such as the just-in-time production systems developed in Japan.

National systems differ both in their internal stocks of knowledge and in their access to knowledge resident elsewhere. The stock of knowledge inside a national system consists of the embodied individual knowledge of the workforce (typically including, at any point in time, foreign nationals) along with resident organizational knowledge. Access to knowledge from outside is a function of the absorptive capacity of the national system, which depends in part on individual and organizational competencies, including those of universities and government laboratories.

There is no practical way to measure stocks of knowledge, but it is possible to explore the question of absorptive capacity. I have argued elsewhere that technical knowledge can be analysed in terms of four interrelated factors (Alic 1993b):

1. the extent to which knowledge and methods are *formally codified* as opposed to being *tacit*;
2. whether the knowledge is *individual* or *organizational*;
3. the extent to which knowledge and methods are *openly available* rather than closely held or *proprietary*;
4. the *mobility* characteristics of the knowledge.

The last factor – mobility – determines the nature of the linkages between national systems and the global technology base and international economy.

On the basis of the classification above, we can make the following
statements concerning mobility and absorptive capacity:

1. *Formally codified knowledge* can be transmitted via print, computer
   messages, and other media. Codified knowledge from anywhere in
   the world will be available to any firm in any country provided that
   (a) the knowledge is non-proprietary, and (b) the firm's employees
   have the expertise to understand and apply the knowledge.
2. *Tacit knowledge* moves primarily when people move. Firms can acquire
   tacit knowledge, organizational or individual, by bringing in new
   people. When a U.S.-based automaker sends a group of engineers,
   managers, and technicians to Mexico to help set up a factory, it is
   transplanting organizational knowledge. When a company hires a
   recent Ph.D. in organic chemistry, it may expect not only codified
   knowledge, learned in school, but a set of tacit skills likewise reflecting the latest in the practice of research — insights and intuitions
   that might pay off in the synthesis of valuable new compounds.

Put most simply, having access to the global technology base is a matter
of having people with the education, training, and experience to utilize available knowledge and methods effectively. Despite the attention
given to intellectual property rights, I believe that the tacit portion of
the global technology base is by far the most important.

NORTH AMERICA IN A REGIONALIZED WORLD

There is one final aspect of the North American innovation system to
consider, given NAFTA and the prospect of free trade agreements joining other countries in the Americas. Relative to the European Union
and in view of the possibility of a regional economic bloc coalescing
around Japan, how might an "Americas Economic Bloc" (AEB) stack
up? In such a world, would an AEB be an effective counterweight to
other loosely organized regions? Or would it be a partnership among
the weak?

Fundamentally, an AEB would couple the technological strengths of
the United States and Canada with low-wage labour elsewhere in the
hemisphere. But cheap labor is becoming less important in the world
economy – a basic dilemma for Mexico, Latin America, and the Caribbean, indeed the entire developing world. An AEB, moreover, would
show less balance – more pronounced asymmetries in state of develop-

ment – than regional groupings in Asia and Europe.[13] Greece and Spain, for example, may be relatively underdeveloped compared to Germany, but they are well ahead of Mexico. Nor is Mexico the only Latin American economy to have been hard hit by debt and economic slowdown since the early 1980s or to have a development history that compares unfavourably with the Asian NIEs. Argentina has deindustrialized since the first part of the century. Brazil, which at the beginning of the 1960s seemed to have much better prospects than South Korea, could not capitalize on its potential.

Of course, Central and South American countries are rich in natural resources and for decades, indeed centuries, have traded raw materials and agricultural products for manufactured goods. But much of the technology and managerial expertise in an AEB would have to come from the United States and Canada, while absorptive capacities elsewhere would be little better than those in Mexico, in many cases worse. A number of Latin American nations have honourable if modest scientific traditions, and a few have managed to do well technologically in targeted sectors (e.g., small aircraft in Brazil), but their R&D/D&D infrastructures are neither broad nor deep: Canada spends more on R&D than does all of Latin America. Mexico, Canada, and much of the rest of the hemisphere, finally, trade heavily with the United States. It is the United States that trades with the world. No other country in the Americas would bring to the table a broadly competitive set of industrial sectors. No other potential AEB country is home to any considerable number of MNEs with substantial experience in world markets and reservoirs of proven managerial talent. The basis for an AEB would have to be

- U.S. technology, with secondary contributions from Canada and elsewhere;
- U.S. management, with significant contributions from other potential AEB countries;
- a large and diverse resource and agricultural base; and
- cheap labour with relatively low skills.

It is much harder to envision an Americas innovation system than a European or Asian innovation system.

Lest this seem an unduly pessimistic or parochial way to conclude, I should stress that while a world divided into regional blocs seems to me a distinctly second-best outcome compared to a largely open and reasonably well integrated global economy, an AEB within such a global economy but not isolated from it could be distinctly good for the Americas. Mexico and the rest of the hemisphere need inflows of knowledge and capital to develop. The United States, too, needs to bring in more know-how from the rest of the world as well as do a better job of diffusing and applying technology domestically.

As the Office of Technology Assessment pointed out in *U.S.-Mexico Trade: Pulling Together or Pulling Apart?*, the United States faces a choice between two future development paths. The first, based on low wages relative to other advanced economies and acceptance of the low productivity growth of the past two decades, would condemn much of the U.S. labour force to a future of declining living standards and dead-end jobs. The alternative, emphasizing human resources, work reorganization, and labour market structures that support higher wages and upward mobility in an economy increasingly dominated by services – and aiming at higher productivity growth to support those higher wages – would create a broader array of opportunities for both individuals and firms. The continent – and the hemisphere – faces a similar set of choices. Free trade does not automatically lead to the more desirable path. If the benefits of economic integration are to be spread broadly, the process will have to be guided and managed. The first step is to understand where we are and where we might go.

NOTES

1 For a survey, see Nelson (1993). Despite what were no doubt the best efforts of the editor and a distinguished steering committee, the country chapters in this volume show only limited signs of a common framework. Freeman and Lundvall (1988) include an earlier selection of papers. Also pertinent among early contributions are Ergas (1987) and Teece (1987). The outpouring of work on differences among national economies, especially the contrasts between Japan's economy and those of Western nations, underlies and parallels much of the recent work on national innovation systems. Viewing innovation systematically raises questions of industrial structure, corporate financing, labour relations, human capital, and managerial practices. Given that a nation's system of innovation is in effect a subsystem of its political economy, much of the literature on differences among national economies is also relevant, at least in principle.

2 Network analysis offers a somewhat different perspective, one that we might note without pursuing: multinational enterprises (MNEs) can be viewed as network structures superimposed on national economic structures.

3 The outputs of innovation can include intangible service products as well as physical objects and systems.

4 This section is based on Alic (1991).

5 The misleading nature of the pipeline model has always been self-evident to practitioners, especially engineers (who generally have less reason

than scientists to try to defend funding for research). See, for example, Schon (1967, esp. 3–18), Morton (1969), and Jones (1970). For the demolition of pipeline models through academic studies of innovation, see Jewkes, Sawers, and Stillerman (1969), Myers and Marquis (1969), and Langrish et al. (1972).

6 Kidder (1981) gives a rich and compelling portrait of development, albeit one in which management and interpersonal relations get more attention than technology.

7 "In hindsight, it is clear that our present level of electronic sophistication is the result of luck, trial-and-error, and the beneficence of nature, aided in small part by a few critical theoretical insights" Yablonovitch (1989, 350).

8 For a marvellously detailed illustration from the not so distant past, see Vincenti (1984).

9 As defined by the U.S. National Science Foundation (NSF), keeper of the country's R&D statistics, development is the "systematic use of the knowledge or understanding gained from research directed toward the production of useful materials, devices, systems or methods, including design and development of prototypes and processes." (See NSF 1996.) Given this definition, a good deal of D&D, or knowledge utilization, should be included. As actually applied, however, NSF's R&D figures seem to miss a good deal of D&D. Census Bureau surveys of companies provide the basis for NSF's statistics. If companies do not think they are doing R&D, they will not report expenditures when surveyed. Managers of small manufacturing firms (and also managers of many service firms) rarely seem to view their firms as engaging in R&D, no doubt because the common usage of R&D has become so strongly associated with the search for new knowledge through research.

10 Canada spends about $8 billion annually on R&D, Mexico about $1 billion. Data on R&D and numbers of engineering graduates can be found in NSF (1996) and UNESCO (1996). Although Mexico graduates more engineers than scientists (some 9,700 first degrees in the natural sciences in 1990), the reverse is true in the United States (105,000 science degrees) and Canada (13,400).

11 This summary follows Alic et al. (1992). Spending figures for recent years come from NSF (1996).

12 This section, dealing largely with Mexico, draws on *U.S.-Mexico Trade* OTA (1992) and Alic (1995). On Canada, see especially McFetridge (1993), de la Mothe and Dufour (1990), and Niosi (1991).

13 See OTA (1992), 107–8, especially Figure 5-1, which is based on Porter and Roessner (1991). Porter and Roessner develop a set of indicators of technological capacity for twenty-nine countries, drawing on both statistical data (e.g., levels of education, capital stock in industry) and expert opinion (e.g., evaluations of managerial capabilities).

REFERENCES

Alic, John A. 1991. "Science, Technology, and Economic Competitiveness."
   Paper prepared for the conference on Alexander Hamilton's Report on
   Manufactures, Hagley Museum and Library, Wilmington, Delaware, 8
   November.
– 1993a. "Computer Assisted Everything? Tools and Techniques for Design
   and Production." *Technological Forecasting and Social Change* 44: 359–74.
– 1993b. "Technical Knowledge and Technology Diffusion: New Issues for U.S.
   Government Policy." *Technology Analysis and Strategic Management* 5: 369–83.
– 1995. "Organizational Competence: Know-How and Skills in Economic
   Development." *Technology In Society* 17: 429–36.
Alic, John A., Lewis M. Branscomb, Harvey Brooks, Ashton B. Carter, and
   Gerald L. Epstein. 1992. *Beyond Spinoff: Military and Commercial Technologies
   in a Changing World.* Boston, Mass: Harvard Business School Press.
de la Mothe, John, and Paul R. Dufour. 1990. "Engineering the Canadian
   Comparative Advantage: Technology, Trade, and Investment in a Small,
   Open Economy." *Technology in Society* 12: 369–96.
El Estado del Arte de la Ingenieria en Mexico y en el Mundo. 1991. Mexico City:
   Academia Mexicana de Ingenieria.
Ergas, Henry. 1987. "The Importance of Technology Policy." In Dasgupta,
   Partha, and Paul Stoneman, eds, *Economic Policy and Technological Perform-
   ance*, 51–96. Cambridge, U.K.: Cambridge University Press.
Freeman, Christopher, and Bengt-Åke Lundvall, eds. 1988. *Small Countries
   Facing the Technological Revolution.* London: Pinter.
Jewkes, John, David Sawers, and Richard Stillerman. 1969. *The Sources of
   Invention.* 2d ed. London: Macmillan.
Jones, J. Christopher. 1970. *Design Methods: Seeds of Human Futures.* London:
   Wiley-Interscience.
Kidder, Tracy. 1990. *The Soul of a New Machine.* New York: Avon. Originally
   published in 1981.
Langrish, J., M. Gibbons, W.G. Evans, and F.R. Jevons. 1972. *Wealth from
   Knowledge.* London: Macmillan.
McFetridge, Donald G. 1993. "The Canadian System of Industrial Innova-
   tion." In Nelson (1993, 299–323).
Morton, Jack A. 1969. "From Research to Technology." In David Allison, ed.,
   The R&D Game: Technical Men, Technical Managers, and Research Productivity,
   213–35. Cambridge, Mass: MIT Press.
Myers, Sumner, and Donald G. Marquis. 1969. *Successful Industrial Innova-
   tions: A Study of Factors Underlying Innovation in Selected Firms.* NSF 69–17.
   Washington, D.C.: National Science Foundation.
Nelson, Richard R., ed. 1993. *National Innovation Systems: A Comparative
   Analysis.* Oxford and New York: Oxford University Press.

Niosi, Jorge. 1991. "Canada's National System of Innovation." *Science and Public Policy* 18: 83–92.

NSF (National Science Foundation). 1995. *Asia's New High-Tech Competitors.* NSF 95–309. Arlington, Va: NSF.

– 1996. *Science & Engineering Indicators – 1996.* Arlington, Va: National Science Board.

OTA (Office of Technology Assessment). 1992. *U.S.-Mexico Trade: Pulling Together or Pulling Apart?* Washington, D.C.: OTA, October.

Porter, Alan L., and J. David Roessner. 1991. "Indicators of National Competitiveness in High Technology Industries." Executive Summary, Phase I Report, and Phase II (Final) Report under National Science Foundation Award Number 8808909, Georgia Institute of Technology, Atlanta, May.

Rosenbloom, Richard S., and Michael A. Cusumano. 1987. "Technological Pioneering and Competitive Advantage: The Birth of the VCR Industry." *California Management Review* 29: 51–76.

Schon, Donald. 1967. *Technology and Change.* New York: Delta.

Teece, David J. 1987. "Capturing Value from Technological Innovation: Integration, Strategic Partnering, and Licensing Decisions." In Bruce R. Guile and Harvey Brooks, eds, *Technology and Global Industry: Companies and Nations in the World Economy,* 65–95. Washington, D.C.: National Academy Press.

UNESCO. 1993. *World Science Report 1993.* Paris: UNESCO.

Vincenti, Walter G. 1984. "Technological Knowledge without Science: The Innovation of Flush Riveting in American Airplanes, ca. 1930–ca. 1950." *Technology and Culture* 25: 540–76.

Yablonovitch, E. 1989. "The Chemistry of Solid-State Electronics." *Science* 246 (October): 347–51.

8 The Regionalization of Production and Competitiveness in East Asia

JOHN RAVENHILL

The relative contribution made by states and market forces to East Asia's impressive economic performance continues to dominate academic discussion of the region, a tendency reinforced by the publication of the controversial World Bank report *The East Asian Miracle* (World Bank 1993).[1] Curiously, the bank's report says almost nothing about the firms or the organization of production in the region. By continuing to focus on the nation-state as the principal unit of analysis, the bank and many of its critics alike have ignored the regionalization of production that has greatly accelerated in the last decade, contributing significantly to the ability of firms from Northeast Asia to maintain their competitiveness.

In this chapter, I examine why regionalized production networks have attained such prominence and attempt to assess their consequences for the competitiveness both of firms and of national economies in East Asia.[2] I then consider the relationship of these networks to intergovernmental agreements on regional economic cooperation and conclude by raising a number of questions about some of the challenges faced by East Asian countries in maintaining or improving their positions within the production networks.

THE EMERGENCE OF PRODUCTION NETWORKS

At first glance, reference to changing patterns of comparative advantage as indicated in the movement in relative factor prices might appear to provide an adequate explanation of the regionalization of production in East Asia. Such an account, however, would be incomplete.

Changing geopolitical context and technological developments also play an important role.

The regionalization of production in East Asia has its foundations in the Japanese colonial period. Japanese production in Taiwan, Korea, and Manchuria was an integral part of the pre-1945 Japanese empire. The postwar roots of interfirm alliances in East Asia date back to the direct investment in Taiwan by Japanese firms in such industries as electronics and machinery manufacturing in the late 1950s. These investments were intended to establish a Japanese presence in the local market. They were followed by a series of equity and non-equity alliances between Japanese and local enterprises in response to local ownership and content regulations promulgated by the Taiwanese government. The same pattern was replicated, to a lesser extent, in Korea in the aftermath of the signing of the Japan-Korea normalization treaty in 1965 (Bernard 1994). In the last decade, such networks have undergone an important spatial extension. Malaysia, Thailand, and coastal China have all become linked to production in Northeast Asia, so that we may now speak of *regionalized* manufacturing activity in a number of industries.

Three sets of factors, which interacted with one another, underlay the surge in foreign investment that drove the extension of production networks and provided much of the region's dynamism. The first set of factors were those emphasized by mainstream economists – the changes in relative factor costs within the region. Land and labour costs alike soared in Japan, Korea, and Taiwan in the middle of the 1980s. For companies seeking to increase their production of relatively mature products, the costs of undertaking the investment necessary to increase domestic capacity were far more than those of establishing new facilities elsewhere in the region.

The realignment of currencies brought about by the Plaza Agreement exacerbated the problems faced by exporters. The yen was revalued by close to 40 per cent in the years from 1985 to 1987; the NT dollar (Taiwan) by 28 per cent in the same period; and the Korean won by 17 per cent from 1986 to 1988. Currency appreciations of this magnitude were sufficient to overcome inertia and prompt companies to relocate some aspects of their manufacturing in lower-cost countries and to change patterns of trade. Strategies previously pursued, particularly the primary reliance on domestic production of exports for the American market, were no longer viable.

The second group of factors were political. The Plaza Agreement was significant not just in itself but for what it symbolized: the increasing political contentiousness of economic relations between the countries of Northeast Asia and the United States. The original tensions over trade imbalances and market access between Japan and the United States extended to Korea and Taiwan as the latter quickly exploited the advantages they gained in the immediate post-Plaza period by not following Japan in revaluing their currencies to the same extent against the dollar. A surge in exports from Korea and Taiwan to the U.S. in 1987 and 1988 caused the Reagan administration and Congress to increase pressure for a reduction in their trade surpluses. As had occurred with Japan, Washington used the leverage it gained from being the single most important export market to coerce South Korea and Taiwan to allow their currencies to float upwards against the U.S. dollar. Besides the loss of competitiveness arising from currency appreciation, their trade surpluses were squeezed from both directions: the Americans' increasing use of voluntary export restraints and other non-tariff barriers restricted their access to the U.S. market; meanwhile, Washington pressured them to open their domestic markets to American exports. Both Korea and Taiwan were "graduated" from the U.S. Generalized Scheme of Preferences in January 1988. Interstate tensions in turn generated domestic political forces that interacted with and reinforced underlying economic changes. For instance, the Japanese government increasingly pressured corporations to increase both their foreign direct investment and their sourcing from overseas subsidiaries.

The third set of factors has to do with changes in the production process and the advent of the microelectronics revolution. Microelectronics technology does not merely describe a series of clearly identifiable end-products; it constitutes a basic innovation applicable in almost all aspects of product and process design (Lundvall 1992). Microelectronics facilitated the widespread introduction of flexible production techniques. These, in turn, have decreased the significance of economies of scale, thereby opening up markets for a whole range of non-standardized products. Smaller companies have been able to gain a footing in increasingly regionalized production chains. The other important dimension of the microelectronics revolution was its facilitation of transnational communication – most pertinently in this instance between parent companies and subsidiaries and with other partners within the region.

The consequence of these interacting forces was a dramatic surge in foreign investment from Japan, Korea, and Taiwan. Japan's investment in manufacturing in other Asian countries in the years 1986–89 exceeded the *cumulative* total for the 1951–85 period. In 1988 Japanese manufacturing investment in countries of the Association of South East Asian Countries (ASEAN) exceeded that in the Asian newly industrializing countries (NICs) for the first time. The principal reason was that the vast majority of Japanese offshore production of consumer goods for the global market was moved from the NICs to ASEAN (subsequently

China has also become an important location for Japanese investment). Meanwhile, the growth in Taiwanese and Korean investment in ASEAN was even more impressive: total investment from the NICs (including Singapore) in Malaysia and Thailand exceeded inflows from Japan by the end of the 1980s. Data on foreign direct investment alone, however, only tell part of the story. The linkages between companies in Northeast and Southeast Asia included technology tie-ups and the provision of managerial and technical assistance that data on the transborder flow of funds fail to reflect.

The regional political economy now consists of clusters of interrelated manufacturing sectors that are better described as networks than as unconnected industries. The basic organizational "unit" is the interaction between firms linked together in chains of production, exchange, and distribution. Firms, or even decentralized divisions within firms, maintain a degree of autonomy in the chain, but all their significant activity is in some way coordinated with other organizations in the network.[3] This shift has its origins in the vertical interfirm manufacturing and distribution chains and in the horizontal intermarket industrial groups (*keiretsu*) that emerged in postwar Japan.[4] The diffusion of just-in-time production and value-added networks in Japan has facilitated greater interfirm coordination. This trend towards networks was also strengthened by the rise of component suppliers as technological innovators in their own right and by the way microelectronics technologies lend themselves to research and development (R&D) based on intersectoral collaboration and producer-user interaction (Kodama 1991).

The networks are largely built around pre-existing corporate alliances, both within Japan and between Japanese and Taiwanese/Korean producers. Such alliances are not static, however. While ongoing alliances originally were spatially extended to Southeast Asia in the form of links with intrafirm overseas affiliates or with the affiliates of related firms, they have the potential to incorporate indigenous companies or local-foreign joint ventures. This was the case between Japanese and Korean/Taiwanese firms in the 1960s and is also seen in the use of kinship ties by Taiwanese entrepreneurs to locate suitable partners in establishing affiliated companies in Southeast Asia. Although the networks are built around production and technological innovation that is concentrated in Japan, they offer opportunities for technological enhancement and skills upgrading to firms based in other countries that are able to take advantage of the linkages. Even though the low levels of technological capabilities of most domestic firms in Southeast Asia initially limited their participation in these networks, evidence is accumulating of their increased role and of the benefits they have derived from technology transfers from foreign partners.[5] The network as an organizational form is not merely "transactional"; it also implies a degree of ongoing inter-action, coordination, and a certain amount of information sharing that may benefit the weaker firms in the network.

NETWORKS AND COMPETITIVENESS

Any discussion of the impact of the changing division of labour on com-petitiveness within the region should first address the question: the competitiveness of whom? The relocation of some stages of the pro-duction process and/or the transfer of technology from one company and/or location to another company and/or location affects the com-petitiveness of a variety of actors, not necessarily in the same direction. To address the question requires a definition of competitiveness. The competitiveness of firms is simply their ability to produce and sell prod-ucts at an acceptable level of profitability in international markets. The competitiveness of nations is a much more problematic concept that is often susceptible to fallacies of aggregation. The definition put forward by the Berkeley Round Table on Economics is a useful one: "national competitiveness is the ability of a country to produce goods and serv-ices that meet the test of international markets while its citizens enjoy a standard of living that is both rising and sustainable" (Tyson 1993, 1).

No necessary correspondence exists, of course, between the competi-tiveness of firms engaged in the regionalization of production and the competitiveness of the economies of their home countries. The litera-ture on transnational corporations has discussed the effects of moving production offshore at length, so there is no need here for significant elaboration of the issues involved. Much depends upon the counterfac-tual: "what would have happened to the domestic economy and to the skills and living standards of domestic workers if the company had not engaged in foreign direct investment"? Would export and possibly do-mestic markets inevitably have been lost? Would there have been addi-tional domestic investment so that the productivity and skills of domes-tic workers would have been upgraded – as has been argued would have been the case had U.S. companies not transferred abroad labour-inten-sive stages of production?

Beyond the counterfactual, the effects of the regionalization of pro-duction on the home economy will be determined in part by the type of relationship established between the subsidiaries of the corporation located in its home country and the regional production network. Are other parts of the production network dependent upon inputs supplied from within the home country? Have the domestic plants of the com-pany been upgraded so that they now produce components and capital goods rather than undertaking the more labour-intensive parts of the production chain (with an expected upgrading of the skills of the domestic labour force)? From the perspective of the host country and/or companies linked to the production networks, the key questions are, to what extent is technology and knowledge of production techniques transferred, and are labour and management skills upgraded? In part, the bargaining leverage and skills exercised by the host country governments may determine the answer to these questions.

The networks of production that have been extended to Southeast Asia and southern China are hierarchical in that they build to a considerable extent on Japanese innovation and on the competitiveness of Japan's machinery and component manufacturers. The supply of key technologies (e.g., compressors in the manufacture of air conditioners, display technologies used to produce an array of computing and office automation equipment, or derailleur gears for bicycles) is controlled overwhelmingly by Japanese companies. Similarly, a range of intermediate inputs – from computerized sewing equipment to automatic insertion devices – must be sourced exclusively or primarily in Japan. Even though companies in Taiwan, Korea, or Hong Kong may be able to produce a range of capital goods for export-oriented production, the latest technology that facilitates ongoing export competitiveness continues to come predominantly from Japanese (and, to a lesser extent, U.S.) suppliers.

Even though many of the products now being produced in the East Asian NICs and in ASEAN countries are regarded as "mature" (e.g., air conditioners, colour TVs, and microwave ovens), their technologies continue to be developed through the incorporation of ever more sophisticated microelectronics components, maintaining a trend first observed when supposedly technologically mature product groups such as automobiles and TVs began to be produced in Japan in the 1960s (Peck and Wilson 1982). Given the speed with which knowledge of new products is acquired by consumers in what is truly a global marketplace, successful exporting requires that products embody the latest options and technologies. Often these technological improvements require the application of advanced skills in engineering and materials sciences that are beyond the capacity of the countries in which the final products are now manufactured.

Generalizations about the impact that the new production networks have on domestic economies are hazardous, as the networks take various forms and differ, for instance, according to the origins of their lead firms. Hierarchically organized networks of production can both create and limit opportunities for local participation. The opportunities they offer depend in large part on the range of local skills available. Where there is no (or only a limited) indigenous industry antedating foreign investment, as was the case in Southeast Asia, it is likely that assemblers will initially rely largely on overseas procurement of key inputs and on persuading their home-country suppliers and subcontractors to themselves establish local subsidiaries. As surveys of Japanese electronics and machinery companies indicate, local firms can act as suppliers of uncomplicated items; with the continuing rise of the yen, Japanese companies are keen to increase local procurement. However, when Japanese companies set up tightly integrated production processes elsewhere in East Asia, they make use of just-in-time deliveries and require ongoing communication, constant exchange of personnel, and high levels of skill and integrated organization within all related firms. They have therefore often excluded local firms from participation on the grounds that they are unable to meet Japanese skill and quality standards, and on the assumption that communication between firms will be smoother and devoid of misunderstandings if all participant firms are Japanese. In such circumstances, Japanese production practices do contribute to enhancing the local skill base, but do so in ways that are largely organization specific, with relatively few linkages to local (in the sense of domestically owned) firms.

This type of network builds on the vertical and horizontal interfirm relationships that exist in Japan, but extends them to different countries in the region to produce a vertically integrated system of parts production and assembly, particularly in electronics and machinery-related sectors. For example, Japanese parts manufacturers have established facilities to produce electronic components for firms engaged in the large-scale assembly for export of low-end consumer electronics in Southeast Asia. Manufacture of these components has become regionally concentrated in Malaysia. This production not only supplies Japanese or third-country assemblers in Malaysia itself, but has become the supply base for low-technology components for the Taiwanese and Hong Kong consumer electronics industries as well. Taiwanese and Korean companies that are established suppliers for the Japanese assemblers also have set up subsidiaries in Southeast Asia to maintain their relationships. The presence of the Taiwanese and Korean subsidiaries provides a further socio-political benefit for Japanese (and also U.S.) corporations that source components from them: the latter need not become directly involved in some of the most labour-intensive and often labour-exploitative manufacturing activities.

For firms and economies with a greater skill base, more scope exists for the transfer of technology and the involvement of domestically owned firms in the production networks. For example, Korea's large, integrated conglomerates (*chaebŏl*) possess sufficient capacity to engage in capital-intensive mass production of standardized high-technology products.

There have been two different bases for alliances formed between Japanese companies and the *chaeböl* that provide for technology transfer. The first is for Japanese manufacturers to make use of Korean capacity to manufacture mature standardized products such as microwave ovens, thereby obviating the need for increasing their own capacity in products with limited life spans. In return for producing Japanese brand names on an original equipment manufacture (OEM) basis, Korean companies receive technology and quality-control know-how. The second motive for the provision of technology is to lock Korean companies into Japanese standards and specifications, using the broader production alliance to set global industry standards. An example of this is the agreement whereby Toshiba, the world's largest producer of dynamic random access memory chips, transferred its "flash memory" technology to Samsung, Korea's largest semiconductor producer. Toshiba, locked in fierce competition with the American firm Intel, hoped that this licensing arrangement would facilitate the acceptance of its format as the industry standard (*Nikkei Shinbum* 1992, 12). The alliance in turn provided Samsung with favoured access to the new technology in Korea and positioned it to compete globally.

An example from Taiwan illustrates another motive for technology transfer through production networks. Fujitsu, Canon, and NEC preferred to provide prototypes of new computer products to Acer in Taiwan for manufacture on an OEM basis for sale in the U.S. rather than commit new investment and existing domestic production facilities to the new products. Through use of OEM, the Japanese companies are often able to bring new products to the market more quickly than would otherwise be the case; employing OEM suppliers also gives the Japanese companies flexibility through their ability to change suppliers rather than having to reorient manufacturing facilities (USITC 1993).

Subsidiaries of Japanese companies located in Asia did appear, in aggregate, to behave somewhat differently from those of U.S. companies in the first half of the 1990s. Japanese subsidiaries were far less likely to employ local managers, to employ local personnel in senior technical roles, or to have nationals of the host country on their boards. Even where local managers were employed, they were often "shadowed" by Japanese personnel and relegated primarily to the performance of public relations roles for the company. The relatively low levels of employment of locals in key management and technical positions reduced the prospects for the transfer of tacit technical knowledge to the host economy through personnel gaining experience and knowledge in Japanese subsidiaries and then capitalizing on these gains by breaking away to establish their own companies. Moreover, because Japanese managers are less likely to speak local languages and to maintain social networks that include personnel from domestically owned companies, they are likely to be less well informed about the production and technical capabilities of locally owned firms.

Several studies have found that decision making within Japanese transnational companies (TNCs) tends to be hierarchical and centralized, with managers of subsidiaries given little autonomy in key areas of decision making such as the sourcing of capital goods and components (Kreinin 1988; Guyton 1996). This lack of autonomy for local management leads to a third difference in local sourcing patterns. Although there are no data that would enable systematic comparisons controlling for date of establishment, industrial sector, and so on, various studies have suggested that the subsidiaries of Japanese corporations, whether operating in industrialized or less-developed countries, tend to depend more heavily on imported capital goods and components from their home country than do subsidiaries of other TNCs.[6] Moreover, Japanese companies have a greater propensity to internalize their ownership-specific advantages through the replication of their production networks when investing overseas. A study by JETRO in 1994 found, for instance, that nearly a quarter of the sixty-two Japanese affiliates in Malaysia interviewed had invested locally in response to the request of a Japanese assembler (JETRO 1995). In turn, the replication of production networks produces another intercountry difference in foreign direct investment (FDI): small and medium-sized enterprises (SMEs) have a greater share in Japanese FDI than in that of U.S. companies. In general, these smaller companies are less likely to be driven by such ownership-specific advantages as proprietary technology than by the advantages that they enjoy by virtue of the nationality of their management and their established trading links with the large assembly companies; their investment is also more likely to be driven by location-specific advantages such as low labour costs. For the host economy, investment by these SMEs is more likely to have a crowding-out effect on local entrepreneurs, since these companies occupy relatively low-technology niches that start-up local enterprises might reasonably aspire to fill. There is some evidence, mainly anecdotal, that just such a crowding-out effect on local firms has occurred in Malaysia (Ali 1994; Rasiah 1995). In addition, SMEs are even more likely than their larger counterparts to maintain management and key technical positions in the hands of home-country nationals.[7]

In East Asia, at least, the likelihood of technology transfer from foreign subsidiaries to the local economy has been lower for Japanese than for U.S. subsidiaries. This conclusion follows from several of the points made above: the dominance of Japanese nationals in key management and technical positions, the lack of autonomy the affiliates enjoy in sourcing, and the development of supplier networks involving local investment by Japanese SMEs. There are two dimensions here: the diffusion of technology from subsidiaries to local companies and the transfer of technology from parent companies to locally based subsidiaries. In her survey of Japanese affiliates in Malaysia, Guyton (1996) found that Japanese companies were more likely to work closely with locally based Japanese suppliers on product specification and design than they were with locally owned companies. Moreover, there appeared to be less transfer of technology from parent company to local subsidiary: Malaysian employees of Japanese subsidiaries whom she interviewed who had previously worked for U.S. or European subsidiaries reported that the U.S. and European parent companies had transferred more technology more quickly to local subsidiaries than was true of their current Japanese employers. In part this difference appears to result from the lack of English-language technical documentation within the Japanese firms and from their preference for a protracted process of on-the-job training. A further important factor impeding the transfer of technological capabilities to local subsidiaries is the continuing centralization of research and development operations within Japan. Various surveys have shown that Japanese companies seldom give their subsidiaries in Southeast Asia responsibility for more than incremental process improvements: product research and development is rare.

There are obvious dangers in generalizing across different firms, networks, and sectors, especially where relationships among firms are evolving as rapidly as they are in East Asia. Such dangers are made all the more real by the inadequacy of the data available: it is seldom possible to make careful comparisons by nationality of subsidiary while controlling for date of establishment, size, or sector of operation. These caveats notwithstanding, the differences between Japanese and U.S. subsidiaries listed above do suggest that from the host-country perspective, the likelihood of garnering benefits in the form of technology transfer is higher with U.S. than with Japanese investment. But even though the distribution of benefits in terms of firm and national competitiveness from participation in production networks may vary according to the nationality of the lead firms in the networks, little reason exists to doubt that such networks are largely a positive sum game. A great advantage of participating in the networks, from the perspective of domestically owned firms in other parts of the region, is that they facilitate access to the Japanese market, a particularly difficult one for outsiders to penetrate. And with the appreciation of the yen, Japanese subsidiaries have been keen to increase their sourcing from local companies and to provide them with the technology needed to meet production standards.

In Japan, the movement of low-end manufacturing offshore provoked fears that there would be a "hollowing out" of the domestic economy and a loss of production expertise (Yoon 1990). Little evidence exists, however, from the perspective of the domestic economy as a whole, to substantiate these fears. Japan has enjoyed burgeoning surpluses in trade in manufactures with other East Asian countries. The Japanese market has remained relatively closed to manufactured exports from other parts of the region, while Japanese sales of components and capital machinery have flourished (Ravenhill 1993). Studies of foreign subsidiaries of Japanese corporations have shown that they tend to import a larger percentage of inputs from their home country than do branches of TNCs domiciled elsewhere. The average reliance on imports from Japan by Japanese affiliates in all manufacturing sectors (including food and fuel products where there is a high percentage of local procurement) in Asia in the late 1980s was over 40 per cent. Japanese affiliates in machinery manufacturing in Asia sourced close to half of their inputs from Japan (MITI 1991). The dependence on Japan for capital equipment is even higher – more than 75 per cent for affiliates in ASEAN countries in the late 1980s. Such "national" data are of course becoming increasingly meaningless as Japanese assemblers source from local subsidiaries of other Japanese (and Korean and Taiwanese) companies.

For many Japanese corporations, transfer offshore of the manufacture of basic consumer goods has led directly to the sale of machinery and components to subsidiaries or to independent companies in the region. Many corporations have benefited from a process in which production has been upgraded from less-sophisticated finished goods to consumer goods incorporating more advanced technologies and to the manufacture of intermediate goods that often generate economies of scope. As an illustration, take the Japanese electronics industry. Although the value of exports of consumer electronics in 1994 was 60 per cent less than that in 1985, growth in the exports of industrial electronic equipment and in electronic components substantially outweighed this loss. The total value of electronics exports in 1994 was 15 per cent above the 1985 level. Of particular note is the rapid growth in components exports, which more than doubled in value from 1985 to 1994. Exports of industrial electronic equipment also increased (Electronics Industries 1995). Even though the value of production of finished electronics for the domestic market will almost certainly fall back further (because the higher yen will drive more production offshore), the regionalization of production to date generally appears to have improved the competitive position of the Japanese electronics industry by forcing it into upgrading, and it can be said to have improved that of the Japanese economy in the aggregate.

Generalizations about the impact that the regionalization of production has had on companies from other countries in the region, and on their national economies, are particularly risky given the diversity of network arrangements, size of firms, and levels of national economic development. Much depends on the terms on which firms have been incorporated into networks – for example, the limitations that they have accepted on the use of technologies transferred. From both a firm-level and a national perspective, there is always the potential danger of becoming excessively dependent on one party for inputs or for access to markets. Perceptions of the benefits and costs of the new linkages may well differ depending on where one sits. State élites will often be more concerned about the possibilities of excessive dependence, or the desirability of competing in prestigious high-end product markets, than will managers of individual firms that see an immediate profit to be made. The extent of benefits derived from incorporation into such networks will, of course, be determined by the skills of managers and engineers and their ability to exploit the new opportunities available to them, as well as by the size and complexity of a country's existing industrial base.

In China, particularly in the greater Shanghai, Beijing-Tianjin, and northeast regions, a large industrial base was developed as part of the pre-1978 "auto-centric" development strategy. Tensions with both the United States and the Soviet Union also helped foster a core of sophisticated, knowledge-based institutions linked to military production. Thus, unlike other countries in the region, China's recent promotion of export-oriented production is not so much a process of "industrialization" as it is one of "re-industrialization," whereby existing industrial plant and capacity are upgraded and reoriented (Goodman 1992). There are numerous points at which Chinese industry can participate in regional production networks. In contrast, in Southeast Asia, where backward linkages with local companies remain extremely limited, the potential for technology diffusion is poor.

In Korea and Taiwan, the regionalization of production has enhanced competitiveness through the diffusion of some advanced Japanese technologies as well as through the upgrading of local production as low-value-added, labour-intensive processes are transferred to Southeast Asia. As centres of regional expertise have developed (e.g., the production of computer monitors in Taiwan), and the pool of expert technicians has grown, so Japanese companies, suffering from a shortage of domestic technical staff and consequent high salaries, have begun to establish regional centres for research and development outside Japan, especially in Taiwan, Korea, and Singapore. The decision of non-regional firms to take advantage of the regional production capabilities in electronics and telecommunications-related products has strengthened this trend towards the emergence of local centres of expertise. Philips, Europe's largest electronics company, for example, decided in 1988 to establish its worldwide centre for design and manufacture of computer visuals in Taiwan. The emergence of these localized centres of expertise is testimony to the way in which technological spillovers and other externalities tend to be geographically bounded (Krugman 1991). The transfer of some of the more skill-intensive operations from Japan illustrates the considerable scope that exists for companies in countries with more advanced technological bases to carve out niches for themselves in the regional production networks, and the possibility for concentrations of expertise other than at the apex of production networks (in a manner akin to the evolution of the relationship between assemblers and their suppliers within Japan).

For the most part, however, the hierarchical nature of the networks remains unchanged. Key technologies and components continue to be sourced from Japan (and, to a lesser extent, the United States). A recent study of the Korean electronics industry, for example, showed that in 1987 the industry imported 36 per cent of components from Japan (Bloom 1992, 73). This figure may considerably understate the import dependence of the industry. A Bank of Korea study found that only 38 per cent of the value of semiconductors was added locally (Bank of Korea 1993). Korean and Taiwanese electronics companies alike are heavily dependent on OEM production, inevitably tying them to the networks of Japanese and American companies for the sales of their products. Where firms in Korea and Taiwan have to purchase technologies from companies that are also their competitors in markets for final products, they may find that the latest technologies are withheld from them.[8]

While corporations domiciled outside the region may be excluded from some manufacturing networks, they are members of other corporate alliances that link American and/or European firms with Japanese, Korean, or Taiwanese counterparts. One of the most notable trends arising out of the regionalization of production in East Asia is the establishment by American and European companies of subsidiaries, initially in Japan, but increasingly in Taiwan, in an effort to take advantage of the new networks. In part, their role is intelligence gathering, but increasingly the reason for their location is also to be close to what has become the world's leading centre for manufacturing and for R&D in a wide range of sectors linked to the manufacture of electronics products. For countries like Taiwan, the nationality of the firms involved is less important than that they choose to carry out some of their more sophisticated R&D and production operations on the island.

For corporations domiciled outside the region, perhaps the major threat to competitiveness is that the pervasive Japanese presence may lead to the adoption of Japanese standards for various technologies and processes, standards which the corporations may find it difficult to meet.[9]

NETWORKS OF PRODUCTION AND REGIONAL INTEGRATION ARRANGEMENTS

A prominent feature of the East Asian political economy is that, in contrast to North America or Europe, regional economic integration has been both firm and production led, as opposed to being initiated by governments. Governments have, of course, played a role but it has been one that was at best facilitating. The liberalization of foreign investment regulations in Southeast Asia in the mid-1980s (e.g., the dilution of Malaysia's New Economic Policy) undoubtedly encouraged the inflows of foreign investment that occurred in the second half of the 1980s. Elsewhere, in their construction of production networks, corporations have proved remarkably adept at circumventing the barriers to intraregional collaboration that governments have placed in their way (e.g., Taiwan's prohibition of direct trade with China).

Three levels of officially sponsored integration may be distinguished in East Asia: the subregional, most notably the emergence of transborder growth areas; the regional, as for instance the ASEAN Free Trade Area (AFTA); and the supraregional, specifically the Asia-Pacific Economic Cooperation (APEC) grouping.

To date, the subregional arrangements have had the most significant impact on furthering the regional division of labour and increasing the competitiveness of local firms and economies. The most successful of the transborder arrangements – the Hong Kong-Guangdong and Singapore-Johor-Riau (SIJORI) areas – have been largely private sector driven. For instance, companies based in Singapore began investing in Johor in the early 1980s as wage rates in Singapore rose; the process accelerated as the Singapore labour market tightened in 1987/88. The SIJORI growth triangle only took on an official identity in 1989 when, following a meeting between the heads of state of Indonesia and Singapore, Indonesia announced a package of measures liberalizing procedures for foreign investment in the Batam island of Riau. The growth areas have been driven primarily by economic complementarities, in particular the availability of a comparatively low-cost labour force in close geographical proximity to a relatively more sophisticated manufacturing base (Hong Kong and Singapore). Governments have played an important but largely facilitating role. Of particular note are the guarantees offered foreign investors, in southern China through the establishment of special economic zones and in SIJORI through the bilateral Singapore-Indonesia Agreement on the Promotion and Protection of Investments. Governments have also played an important role in providing infrastructure, including transport links and fully serviced industrial estates (Yuan 1991; Heng and Low 1993).

Again, the evidence to date suggests that the new networks of production facilitated by these transborder growth areas have been positive sum. Certainly a hollowing out of manufacturing has occurred in Hong Kong, but the loss of low-paid employment in manufacturing appears to have been compensated by the growth of the service sector. In Singapore, little decline has occurred in the percentage of the labour force in manufacturing; rather, an upgrading of labour force skills has taken place. For the areas receiving investment, little evidence exists to date of any significant transfer of technology (although it is early in the process and much more research remains to be done); instead these areas have served primarily as outward processing platforms, akin to the export processing zones popular in the 1980s.[10]

The success of these subregional cooperation zones has prompted a proliferation of proposals for the establishment of similar arrangements in other parts of Southeast Asia – including a northern triangle linking northern Sumatra with Penang and southern Thailand; a 1992 proposal by Thailand for a "golden quadrangle" to link Laos, Myanmar, Thailand, and Yunnan Province; and other geometric designs that are testimony to the fertile imagination of the region's bureaucrats. Lacking infrastructure to link the various components and in the absence of significant private sector interest, these areas (with the possible exception of the northern triangle) are unlikely to get off the drawing board.

In contrast to the subregional economic areas' success in enhancing the competitiveness of both local firms and, more generally, the local economies, the officially sponsored regional and supraregional initiatives to date have had a very limited impact. The ASEAN Free Trade Area was initiated primarily in response to fears that ASEAN's voice would be neglected in a world increasingly dominated by regional trading blocs such as the North American Free Trade Agreement (NAFTA) and the European Union, that a broader East Asian or trans-Pacific grouping would dilute the Southeast Asian identity, and that a failure to promote regional economic integration would lead to a diversion of investment away from the region to China – and possibly also to Mexico with the formation of NAFTA (the last concern being somewhat relieved by the stringency of the rules of origin in NAFTA). Despite some progress in implementation, AFTA remains more a statement of intent than a reality. Contrast, for instance, the dozen or so pages of the Singapore Declaration of 1992 (which established AFTA) with the length and density

of the NAFTA agreement. For ASEAN, the danger is that other developments will overtake AFTA, including the unilateral lowering of tariffs by
its member states and the possibility that one or more of its parties will
seek special arrangements with other trading groups (e.g., the desire of
Singapore to forge a link with NAFTA) (Ravenhill 1995).

The most ambitious of the new intergovernmental forums, the Asia-
Pacific Economic Cooperation grouping, is also still in its formative stages.
It remains to be seen whether the commitment to free trade by 2010 for
the industrialized countries and 2020 for the less-developed countries,
made at the Bogor leaders' meeting in 1994, will be realized. APEC's
working parties may, through their promotion of harmonization and
standardization, help reduce the transactions costs of commerce among
its member states. And APEC also has its uses as a vehicle to maintain
pressure for non-discriminatory trade liberalization. Beyond these functions, it is difficult to see APEC having a significant impact on the competitiveness of East Asian economies in the immediate future.

THE CHALLENGE TO REMAIN COMPETITIVE

Issues of competitiveness and innovation have to be addressed at various levels of abstraction, ranging from individual firms, to local, national, and regional networks of innovation, to the role of the state in
promoting innovation and diffusing technology, to global alliances between transnational corporations. In attempting to address the issues
of competitiveness and innovation in East Asia as a whole, this chapter
inevitably has been pitched at a high level of abstraction by concentrat-
ing on the emergence of production networks. In doing so, a number
of issues for further research have been raised.

Certainly the increasing mobility of capital and the new complexities
of linkages through production networks present new challenges to
states seeking to maintain the competitiveness of their domestic firms
and their national economies. The nature of the challenge differs, of
course, depending upon the level of sophistication of the domestic
economy. Space precludes but a mere mention of some issues for further investigation.

For the less-developed states in the region, the key question is how
they can increase their attractiveness to transnational capital while at
the same time seeking to maximize the gains, in the form of technology
and skills transfer, that arise from participation in production networks.
The quest for foreign investment to link into production networks for
export to third-country markets appears increasingly as a zero-sum game
in East Asia, with Southeast Asia particularly concerned about an apparent loss of investment to China in the first half of the 1990s. In re-

sponse, governments have further liberalized the conditions for foreign investors by removing requirements for local participation. Yet it was precisely the restrictions on foreign investment that many observers believe contributed to the transfer of technology to Japan and Korea that helped make domestic industries competitive on international markets within a remarkably short time. Whether domestic economies in East Asia can become as competitive where the principal vehicle for industrialization is the transnational corporation as they would be when growth is driven by domestically owned firms remains to be seen. Singapore certainly suggests that such a route is possible.

Much work remains to be done on the factors that attract foreign investors; these include concessions in the form of tax holidays, the overall political climate for foreign investment, the skills of the labour force, and the development of infrastructure. Mention of these issues points to a challenge for those Southeast Asian countries that wish to compete on a basis other than low-cost labour: education systems in some countries (e.g., Thailand and Indonesia) are poor; R&D activities, whether performed by government or domestically owned firms, are virtually non-existent (true also of Malaysia); and some governments, especially in Thailand, seem incapable of providing the collective goods (such as transport infrastructure) that are necessary to maintain the attractiveness of their economies to foreign firms. A process of continuous upgrading will be required if these economies are to resist the challenge from new entrants, such as Vietnam, that will compete primarily on the basis of low labour costs.

Korea and Taiwan both face the challenge of maintaining labour and price stability under democratization and of upgrading domestic skills as labour-intensive activities are transferred offshore. Again there are many questions requiring further research here, such as the importance of innovation networks in Taiwan, the role of government in promoting technology diffusion, and the relative advantages for innovation and competitiveness of an industrial structure based primarily on small firms (Taiwan) versus one based on giant conglomerates (Korea's *chaebŏl*). And any consideration of the challenges facing Japan would require a whole study in itself.

NOTES

1 For a critical review, see Amsden (1994).
2 This paper relies extensively on work completed jointly with Mitchell Bernard of the Department of Political Science, York University, Toronto. See Bernard and Ravenhill (1995a, 1995b).

3 For a discussion in the context of Japan's domestic political economy, see Imai (1992).
4 For a general discussion, see Gerlach (1992).
5 For evidence from Malaysia, see Rasiah (1995).
6 On Malaysia, see Guyton (1988); on Singapore, see the survey by Poh Kam Wong cited in Dobson (1993) and Dobson's own survey of four TNC subsidiaries (Dobson 1993).
7 This argument applies *a fortiori* to Taiwanese investments – see Schive (1990).
8 For examples from Korea, see Simon and Soh (1994).
9 For suggestions of such a possibility, see Doner (1992).
10 For discussion of the lack of technology transfer to the export-processing zones, see Warr (1989).

REFERENCES

Ali, Anuwar. 1994. "Japanese Industrial Investments and Technology Transfer in Malaysia." In Jomo K.S., ed, *Japan and Malaysian Development: In the Shadow of the Rising Sun.* London: Routledge.
Amsden, Alice H., ed. 1994. "The World Bank's *The East Asian Miracle: Economic Growth and Public Policy.*" *World Development* 22 (4): 613–70.
Bank of Korea. 1993. *List of Import-Inducing Effects of Korea's Major Goods.* Seoul: Bank of Korea.
Bernard, Mitchell. 1994. "Post-Fordism, Transnational Production and the Changing Global Political Economy." In Richard Stubbs and Geoffrey R.D. Underhill, eds, *Political Economy and the Changing Global Order*, 216–29. London: Macmillan.
Bernard, Mitchell, and John Ravenhill. 1995a. "Beyond Product Cycles and Flying Geese: Regionalization, Hierarchy and the Industrialization of East Asia." *World Politics* 47 (2): 171–209.
– 1995b. "The Pursuit of Competitiveness in East Asia: Regionalization of Production and Its Consequences." In David P. Rapkin and William P. Avery, eds, *National Competitiveness in a Global Economy: International Political Economy Yearbook*, 103–20. Boulder, Colo: Lynne Rienner.
Bloom, Martin D. 1992. *Technological Change in the Korean Electronics Industry.* Paris: OECD.
Dobson, Wendy. 1993. *Japan in East Asia: Trading and Investment Strategies*, 52–3. Singapore: Institute for Southeast Asian Studies.
Doner, Richard. 1992. *Japanese Foreign Investment and the Creation of a Pacific-Asian Region.* Del Mar, Calif: National Bureau of Economic Research.
Electronic Industries Association of Japan. 1995. *Facts and Figures on the Japanese Electronics Industry: 1995 Edition.* Tokyo: Electronic Industries Association of Japan.

Gerlach, Michael L. 1992. *Alliance Capitalism: The Social Organization of Japanese Business*. Berkeley: University of California Press.

Goodman, David S.G. 1992. "China: The State and Capitalist Revolution." *Pacific Review* 5 (4): 350–9.

Guyton, Lynne. 1996. "Japanese Manufacturing Investments and Technology Transfer to Malaysia." In John Borrego, Alejandro Alvarez, and Jomo K.S., eds, *Capital, the State and Late Industrialization: Comparative Perspectives on the Pacific Rim*. Boulder, Colo: Westview Press.

Heng, Toh Mun, and Linda Low, eds. 1993. *Regional Cooperation and Growth Triangles in ASEAN*. Singapore: Times Academic Press.

Imai, Ken-ichi. 1992. "Japan's Corporate Networks." In Shumpei Kumon and Henry Rosovsky, eds, *The Political Economy of Japan. Vol. 3, Cultural and Social Dynamics*, 198–230. Stanford: Stanford University Press.

JETRO (Japan External Trade Organization). 1995. *JETRO White Paper on Foreign Direct Investment 1995*. Tokyo: JETRO.

Kodama, Fumio. 1991. *Analysing Japanese High Technologies*. London: Pinter.

Kreinin, Mordechai E. 1988. "How Closed Is Japan's Market? Additional Evidence." *World Economy* 11 (4): 529–42.

Krugman, Paul. 1991. *Geography and Trade*. Cambridge, Mass: MIT Press.

Lundvall, Bengt-Åke, ed. 1992. *National Systems of Innovation: Towards a Theory of Innovation and Interactive Learning*. London: Pinter.

MITI. 1991. *Wagakuni Kigyono Kaigai Jigyo Katsudo*. Tokyo: MITI.

Nikkei Shinbum. 1992. 11 December.

Peck, Merton J., and Robert W. Wilson. 1982. "Innovation, Imitation and Comparative Advantage: The Performance of Japanese Color Television Set Producers in the U.S. Market." In Herbert Giersch, ed, *Emerging Technologies: Consequences for Economic Growth, Structural Change, and Employment*, 195–211. Tübingen: J.C.B. Mohr.

Rasiah, Rajah. 1995. *Foreign Capital and Industrialization in Malaysia*. New York: St Martins Press.

Ravenhill, John. 1993. "The 'Japan Problem' in Pacific Trade." In Richard Higgott, Richard Leaver, and John Ravenhill, eds, *Pacific Economic Relations in the 1990s: Cooperation or Conflict?*, 106–32. Boulder, Colo: Lynne Rienner.

– 1995. "Economic Cooperation in Southeast Asia: Changing Incentives." *Asian Survey* 35 (9): 850–66.

Schive, Chi. 1990. *The Foreign Factor: The Multinational Corporation's Contribution to the Economic Modernization of the Republic of China*. Stanford, Calif: Hoover Institution Press.

Simon, Denis Fred, and Changrok Soh. 1994. "Korea's Technological Development." *Pacific Review* 7 (1): 89–103.

Tyson, Laura D'Andrea. 1993. *Who's Bashing Whom? Trade Conflict in High-Technology Industries*. Washington, D.C.: Institute for International Economics.

USITC (United States International Trade Commission). 1993. *East Asia: Regional Economic Integration and Implications for the United States.* Washington, D.C.: USITC. Publication no. 2621.

Warr, Peter G. 1989. "Export Processing Zones: The Economics of Enclave Manufacturing." *World Bank Research Observer* 4 (1): 65–88.

World Bank. 1993. *The East Asian Miracle.* Washington, D.C.: World Bank.

Yoon, Young-Kwan. 1990. "The Political Economy of Transition: Japanese Foreign Direct Investments in the 1980s." *World Politics* 43 (1): 1–27.

Yuan, Lee Tsao, ed. 1991. *Growth Triangle: The Johor-Singapore-Riau Experience.* Singapore: Institute of Southeast Asian Studies.

9 The European Information Society and Regional Cohesion

LUC SOETE

INTRODUCTION

The potential economic and social benefits to Europe's regions offered by the new information and communication technologies (ICTs) identified with the emerging Information Society are varied and great. The "death of distance" associated with these new technologies leads one quite naturally to focus on the new growth and development opportunities in the geographically *less-favoured regions* (LFRs) – those areas that have hitherto suffered most from such geographical barriers to development. It is clear, however, that grasping these opportunities is not automatic.

In order to access the benefits of the Information Society, the LFRs must have in place a number of pre-requisites. Most obvious is the infrastructure for accessing information. In the past, a universal service provision has been used in the attempt to resolve the problem of affordable access to telephone service. An updated version of universal service for advanced telecommunication services must now be designed. In contrast to past experience, however, such a version will have to be designed within the increasingly liberalized framework within which new information services will be provided. Hence, the issue of liberalization and its possible countervailing impact on regional and peripheral development must also be examined.

Within the context of regional cohesion, the important distinction between less-favoured regions and peripheral regions needs to be made. Analyses of and policies for both sets of regions tend to be erroneously consolidated under the heading "regional cohesion." A clear distinction between these two areas does, however, exist. Less-favoured regions have problems related to their economic position – in other words, they face problems of poverty and development. Peripheral regions, on the other hand, have problems related to their geographical position – their problems relate to distance. Thus, policies for these two regions must reflect the specific structural problems that pertain to these regions. For example, less-favoured regions often have high population densities, while peripheral regions usually have low population densities. The problems associated with these two different characteristics will therefore be very different. In less-favoured regions, it would likely be less problematic to supply an information infrastructure than in peripheral regions. Telecommunications companies would be willing to invest in LFRs because of the number of inhabitants and therefore the ability to recover costs and make a profit. In LFRs there are also agglomeration effects. The higher the population of an area, the larger the range of skills in the labour force and the larger the market for goods and services.

CENTRALIZATION AND DECENTRALIZATION IMPACTS

Most analyses of the Information Society with respect to cohesive core regions have focused on the potential decentralizing impacts of the technologies. Often described are how information-based goods and services in combination with widely diffused electronic networks will allow regions to overcome the problems associated with distance. People may be socially included through their participation in virtual communities or communities of interest; their democratic rights may be enhanced, since they will be able to communicate with politicians and participate in decision making; their social services may improve through, for example, tele-education and tele-services; their economic situation may be improved through new working opportunities; they may have a wider media choice; and cultural pluralism will be facilitated. Thus, not only might centralized communities prosper but so might decentralized communities that have been disadvantaged in the past. Many see this as the future for the Information Society. However, it should be acknowledged that this is only *one* vision.

In an alternative vision, information and communication technologies could reinforce centralization in information-rich core regions and be used to control, rather than liberate, remote regions. Thus, the less-favoured regions might be excluded from the Information Society and their position could worsen. Further, local producers could lose their presence in local markets as larger firms gain the ability to service customers "from a distance." Excluded regions are often described as having low income levels and inferior potential for development. How could this happen? The most obvious way is through the lack of affordable access to information infrastructures. But this is not the whole story. Other equally important factors may impede their participation in the Information Society. For example, firms may not have the knowledge required to turn new opportunities into concrete realities or managers may not have the skills needed to adopt new working practices.

Many have pointed to the "death of geography" – the ability of ICTs to shrink distance. This suggests that core regions may lose their traditional advantages over less-favoured and peripheral regions. However, as pointed out by K. Morgan (1996), "the reported death of geography is often greatly exaggerated." Indeed, some researchers argue that the principal dilemma in economic geography today is how to explain the resurgence of core regional economies at a time when the forces of globalization (in the shape of transport and telematic innovations for example) appear to have reduced the world to a "placeless" mass. The continuing significance of core regional clusters – in Silicon Valley, Baden-Württemberg, Emilia-Romagna, the City of London, and so forth – is said to be based on the strong association between learning and clustering. Such clusters are said to embody a whole series of traded interdependencies (e.g., sophisticated labour markets and localized input-output linkages) and untraded interdependencies (e.g., tacit knowledge and networks of social capital). These assets are not easily transferred from one region to another. The key point is this: the greater the complexity, irregularity, uncertainty, and tacitness of transactions, the more sensitive they are to spatial distance. Indeed, there tends to be a high premium on physical proximity. Notwithstanding the distance-shrinking power of ICTs, the fact remains that physical proximity remains very important for complex activities such as, for example, strategic management and research design and development.

Others have speculated that Europe's LFRs might gain only limited benefits from newly mobile service functions. They note that many high value-added activities remain in core regions and point to a further concentration of these activities in a few city-regions. In addition, they point out that many core regions are realizing the importance of the new mobile jobs and are seeking to keep them in the core regions. Furthermore, since ICTs allow for greater mobility of activities, core regions may also have to compete with countries outside of Europe. The Indian subcontinent, Eastern Europe, and Southeast Asia, for example, are able to perform software activities at a fraction of the cost of Europe's LFRs companies. These countries set up export processing zones with little or no taxation and with low labour costs.

POTENTIAL BENEFITS TO LESS FAVOURED REGIONS

All of the points above do not imply that LFRs cannot benefit from ICTs. A number of particular features of the Information Society can contribute to the development and greater integration of peripheral and less-favoured regions. The following benefits are often noted:[1]

- *new market opportunities* (e.g., ICTs can offer new growth opportunities to local firms through better and improved access to more centrally located growth markets);
- *new location opportunities* (e.g., ICTs can provide opportunities for the location of new information-processing activities, such as "call centres");
- *new access opportunities* (e.g., ICTs can improve remote access to tele-services such as tele-health, tele-education; access to other cultures and media; and access to the democratic process, including access to politicians, political decisions, and relevant information); and
- *new social integration opportunities* (e.g., ICTs can reduce social isolation through access to, say, virtual communities).

These opportunities are well known. The Information Society does have the potential to benefit less-favoured regions. However, none of these benefits are automatic. And none are without risk.

"UNIVERSAL SERVICE," AND INFRA-STRUCTURE DEVELOPMENT

Because of the disparity in accessibility between core and other regions, it is not surprising that the regional cohesion dimension of the Information Society has generally been discussed within the framework of updating the present universal service obligation with respect to basic telephone services so that it would apply to the new information services.

The support for information infrastructure in peripheral regions and LFRs has traditionally been a central feature of European cohesion policies. For example, the STAR program (Special Telecommunications Action for Regional Development) provided funding from 1987 to 1991 to accelerate the rate of investment in advanced telecommunications infrastructure in the LFRs of seven member states. The objective of the program was to stimulate demand and development. TELEMATIQUE followed the STAR program, with the goal of developing complementary assets. Such policies have aimed at guaranteeing access and improving affordability to advanced information infrastructures in terms of the so-called universal service provision (USP) set out in a European Council resolution (22 July 1993) (Sandler 1993).

USP guarantees access to a minimum level of postal and telephone services to everyone in all member states. However, the Information Society covers a much wider range of services than these. The question must therefore be raised as to how the definition of USP must be broadened to take into account the fact that the old basic provisions might no longer fulfil basic communication needs in the newly emerging Information Society.

The proposed "open network provision" (ONP) directive[2] proposes an extremely low minimum transmission rate, specified at 2.4 kbits per second, adequate for voice transmission but not for fax, on-line access, or data transfer, where the current minimal norm for modem speed is 14.4 kbits. Obviously, in an increasingly information-dependent society, a notion that will remain essential is a universal service guaranteeing some level of equal voice and data access, neutrality with respect to users, continuity, availability, and adaptability to specific needs. The current notion of universal service has been defined as the "basic service offered to all in the Union at affordable tariff conditions and at a standard quality level." The question to be raised is how this definition should be changed in consideration of the coming Information Society and its impact on European cohesion.

The universal service debate should focus on the functionality of services and alternative technologies rather than on minimum technical standards. From this perspective, there is a need to investigate in greater detail whether, in order to avoid exclusion and preserve regional cohesion, the existing concept of universal service should not be shifted in the direction of a concept of universal community service, extending the universal service provision to include basic access to new information services but be limited in its obligation of universality to the educational, cultural, medical, social, and economic institutions of local communities.

LIBERALIZATION

The issue of liberalization and its possible adverse impact on regional and peripheral development must also be considered. Liberalization in the form of deregulation and increased competition helps to stimulate private investment in public telecommunications networks and in doing so reinforces a general downward trend in some tariffs. The introduction of competition creates pressure on incumbent operators to bring prices of telecommunications network services more in line with costs. As a result, telecommunications network operators attempt to maximize the benefits of new investments. In other words, investments are made in the most profitable market segments, in general, in those services geared towards large businesses. Since large businesses are usually located in major city centres, such areas will be the primary target for new investments. Thus, the benefits of liberalization will not necessarily be evenly distributed across all regions of the European Union (EU).

The differences between less-favoured and peripheral regions are also relevant to policies on information access. In less-favoured regions, the potential for catching up in information and communication infrastructure is often significant; new entrants might be willing to invest in view of the large latent demand associated with high-density areas. There is frequently scope for recouping costs and turning a profit. The lack of development of these regions does not imply that there would not be significant economies of scale to be reaped. Liberalization is likely to make the potential advantages of scale and concentration far more transparent. Insistence on a universal service option will, however, often undermine such commercial opportunities. Whereas connecting the central high-density areas in a less-favoured region might hold commercial promise, the additional obligation to universal service might render the whole process unprofitable.

In peripheral regions, by contrast, active participation in the future Information Society will crucially depend on universal service provisions. Given their peripheral location and low relative population density, taking advantage of the death-of-distance features of ICTs will depend on the universality and quality of the information infrastructure available. New commercial opportunities leading to more intense competition in price and quality will first focus on those activities with the most commercial potential – often the "cherries" of little relevance to the regions themselves.[3]

Thus, the importance of universal access varies among regions. Seen from this angle, a generalized European directive on an extended universal service provision is unlikely to contribute in any real sense to regional cohesion. Instead, regional policies should be targeted to those areas/regions where the benefits of liberalization are unlikely to filter through.

BEYOND UNIVERSAL SERVICE

There is little doubt that physical investment is essential for regional growth and that its lack has often formed a major bottleneck for peripheral and less-favoured regions. However, it is becoming increasingly recognized that alongside such tangible ICT investment, intangible investment, including investment in human capital, has become equal if not much more important for economic growth in the knowledge-based economy of the 1990s.

As a recent report by the Organization for Economic Cooperation and Development put it, "knowledge plays today in all its forms a crucial role in economic processes. Intangible investment is growing more rapidly than physical investment. Individuals with knowledge get better paid jobs, firms with more knowledge are winners on markets and nations endowed with more knowledge are more productive" (OECD 1996). This is also applicable at a regional level. The full exploitation of the technological capacity of the new ICTs requires the adaptation and development of regional human resources and of the institutional structures that support regional innovation and organized learning.

The implications of these trends for regional cohesion policies go in the direction of putting ever more emphasis on knowledge accumulation and the new growth opportunities associated with research and technological development. This goes beyond strengthening the information infrastructure or universal service provision and includes technological diffusion and transfer, support for human resources, and adapting regional institutions to new conditions.

TECHNOLOGICAL DIFFUSION AND TRANSFER

Clearly, a major challenge in developing technological capabilities is to stimulate the demand that will make investment in the infrastructure for the new ICTs worthwhile. Despite quite a lot of support for innovation and investments, the level of acceptance of ICT-based services, for example, has generally been disappointing. The prospects for success appear to be strongest where the innovations involve some significant change in organizational behaviour, particularly if it leads to a boost to competitiveness or the value added for the firm concerned. Thus, integration of subcontractors into the operations of a larger firm via electronic data interchange (EDI) is far more likely to lead to sustained use of ICTs, because it involves both a new way of operating and has a strong economic rationale.

At the same time, regional growth dynamics strongly depend on the way new forms might pick up particular growth opportunities. These new entities will often require advice, information, and support. The CRAFT initiative within the Brite-Euram RTD Support Programme has been instrumental in helping small and medium-sized enterprises to link up with technological research centres.

HUMAN RESOURCES

In many LFRs, higher-education institutions concentrate on providing a general education rather than high-level, vocationally oriented training. While a general education is essential, most successful economies also have a highly developed vocational education provision. In many cases, though, there is still a need for the development of vocational training in close interaction with the actual needs of local enterprises. However, the desire to focus on such immediate needs should not lead one to ignore the need to develop vocational education in a more proactive fashion, going beyond the region's immediate requirements. While the current needs of local enterprises are not always clear, the future needs are even less easily assessed.

Applications of new knowledge can be found in almost all firms and sectors. However, getting the best out of the technologies usually requires customizing the systems to users' needs. In addition, knowledge implementation usually means changing current procedures and working practices. In some cases, quite basic research may be needed in order to facilitate the application of new technologies to production processes, especially in the long-established industries often found in LFRs, such as viticulture or the garment industry. Local industries, therefore, need to be able to call upon readily available expertise in order to innovate successfully. While such expertise is rarely of local origin, easy access implies the geographical proximity of technological training, assessment, and information facilities.

There are, however, no universal solutions. In some LFRs, there is still the *reactive* need for the establishment of regional technology transfer centres, linking up existing and new research institutes, educational institutions, and firms. In other regions, there is a need for more *proactive* approaches and for existing regional technology transfer centres to integrate training more effectively with the transfer of technology, on-line market information, and other forms of consultation and advice on specific issues relating to the modernization and restructuring of local firms. Given the growing complexity of technology, regional technology transfer centres will never be able to provide all the requested technological and market information. However, they could become crucial information and knowledge brokers, bringing firms in contact with other technology institutes and centres outside the region. This will require that more emphasis be put on the coordination of activities than on the creation of new, regional innovation institutions.

ADAPTING REGIONAL INSTITUTIONS

The ways in which a region's institutions are structured is a major factor in determining how receptive a region is to the new technologies. The relationships between regional government and industry and such other major actors as the universities and the economic development authorities significantly shape regional innovation. In general, diverse but well-integrated and adaptable institutions tend to lead to greater innovation. Rigid institutional structures based upon old or declining industries, or located in areas in which there has been little diversity of industrial culture, tend to be less innovative, particularly if they are in peripheral areas.

NOTES

1 See also Nexus Research Co-operative (1996).
2 See COM(94) 689 final, 1/02/1995, in the Commission Communication on the Consultation on the Green Paper, May 1995.
3 See the European Commission Information Society Project Office WWW homepage at http://www.ispo.cec.be/infosoc/legreg
4 See http://www2.cordis.lu/sme/src/2sme_int.htm

REFERENCES

European Commission. 1995. Consultation on the Green Paper on Communication. May.

Morgan, K. 1996. "The Information Society Opportunities for SMEs in Objective Regions." Paper prepared for Objective Desk Officers, European Commission, Brussels, 23 May.

Nexus Europe. 1996. "An Assessment of the Social and Economic Cohesion Aspects of the Development of the Information Society in Europe." In *Synthesis and Recommendations, Final Report.* Vol. 5. Centre for Urban and Regional Development Studies, University of Newcastle. January.

OECD. 1996. "Employment and Growth in the Knowledge-Based Economy." OECD document, April.

Sandler, P. 1993. "Universal Service in the European Union Today." Paper prepared for the European Commission, Brussels, 22 July.

PART FOUR

Emerging Issues in Innovation Systems

10 Competitiveness and Complex Economic Integration in the North American Region

RICHARD G. HARRIS

INTRODUCTION

Competitiveness has traditionally been addressed at the national level, and a fundamental issue in economics has always been the wealth of nations. The past decade has seen an unprecedented move towards the economic integration of large regions of the globe. The link between the regional trading blocs and national competitiveness has thus far received less attention than it merits. The completion of the North American *economic region* was given considerable impetus with the North American Free Trade Agreement (NAFTA). In this chapter, I review the issue of the competitiveness of North America in light of the integration that is proceeding.

The link between competitiveness (defined more precisely below) and the process of economic integration is one which economic theorists have had difficulty in making precisely. The traditional theory of economic integration has tended to support the idea that national economies that are similar in terms of income, size, economic structure, and developmental levels are the ones that will most naturally become integrated. The three economies of North America clearly do not fall within this category – Mexico, the United States, and Canada represent quite different economies in terms of the variables mentioned.

A critical point, and one reinforced in this paper, is that in the face of such substantive differences among the countries in the region, there are some serious impediments to economic integration. However, the argument will be made here that from the perspective of the competitiveness of the North American continent there is considerable strength in this diversity. After outlining these arguments, the chapter will conclude with a discussion of why "North America," in contrast to other regional groupings, might make sense from an economic integration point of view.

DIVERSITY IN THE CONTINENT

The economies of Mexico, the United States, and Canada are incredibly diverse across a wide range of economic and social indicators. Economic integration – which is generally measured on a continuum running from free trade areas, to customs unions, to full economic union, and finally to full political union – is usually thought of as being both feasible and beneficial to all parties the 'more similar' the integrating regions are. It is useful to remember some of the basic facts when thinking about North American economic integration.

Global Perspective

North America has 7 per cent of the world's population and produces 28 per cent of the world's output. On a per capita basis, it produces about five times the world's average per capita output.

Market Size

In 1988, the year in which a NAFTA was first seriously contemplated, the absolute incomes of Canada, Mexico, and the United States were $513 billion, $201 billion, and $5,198 billion respectively.[1] Canada's economy has always been approximately one-tenth the size of the U.S. economy in terms of total economic activity; Mexico's is less than one-twentieth the size of the U.S. economy. The United States is the world's largest economy, while Canada ranks sixth or seventh among the OECD (Organization for Economic Cooperation and Development) countries. The North American integration, therefore, is among economies of vastly different economic size. In terms of population,[2] the United States, with 251 million people, is the third-largest country in the world, though very slow growing (a doubling time of ninety-two years at current rates). Mexico, on the other hand, has a population (1990) of 89 million but is doubling every fifty years. Canada is a "small country" in terms of population at 26 million and is extremely slow growing, assuming no significant changes in its immigration policy.

Income Levels and Productivity

Per capita gross domestic product (GDP), adjusted for purchasing power parity, in Canada, Mexico, and the United States in 1989 was, respectively, $19,995, $2,335, and $20,694. The world average in 1989 was $3,865. Canada and the United States are two of the richest industrial countries, while Mexico is still generally regarded as a developing economy, although it appears to be rapidly making the transition to a newly industrializing economy. Income differences are closely related to differences in productivity per worker. Relative to the United States, in 1990 Canada had a productivity level of 93 per cent and Mexico (where productivity is much harder to measure) one of about 25 per cent.

Openness

While all three economies are important participants in the world trading system, they naturally tend to have different levels of dependence on foreign trade. One measure of this is the *openness index*, defined as the ratio of exports plus imports to GDP. In 1989 for Canada, Mexico, and the United States, the openness indexes were 46, 29, and 15, respectively.

Trade Patterns

Canada and Mexico both trade predominantly with the United States. On the order of 75 per cent of Canadian exports are bound for the United States. Canada is the largest trading partner of the U.S., taking about 17–18 per cent of its exports, followed closely by Japan and then Mexico, a distant third, although Mexican manufactured exports to the U.S. have been growing rapidly recently.

Wealth

Wealth statistics are extraordinarily elusive, but a useful first approximation is indicated by the capitalized value of shares in the respective national stock markets. In 1990 the capitalized value of all world share markets was $9.5 trillion. The U.S. markets were by far the largest at just over $3 trillion. Canada, while the fifth largest in 1990, was virtually insignificant at $242 billion (or $0.24 trillion). Mexico's total capitalization in the same year was $33 billion. All three countries are large foreign debtors, although in relative terms Canada and Mexico are more indebted than the United States.

These aggregate statistics only hint at the extraordinary degree of diversity among the three economies. With respect to demographics, for example, Mexico has an extraordinarily young population with 42 per cent of its total population under age fifteen compared with only 12 per cent for Canada. Educational attainment for the three is also quite different. In comparing Canada and the United States, government plays a different role in the economy. Canada is much closer to the European welfare state model than is the U.S., although both countries have large fiscal deficits. The Canadian welfare state has produced a more equitable income distribution than has the United States, whose income distribution was among the least equal in the OECD group.[3] Mexico, typical of many developing countries, has a very large part of its population in extreme poverty by developed-country standards, as well as possessing a fairly well off and well-educated élite.

MEASURING COMPETITIVENESS

It is helpful to review briefly what we mean by the term "competitiveness," as it tends to be used in a variety of different ways.[4] One of the most common uses of the term is in relation to relative national positions with respect to international trade balances. This very old mercantilist idea is deeply rooted in the way most business people view economics, and comes from the common fallacy of viewing countries as if they were giant corporations engaged in battles for market share. This perspective implies that one country is doing better than another if it has the larger trade surplus. Most economists cringe at this idea, although it has its uses in debate. Another sort of picture is given by the relative performance of individual national companies within the same sector. Thus, the United States is said to be more competitive than Japan in computers if U.S. firms account for a larger share of total world sales of computers – the major empirical indicator used, for example, by Porter (1990). This definition is also problematic because of the difficulty in defining what it means for a particular firm to be "U.S." The end-product sold by the U.S. firm may have most of its parts produced in Japan and the European Union, and it may have been assembled in Thailand, marketed by Canadians, and financed by Germans. Robert Reich's point about "who is us" (1991) is well taken.

There are two indicators of competitiveness with which economists are most comfortable when making international comparisons. The first is growth in productivity – in particular what is called *growth in total factor productivity*. An economy with a higher rate of growth in total factor productivity than another will over the long run tend to have a much higher standard of living. The other indicator is what is known as *PPP adjusted per capita incomes* – basically a measure of the standard of living per person measured in terms of a standard basket of goods adjusted for the local cost of living. However bad these measures may be, they are generally the best we have. It is important to emphasize that they do not include other elements important to quality of life – the environment, life expectancy, commuting times, recreational opportunities, and the like. There is little agreement about which of the two basic measures – growth in productivity or income levels – is the most appropriate, in part because of what is known as the *convergence hypothesis*. Roughly, this hypothesis states that a lot of economic growth can be explained by "catch-up"; that is, economies that are behind the leaders will tend to grow faster than the leaders did because by adopting the methods of the leaders they can get to the same technological frontiers without having to spend time on research and development. Thus, poorer countries ought to grow faster than rich countries. If the catch-up factor is important, then one has to correct growth rates for this effect. Economic growth in China may be very high, for example, but this does mean that it is competitively superior to the slower growing OECD countries, which may well be responsible for most of the technological developments upon which Chinese growth is dependent.

It is fair to say that most of the competitiveness literature is not about final outcomes but about differences among countries with respect to some intermediate variable, such as the number of jobs in manufacturing, the percentage of gross domestic product (GDP) devoted to R&D, the average level of education, attainment scores on math tests, the number of lawyers or doctors per 1,000 in the population, and so on. Generally, these types of discussions presume some theory connecting the variable in question to more broad-ranging indicators such as growth rates or standards of living.

BARRIERS TO ECONOMIC INTEGRATION

Given the diversity within the region, there are some obvious problems with trying to integrate Canada, Mexico, and the United States. The NAFTA agreement is the first step in what will be a lengthy and difficult process. As is often mentioned, however, NAFTA is not "just a trade deal" – it goes some way to being what is conventionally called a deeper economic integration, covering services, investment, dispute settlement, environment, and so on, although stops well short of what the Europeans are aiming for in their single-market program. Rather than reiterating what should by now be familiar details regarding trade policy given the NAFTA debate of the early 1990s, I prefer to outline what I believe to be the four basic obstacles to achieving a deeper economic integration, by which I mean more substantive policy harmonization in such areas as regulation, financial markets, environment, labour standards, labour mobility, taxation, and monetary union.

The Small Country Problem

Both Mexico and Canada are countries which by virtue of their size and history have deeply rooted fears of U.S. economic domination. A large part of this fear stems from the belief that economic domination will lead to political domination. Neither the Canadians nor the Mexicans need to be told how important this fact of political life is in their respective countries. The practical implication of this fear is that the task of making NAFTA into something more substantive from the point of view of deeper integration will encounter great political difficulties from both the Canadian and Mexican sides unless mechanisms are put in place that effectively guarantee the national economic rights of the minorities against a U.S. majority. The real problem, though, boils down to agreeing on a definition of an "economic right." Can Canada have its own environmental standards and Mexico its own labour standards to name two obvious examples? Alternatively, are the benefits of deeper economic integration worth the sacrifice in sovereignty?

Asymmetry in Developmental Levels between Canada-U.S. and Mexico

Asymmetry in developmental levels runs two ways. In Mexico it translates into worries that the high productivity industrial North will obliterate any efforts by Mexico to build a competitive manufacturing sector. Lowering its trade barriers or relaxing entry restrictions in service industries may result in a wholesale takeover of Mexican enterprise by U.S. (and Canadian) firms. In the North the worry is that all industry will move to Mexico because of its substantial wage advantage; this is the low-wage or cheap labour argument. It is noteworthy that this latter concern is largely that of labour and not capital (or management). Mexican worries tend to be shared by both business and labour interests. Both of these concerns were overcome, or more accurately ignored, in the ultimate deal making on NAFTA. They are, however, still there and politically potent.

The Distribution of Income

A general worry in the industrial countries related to the globalization of the world economy is that the distribution of income will worsen if it follows its current tendency to move towards the income distributions typical of developing countries and thus becomes more unequal. This is most evident in the United States, where real wages to unskilled workers have decreased and the returns to more highly educated workers have increased. In the United States, from 1945 to 1973 the median income of full-time 45- to 54-year-old men went from $16,702 to $31,862 (using 1988 U.S. dollars). Over the next fifteen years the same income statistic grew by only $900. This is one example of the well-documented slowdown in the growth of real wages that occurred in the United States and elsewhere. Bluestone and Harrison (1988) noted that earnings inequality from 1950 to 1980 increased in the United States, and attributed this to the growth of low-paying jobs. They noted that during the 1970s about one of every five additional wage earners found a job (or jobs) paying as little as $7,000 (per year in 1984 dollars), and since 1979 that fraction has risen to nearly six in ten. Labour economists have studied the determinants and structure of earnings in great detail. One consistent finding is that an increased earnings premium emerged during the 1980s to educated workers. Murphy and Welch (1992) found that 25- to 34-year-old male high school graduates' median earnings declined by 12 per cent from 1979 to 1987; they also found that for male college graduates in the same age group, there was an 8 per cent increase in median earnings.

In Europe and Canada the same patterns in wages have not emerged.[5] However, there have been significant increases in the long-term rate of structural unemployment. One common explanation for this is that the impact of globalization in these economies, with their strong labour market regulations and income support programs, is reflected largely in unemployment rates rather than in changes in wage distribution. In either case, North American economic integration carries with it the concern that these trends will only be exacerbated. It should be emphasized that the presumed links between globalization and wages are still controversial; nevertheless, the worries are real and are going to prove a significant political barrier to deeper integration in the continent.

A related barrier to integration pertains to governments' response to these changes in income distribution. In both Canada and the United States, there are many who feel strongly that government should implement policies that would ensure that the gains and burdens of globalization were shared; this could be done through better income support programs, retraining, and more progressive taxation. Those of this opinion, however, fear that North American economic integration might constrain governments from implementing such policies.

Tensions between Widening versus Deepening NAFTA

There are two basic views as to which way NAFTA should evolve. One view is that more effort must be put into deepening the level of economic integration beyond that in the existing agreement. A number of issues are usually raised in this regard: the need to replace anti-dumping with harmonized competition policy; the need to develop a consistent subsidies code for use in countervailing duty cases; the need for better harmonization of environmental and labour standards; and finally increased efforts to secure improved mobility of labour. The motivation for pursuing deeper economic integration such as this is almost always to achieve large productivity gains. This view is quite different from the one held by those who emphasize the need to widen NAFTA – that is, extend it to a greater number of countries. The usual candidates are Latin American economies and some even see NAFTA merging with APEC (Asia-Pacific Economic Cooperation) to form a cross-Pacific free trade area. The motivation in this case is what is referred to as *open regionalism* – the need for non-discriminatory access of third parties to the NAFTA mechanism – indeed, some even see most-favoured-nation (MFN) treatment as the principle that should be applied.

I must admit to being torn between these two views. The latter view – that of turning NAFTA into a mini-GATT (General Agreement on Tariffs and Trade) – is probably a non-starter. The aims intended in this type of multilateralist agenda are better secured through the GATT. The real problem in North America is finding a way to get a more substantive form of economic integration and at the same time develop political mechanisms to legitimize that integration. That being said, the mere existence of these two sets of contradictory agendas for trade policy will prove to be an impediment to deeper economic integration within the continent. A classic example of this tension is the inability thus far of the United States to give up in any way on its sovereignty over administrative trade actions – that is, anti-dumping and countervail. Economists are uniformly of the opinion that anti-dumping is a pernicious policy that needs to be replaced with more conventional legislation on predatory pricing, which is common to all firms within the free trade area. Failure to do so has meant that the unrestrained use of anti-dumping as a device for harassing foreign firms results in an anti-competitive outcome and one that is highly discriminatory. Those who argue for widening often do so out of exasperation with the lack of progress on issues such as anti-dumping with the U.S. government.

STRENGTH THROUGH DIVERSITY

Despite the great diversity in the three economies of the North American continent and what seem to be overwhelming obstacles, both political and economic, to deeper economic integration, there are a number of reasons to be optimistic about the impact that closer economic integration might have on the competitiveness of the region.

The Static Efficiency Impact of Trade Liberalization

This is the effect economists point to most often in studying free trade areas. For the three NAFTA countries, it is widely estimated that the reduction of trade barriers, both tariff and non-tariff, will have an impact on trade creation that will exceed the potential trade diversion effects and thus be, on balance, net income creating for the region as a whole. The estimates from formal quantitative economic models generally point to the conclusion that Mexico has both the most adjustments to make and the most benefits to gain relative to a situation of no NAFTA.[6] The net effect should be towards greater intraregional trade, lower prices to consumers, and more exports out of the region as a whole. These type of estimates, however, miss a number of longer structural features of integration which could potentially enhance productivity and dynamism in the region. I turn now to some of these effects.

Complementarity in Resource Endowments

One of the benefits to the NAFTA region is the reorganization of economic activity fostered by the great complementarity in the factor endowments of the three economies. This carries with it the implication that less of the output from each one of the three countries is potentially competitive with that of the other two, reinforcing the productivity-enhancing impact of NAFTA. Mexico is well endowed with a temperate climate, substantial reserves of oil, and a large unskilled labour force. Canada has strong endowments in the area of forest products, minerals, agriculture, water, and skilled human resources in services (including education and health) and manufacturing. The United States has a strong research and development performance, skilled labour, and a large and diversified service and manufacturing sector.

Strengthening the Consumer Market

A potential major benefit of the integration of the three economies is a strengthened and diversified market for the firms in the region. Stability in total market demand, both in terms of income and age group, will be enhanced by bringing Mexico, a lower-income and much younger country, into the overall North American market. Companies that specialize, for example, in products that appeal to younger consumers will find an alternative market as the consumer market in Canada and the U.S. ages. Companies with an established niche in these areas can benefit from their reputation and experience. Other examples include Canada's forest industry, whose wood products could meet the demand of a housing market driven by a younger population in Mexico. In the case of Mexico, an aging and retiring population in Canada and the United States should prove to be an important and growing market for tourism. Both of the smaller economies gain by improved access to the much larger U.S. economy, as its more diversified economic base imparts a greater degree of stability to the aggregate demand for any particular good or service.

Labour Cost Advantages

In a number of sectors, productivity can be enhanced by strengthening the vertical linkages with sectors in which Mexico has a clear cost advantage and/or that have been highly protected in both Canada and the United States. The areas most pertinent to this argument are clothing, textiles, leather and footwear, and manufacturing assembly operations. If Canada and the United States can stick to their commitment to guarantee Mexico unrestricted access in these sectors, then a long-standing obstacle to improvements in manufacturing productivity in both advanced countries will be removed. At the same time, such vertical linkages will give Mexico a major opportunity to proceed to the next stage of industrialization, much as Hong Kong, Korea, and Taiwan moved ahead over the 1970–90 period. In some other sectors, competitiveness is determined in part by access to lower-cost intermediate inputs. Canadian and American firms that use inputs produced in labour-intensive industries should find their competitiveness enhanced by a rationalization of manufacturing across the continent.

Building Vertical Linkages in High-Technology Sectors

This will be of particular benefit to Mexico and Canada, each of whose small and necessarily less-diversified industrial base has always made it difficult for labour in highly skilled and specialized occupations. With improvements in information technology and reduced barriers to the movement of services and goods across national borders, people should have increased options in the choice of occupation, skill level, and location. In this sense, then, there will be greater opportunity for people in the smaller economies to experience freedom of occupational choice – a major benefit to the competitiveness of the region as a whole through its effect on the human resource base in highly skilled sectors. In the case of firms located in both of the smaller economies, there will be opportunities for greater vertical linkages in areas such as R&D, engineering, sales, and service, thus ensuring a more stable economic base. This in turn should generate lower capital costs and provide more secure and high-quality employment in the firms in these areas.

Complementary Savings Patterns and Demography

The addition of Mexico to the Canada-U.S. industrial base and the slow population growth in the two high-income countries combine to offer a unique investment opportunity, given the likely shift in savings patterns in the two advanced countries. As the baby boomers move into middle age, evidence strongly suggests that their personal savings rates will increase. Assuming our governments can restrain their fiscal deficits, these savings should find their way into largely domestic capital formation. Some will go offshore, but the evidence indicates that savings have a strong tendency to stay "at home." Given the aging populations in Canada and the United States, these savings would be channelled to areas with reduced labour forces, thus forcing a very high capital intensity and hence reduced returns to investment. NAFTA with Mexico will offer a clear alternative to this scenario over the first two decades of the next century. With Mexico's large supply of labour and a low capital intensity of production, the increased savings in Canada and the United States can find more productive use within Mexico. Secure and permanent economic integration, however, is the only way that this could happen successfully. People will only place their savings within Mexico if (1) they believe those savings are relatively safe from either punitive taxation or expropriation, and (2) the returns on that capital are secure because the firms that do the investing in real capital have secure access to product markets in which to sell their goods and services. This is a clear win-win proposition, since this investment also has the effect of raising labour productivity and thus real wages in Mexico. An important side benefit for the border states in the United States is that higher Mexican wages may stem the flow of illegal migrants across the Mexican-U.S. border.

Raising the Returns on Investment in, and the Stock of, Human Capital in the Continent

It is now widely recognized that in modern industrialized economies *human capital* – that is, the cumulative acquired skills of the active labour force – represents quantitatively the most important factor input to production. An implication of this fact is that increases in the quantity of, and returns on, human capital are potentially more responsible for raising incomes than anything else. The evidence is also quite conclusive that the average returns on investment in human capital are higher in developing countries than in the advanced industrialized countries.[7] Integration, and the specialization that it promotes, can have a potentially significant effect on both the returns on investment in new human capital and the number of individuals choosing to invest in human capital. There are a couple of important channels at work here in the North American context. First, within Mexico the large stock of very low skilled labour implies that the potential exists for raising the stock of human capital fairly quickly, much as was accomplished in the Asian "tigers" thanks to the high incremental returns on new investment in human capital. The investment occurs because the new jobs in manufacturing resulting from NAFTA (1) create the demand for skills, encouraging people to get more training and education, and (2) create skills acquired through experience and learning-by-doing. This leads to higher incomes and thus a higher aggregate income in the region and so on.

In Canada and the United States, the effect of NAFTA on human capital formation is potentially quite different. Skill acquisition is subject to *creative destruction*. Opening up both economies to low-wage competition from Mexico will raise the returns to higher-skilled jobs and lower the returns to less-skilled jobs. In the short term, this can have a negative effect on real wages, but if human capital acquisition is responsive to rates of return, new human capital formation should increase over the longer term. Experience suggests, however, that a high rate of return on investment in skill acquisition is only one necessary condition for additional investment in human capital. Given imperfections in markets for human capital, governments must have in place policies which facilitate that investment.

NORTH AMERICA AS A REGION IN THE GLOBAL ECONOMY

An important and interesting question is whether competitiveness in each of the NAFTA countries could have been better enhanced through a unilateral push into the global economy head-on rather than through the North America regional grouping. There is no clear answer to this question, but I am sceptical about the relevance of the global option. Some countries, such as Singapore, seem to have unilaterally pursued such a strategy with success. For countries as large as those in North America, a sort of "borderless free market world" (Ohmae 1990) seems a considerable way off, although we may well be moving in that direction. What then of the regional option? There are two sets of arguments to support North America as a "natural" economic grouping, as opposed to other groupings such as APEC or a Western Hemispheric Free Trade Area.

The arguments of the first set are similar to those of Lester Thurow (1992), that a North American economic bloc is a practical and realistic alternative to blocs being formed in Europe and Asia. Blocs by definition offer preferential access, and this is certainly the case in the European Community. North America, then, makes strategic sense as a response to these global developments. I should say that at the moment this seems far too pessimistic a view, but I must admit that it should be taken seriously.

The second set of arguments in favour of a North American economic space are based on the proposition that integrating within North American is a logical first step towards a truly global economy. Some of these are as follows.

First, with the emergence in the next century of China and India as major economies in the world, it is in North America's interest, in terms of preserving geopolitical stability, to promote economic growth within those regions, and this of necessity means accommodating exports from those regions. After decades of fairly restrictive trade policies against the developing economies, the advanced countries must come to terms with admitting exports from those regions in a non-discriminatory way. The way to do that while dealing with domestic politics remains as elusive as ever, although the last GATT round set some goals in this regard. NAFTA on the other hand provides a more local and highly visible example of the same problem – how to bring Mexico into the partnership and the exports expected from that country while simultaneously accommodating the political pressures Mexican success will inevitability bring. There is a need for some innovative policy in this regard, and the NAFTA experience may prove useful in terms of the lessons it generates for the next GATT round.

Second, "going global" carries with it the implication that a larger part of the national entrepreneurial base must expand its horizons beyond the local national market and ultimately to the world economy. A useful and important first step in this process will be for firms to learn to sell into the North American market. For Canadians, Mexico in particular offers a unique alternative. Canadian business and management, through a long association with American subsidiaries, found that entry to the U.S. market over the last decade was, if not easy, at least a familiar commercial and cultural experience. Going into Mexico should promote a greater understanding of the requirements of selling and producing in a less culturally familiar environment. Large firms, of course, now do this routinely in Asia and Europe. However, for small and mid-sized firms, North America, given its geographic proximity, is a more natural territory in which to acquire that type of experience.

Third, there is the potential experience NAFTA carries for governments – federal, state, and local. The great irony is that we cannot truly have a global economy with genuine non-preferential access and complete policy harmonization without global government – that is a very long way off. Learning to coordinate appropriate economic policies across national and subnational boundaries is something governments have yet to learn very successfully. The European Community is one model in this regard but one with which most North Americans do not feel comfortable at this stage – and perhaps forever. Our governments therefore need greater institutional experience in both these areas, and NAFTA presents again a highly useful experiment that might be applied elsewhere. Part of this experience involves getting the voters to redefine who is the "we" – as in "we are in the same boat." While recent bickering within the Canadian federal system suggests this may well be impossible, the reality is that there is no alternative. The global economy is a fact and our governments need to do a better job across a wide range of areas of delivering better-coordinated policies, and this goes well beyond trade policy. In this respect, the United States must act in an appropriate way if this integration program is to be successful. If the U.S. tries to turn NAFTA into a series of "hub and spoke" bilateral trade deals, the concept of NAFTA will quickly lose credibility in Canada and Mexico and their governments' attentions will turn elsewhere.

NOTES

1 Units are 1988 U.S. dollars.
2 Numbers are World Bank estimates, as of 1993.
3 See Sharpe (1993).
4 Like most economists, I tend to have a rather critical view of most of this literature. See Harris and Watson (1992) for a detailed critique of the competitiveness literature.
5 See Sharpe (1993).

6 For a review and critique of these estimates, see Harris 1991.
7 This is not meant to suggest that there has been too much investment in human capital in the advanced countries; generally, estimated social returns on education, for example, are still well in excess of that on physical capital. Severe constraint on income through job loss, say, can act as an effective restraint on acquisition of additional training or education. This type of market failure forms exactly the circumstances where appropriate government policy can be crucial in creating an advantage out of apparent adversity.

REFERENCES

Bluestone, B., and Harrison, B. 1988. *The Great U-Turn.* New York: Basic Books.
Harris, R.G. 1991. "Free Trade with Mexico: Opportunity or Threat?" In W. Watson, ed., *The North American Free Trade Agreement.* Kingston: John Deutsch Institute for the Study of Economic Policy, Queen's University.
Harris, R.G., and W. Watson. 1992. "Three Visions of Competitiveness: Porter, Reich and Thurow on Economic Growth and Policy." In T.J. Courchene and D.D. Purvis, eds., *Productivity, Growth and Canada's International Competitiveness.* vol. 1, *The Bell Papers on Economic and Public Policy.* Kingston: John Deutsch Institute for the Study of Economic Policy, Queen's University.
Murphy, K., and F. Welch. 1992. "The Structure of Wages." *Quarterly Journal of Economics* 107 (1): 215–326.
Ohmae, K. 1990. *The Borderless World: Power and Strategy in the Interlinked Economy.* New York: Harper's.
Porter, Michael E. 1990. *The Competitive Advantage of Nations.* New York: Free Press.
Reich, R. 1991. *The Work of Nations: Preparing Ourselves for the 21st Century.* New York: Alfred A. Knopf.
Sharpe, Andrew. 1993. "Living Standards in Canada and the United States: A Comparative Analysis." Mimeo. Canadian Labour Market and Productivity Centre.
Thurow, Lester C. 1992. *Head to Head: The Coming Economic Battle among Japan, Europe, and America.* New York: William Morrow.

11 The Variable Geometry of Asian Trade: Trade and Competitiveness in North America – East Asian Interdependence

STEPHEN S. COHEN AND PAOLO GUERRIERI

INTRODUCTION

The spectacular economic success of the Asian Pacific region has generated a vast literature[1] that has identified many different, and often mutually exclusive, sources for that success and related it to North American competitiveness – as both cause and effect – in positive, negative, and relative terms. Most studies of Asian success, however, have attributed a critical role to international trade. The exceptionally rapid rates of economic growth achieved by the Asian countries are generally associated with their even more impressive achievements in export performance. Though exports of Asian countries have historically been oriented towards Western industrial countries, trade statistics indicate very substantial increases in trade flows within the region in recent years, and hence an apparent shift towards trade integration in the area.

Given the tendency towards regional trade agreements in Europe and North America (the Single European Market; the North American Free Trade Agreement, NAFTA), observers have increasingly speculated that the Asian Pacific region might emerge as a third, powerful trading bloc. Others take an opposite view and argue that concerns over emerging patterns of intra-Asian trade flows are totally misplaced. Their pattern is an entirely natural outcome of the rapid growth of the Asian national economies and their geographic propinquity. Interpreting patterns of Asian trade flows remains highly controversial, as does hypothesizing about their significance for the global trading system or for the competitiveness of the North American economy, the keystone of the structure of Asian trade.

This chapter presents a different interpretation of Asian trade patterns. The data presented here, which draw on a recently compiled trade database, do not show the formation of an exclusive bloc, nor even an emerging one. But they do show that rapid economic growth in the Asian countries and their relative geographic propinquity cannot by themselves explain the growth or the distinct patterns of Asia's intraregional trade. Instead increased intraregional trade has reinforced – not attenuated – a unique trade and production arrangement that causes serious adjustment problems for countries outside the region. This arrangement will have to change in substantial and fundamental ways for Asian regionalism to be "benign" for the international economy.

The paper is divided into three parts. The next section briefly surveys the literature in this area and identifies the two most widely received but contending interpretations of trade flow patterns in Asia. This is followed by an examination of the relevant statistical evidence, drawing on an original trade database, in order to specify the distinct character of Asia's current trade and production arrangement. The third section provides an alternative explanation of this arrangement. It concludes with some remarks on the strategic consequences of the arrangement for the world trading regime.

ASIAN TRADE INTEGRATION: A REVIEW
OF THE LITERATURE

In recent years the apparent movement towards increasing regional trade integration in the Asian Pacific area has attracted much attention among scholars, but very different explanations have been put forth to account for this trend. Furthermore, these analyses have identified different implications for the future evolution of the world trading regime. While it is beyond the scope of this chapter to present a comprehensive review of this literature, two of the principal competing views can be identified here: (1) trade flow patterns point to the likely consolidation of an exclusive trading bloc in East Asia, centred around Japan, with the risk of increasing discrimination against outsiders, particularly U.S. and European exporters; and (2) despite an increase in aggregate intraregional trade, there is little evidence that Asian countries are moving towards a trade bloc and no evidence of any abnormality in the region's trade pattern.[2]

The first line of thinking makes the following general arguments:

1 Shifts in regional trade flows over the past decade and particularly in recent years confirm that trade within the Japan–Southeast Asia region has been rapidly increasing. For example, Japan's trade with the rest of Asia exceeded that with the United States for the first time in 1991. In the latter half of the 1980s, trade among the Asian newly industrializing countries (NICs) grew by 44.7 per cent per year; exports from the NICs to ASEAN (Association of South East Asian Nations) countries grew by 31.7 per cent per year. Similarly, substantial increases were achieved in trade among the NICs, ASEAN and China (JETRO 1992).

2 A further indicator of the trend towards Asian economic integration is the rapid expansion of Japanese direct investment in the Asian Pacific region (Urata 1993). Particularly in the second half of the 1980s, Japan stepped up its direct investment into the Asian countries, investing at more than twice the U.S. and British rates in the region. More recently, the Asian NICs have also emerged as important investors in the area. Direct investment in ASEAN countries expanded at a very rapid pace in the most recent period (JETRO 1992).

3 Greater economic integration in Asia, as evidenced by this increase in intraregional trade and investment, has taken place without the implementation of any formal intergovernmental arrangements; rather, increasing intraregional trade seems to be primarily the outcome of autonomous decisions by firms and the result of market forces.

4 Given the diversity of history, culture, and tradition among the Asian countries, it seems unlikely that they could proceed along integration paths similar to those currently characterizing the European Community and NAFTA; however, there is a growing concern that an Asian trade network will develop into a trading bloc by increasingly discriminating against firms and products from outside the region.

5 Fear of an exclusionary Asian trading bloc will intensify pressure for greater intraregional trade in the European and North American regions. The European Union (EU) in particular is anxious about discriminatory trading arrangements, especially after allowing Central and Eastern European countries access to the EU market. Such fears could drive regions to erect more and more barriers to their own markets and might ultimately divide the world economy into three huge and probably inward-looking and discriminatory trading blocs.

The second set of interpretations provides a very different perspective:

1 It is certainly true that trade within the Japan–Southeast Asian region substantially increased in the second half of the 1980s. While East Asian trade with other regions in the world increased rapidly, its trade with other Asian countries increased even more rapidly. The latter, however, was the automatic outcome of the rapid growth in overall output and trade achieved by Japan and most East Asian countries in the 1980s. Therefore, the increase in the intraregional trade is entirely attributable to the greater participation of Asian countries in world trade flows – specifically, to their rapid growth and geographical proximity (Frankel 1991).

2 It is also true that, by the end of the 1980s, Japan became the world's single most important source of foreign direct investment (FDI). The major beneficiary of these flows, however, has not been East Asia, but North America. Less than 20 per cent of the total Japanese direct investment has been directed towards Asia, although Japanese FDI flows to this region have been rising significantly in recent years.

3 These qualifications suggest that there is no significant long-run trend that points to the formation of a self-contained Asian trading bloc centred around Japan. Indeed, if the influence of geographic proximity and rates of GNP (gross national product) growth are taken into account, by the late-1980s the intraregional share of Asian trade was not very different from that of the early 1970s (Frankel 1991).

4 In the past, the Asian Pacific region's foreign trade was strongly oriented towards Western industrial countries. Recent trade patterns suggest that extraregional trade, particularly with the United States and Europe, still remains very significant for Japan and East Asia. Given this persistent dependency on extraregional trade, the Asian region is very far from transforming itself into an exclusive, protectionist, regional arrangement.

5 A successful trading bloc must be characterized by at least four main features (Schott 1991): (a) similar levels of per capita income among member countries; (b) geographic proximity of member countries; (c) similar or compatible trading regimes; and (d) political commitment to regional organization. A future Asian trade bloc centred around Japan would not meet any of the above conditions except geographic proximity.

6 Although the regional trading arrangements in Europe and North America meet the above conditions much better than Asia, the role of extraregional trade has been and remains very important for them as well. Thus, it seems fair to say that each region retains a strong interest in an open multilateral trading system and that there is little reason to believe that Europe, North America, and East Asia are each

developing into trading blocs. Therefore, "the major regional initia-tives currently under way are more likely to represent the building blocks of an integrated world economy than stumbling blocks which prevent its emergence" (Lawrence 1991a).

The next section assesses the issue of regional patterns of Asian trade flows and its implications for the future of the international trade re-gime in the light of these two competing interpretations.

ASIAN TRADE INTEGRATION: A REVIEW OF THE EVIDENCE

This section examines the evolution in the trade of and between Asian countries, and situates it within long-term regional trade patterns. The most prominent study used the sum of exports and imports of single countries to represent trends in trade integration (Frankel 1991); an-other chose to look only at exports (Lawrence 1991a); some, however, have used both exports and imports to examine Asian regional trade patterns (Schott 1991). This chapter employs the latter method because it gives the most complete picture of the patterns of integration form-ing in Asia. The analysis relies on a recently compiled trade database (SIE World Trade)[3] comprising United Nations and OECD (Organiza-tion for Economic Cooperation and Development) statistical sources (450 product classes, 98 sectors, and 25 commodity groups) for more than eighty countries (OECDs, NICs, ex-CMEA, and less-developed coun-tries [LDCs]).

According to Table 11.1, which shows shares of various regions and countries in the overall merchandise exports and imports of East Asia in selected years from 1970 to 1992, the Asian intraregional share of both exports and imports has significantly increased (around 17.4 per-centage points for imports and 10.2 points for exports). If trade in manufactures for the same period is considered (Table 11.2), the intraregional share also increased substantially and on the same order of magnitude. During the past two decades, there has thus been an increasing regionalization of Asian trade.

A closer examination of these changes in Asia's trade flows, however, reveals substantially different patterns for export and import flows. The intraregional share of East Asian imports steadily increased during the entire period considered here (from 27.7 per cent in 1970 to 45.1 per cent in 1992 in total merchandise trade, and from 35.8 to 52.4 per cent in trade in manufactures during the same years; see tables 11.1 and 11.2). As for exports, however, the dependency of Asian countries on intraregional markets remained stable and rather limited throughout the 1970s and during the first half of the 1980s, increasing only during the second half of the 1980s. Thus, two phases may be distinguished in the evolution of Asian trade over the past two decades: the first covers the 1970s and the first half of the 1980s, while the other includes the early 1990s.

In the first period, Asian countries showed a high propensity to export to extraregional markets. North America and Europe, which received around 51 per cent of the total Asian manufactured exports in the early 1970s, continued to absorb more than 50 per cent during the first half of the 1980s, although there were wide fluctuations in the shares of Asian exports absorbed by the regions given the volatile international macroeconomic and financial environment during this phase. Of the extraregional markets, the United States provided the largest outlet for Asia's exports, increasing in the first half of the 1980s its share of imports from the region in parallel with the strong appreciation of the dollar in that period. It is thus fair to say that at least between 1970 and 1985 the North American market, and especially the U.S. market, was the engine of export growth for most Asian countries, particularly for the Asian NICs (see tables 11.3 and 11.4). During this same period, the share of intraregional merchandise exports remained largely stable, with exports between Asian countries significantly lower than exports between Asia and the rest of the world. In the case of manufactures, the share of intraregional exports was likewise consistently smaller than the share of exports to North America (Table 11.2).

By contrast, the level of intraregional imports increased steadily during this first phase, despite wide, year-to-year fluctuations (tables 11.1 to 11.4). This largely reflected the trade surpluses that accompanied the rapid growth of the Asian economies, especially the trade surpluses with the United States and North America. In the first phase, Asia as a whole continued to penetrate the markets for manufactures of North America, and to a much less degree of Europe, without much reciprocal imports of their goods. Whereas in the 1970s Asian trade balances (standardized) fluctuated around a nil value, with trade surpluses in manufactures compensating trade deficits in raw material and agricultural products, during the first part of the 1980s the trade surplus of Asian countries increased considerably thanks to a soaring positive trade balance in manufacturing trade (figures 11.1 and 11.2). Thus, Asia's cumulative surplus in trade of manufactures increased dramatically in the period from 1980 to 1985, reaching nearly $650 billion. North America, especially the United States, was the main contributor to this surplus (tables 11.5 and 11.6).

The distribution of this external surplus has been highly uneven within Asia, however, with Japan accounting for much of it. During the first phase, Japan continued to be a more important source of imports for the Asian countries than an increasing outlet market (tables 11.1 to 11.4). In the mid-1980s Japan took only 2.9 per cent of the Asian manufactured exports (8.9 per cent for merchandise exports), whereas nearly 28.3 per cent of the Asian manufactured imports came from Japan (15 per cent for merchandise imports) (tables 11.1 and 11.2). This markedly asymmetrical role of Japan has been the source of increasing Japanese trade surpluses with the other Asian countries, especially the Asian NICs, during the entire first phase, particularly the first half of the 1980s. The cumulative trade deficit of the Asian NICs and NECs (newly emerging countries) with Japan, for example, rose to $30 billion in the period from 1980 to 1985 (Table 11.5). In trade of manufactures, the trend was even more accentuated, so that the Japanese accumulated an impressive surplus of $169 billion in the first half of the 1980s (Table 11.6). Thus, Japan, while running a trade surplus with North America, also ran a substantial trade surplus in manufactured goods with its Asian neighbours (especially the Asian NICs) (figures 11.3 and 11.4). At the same time, in parallel with their trade deficits with Japan, the Asian NICs (and to a lesser extent the ASEAN countries) ran compensating surpluses with the rest of the world, especially with the United States and North America (figures 11.5 to 11.8; tables 11.5 and 11.6).

To sum up, a pattern of triangular trade, rather than regionalization, appears to characterize Asian trade flows in this first phase.[4] The Asian countries depended on Japan as a major source of manufactured imports and relied heavily on extraregional markets, especially the North American and European markets, for their exports of manufactured finished goods. This triangular trade was visibly hierarchic: on top, Japan sold mainly capital goods and technologies, and on bottom the United States (and to a lesser extent Europe) bought mainly the final goods. As Asian exports grew rapidly in the second half of the 1970s and the first half of the 1980s, they began to cause serious adjustment problems for countries outside the region. These adjustment problems contributed to increasing trade tensions, first between the United States and Asia, but then also between Europe and Asia, leading to growing protectionist measures directed at exports from Japan (Porges 1991) and, to a lesser extent, from the Asian NICs (Noland 1990).

During the second half of the 1980s, the revaluation of the yen, expectations of its further appreciation, and the growing protectionist attitude in Europe and North America brought on a substantial change in Asian trade flows: the share of trade among Asian countries increased sharply, so that by the beginning of the 1990s the share of intraregional imports reached 45.1 per cent (52.4 per cent for manufactures) and the share of intraregional exports reached 39.8 per cent (36.2 per cent for manufactures) (tables 11.1 and 11.2). In contrast to the steady increase of intraregional imports observed in the first phase, in the second half of the 1980s it was intraregional exports that rose substantially: the share of exports rose from 32.5 per cent in 1985 to 39.8 per cent in 1992 for merchandise trade and from 25.6 to 36.2 per cent in the same period for trade in manufactures (tables 11.1 and 11.2). Consequently, the role of extraregional outlets decreased. According to Table 11.1, the share of Asian exports going to the U.S. dropped from about 34 per cent to 25 per cent in parallel with the strong depreciation of the dollar.

Japan certainly contributed to this increase of intraregional exports by increasing their imports of manufactured goods from the other Asian countries in the second half of the 1980s (Table 11.4). This took place in parallel with the significant appreciation in the value of the yen together with "market opening" measures adopted by Japan in that period. On the other hand, since 1985 a rising share of Japanese manufactured exports has gone to other Asian countries, showing an increasing role of Japanese firms as supplier for the region, especially of intermediate and investment goods (tables 11.3 and 11.4). But the share of manufactured goods imported from countries within the region other than Japan has been rising even more strongly since 1985, so that relative to the share of manufactured goods exchanged between the NICs and the ASEAN countries, the share of manufactured imports from Japan has in fact decreased (tables 11.1 and 11.4). The bilateral relationship between the NICs and ASEAN countries then grew significantly in the second phase, signalling the emergence of a new potential axis in the region (tables 11.3 and 11.4).

According to some analysts, this more recent increase in the regionalization of Asian trade has raised the prospect of the formation of an Asian trading bloc (Dornbusch 1990). The assumption is that the triangular trade pattern and past extraregional linkages, which, as shown earlier, characterized the Asian trade flows in the first phase, are being replaced by new trading relationships, driven endogenously by the rapid growth of the regional market, that will lead to Asian regional integration. This new pattern is fed by Japan's increasing capacity to absorb more manufactured imports from other Asian countries, and by the Asian NICs opening their markets for imports from the ASEAN countries and China.

Although the evidence reviewed here seems to confirm a substantial increase in Asian intraregional trade over the second phase, in order to determine the validity of this view it is necessary to examine the changing patterns of Asian trade in this period in some detail.

To begin with, one must recognize that in the period from the mid-1980s up to the early 1990s Asia as a whole has maintained a high export dependency on, and trade surpluses with, the rest of the world. As shown in figures 11.1 and 11.2, the Asian trade surplus (standardized) fluctuated throughout the 1980s, largely as a result of variations in the continuing, large trade surplus with the United States. After reaching a peak in the mid-1980s, this trade surplus declined rapidly during the second half of the 1980s because of changes in the real exchange rate of the dollar and in the relative incomes of the two areas of the Pacific in that period. Yet at the beginning of the 1990s (that is, at the end of a ten-year cycle of the dollar's external value), the Asian trade surplus was still much higher than at the beginning of the 1980s. Asia's cumulative trade surplus – the sum of trade balances from 1986 to 1992 – more than quadrupled with respect to the cumulative trade surplus for the first half of the 1980s, and it doubled in the case of trade in manufactures, reaching $1.36 trillion (tables 11.5 and 11.6). As in the past, North America, and especially the United States, was the major source of these surpluses. But Europe also significantly contributed to the trade imbalance during the second half of the 1980s, tripling its trade deficit in manufactures and mostly compensating the declining trade surplus towards the United States in the more recent years (Table 11.6). North America and Europe then remained the key markets for Asian countries, as evidenced by the fact that even in 1992 they absorbed nearly the same share of Asia's merchandise exports as they had twenty years before (47 per cent in 1992; 51 per cent in 1970 – Table 11.1).

It is also enlightening to look at the intraregional distribution of Asia's overall trade surplus. In the second half of the 1980s, Japan ran increasing trade surpluses with other Asian countries, especially with the Asian NICs, whereas its trade surplus with the U.S. sharply declined, compensated only partially by the increase in the trade surplus with Europe (figures 11.3 and 11.4). Asia's cumulative trade deficit with Japan rose from about $30 billion in the first half of the 1980s to $163 billion in the period covering the second half of the 1980s and the early 1990s (Table 11.5). In manufactured products, the data reported in Table 11.6 are even more emblematic, since Asia's cumulative trade deficits with Japan rose from $169 to $343 billion. This demonstrates that the Japanese market remained a poor outlet for Asian exports, and that despite the strong appreciation of the yen, the share of Asian exports destined for Japan rose only slightly between 1985 and 1992. Because of this inadequate increase in Japan's capacity to import, the share of Asian manufactured exports destined for the United States was still much higher than the share going to Japan, even in the early 1990s (Table 11.4).

To offset their substantial rising trade deficit with Japan during the 1980s, the Asian countries, and especially the NICs, generated substan-

tial trade surpluses in manufactures with the rest of the world, especially with the U.S. and to a lesser extent Europe (figure 11.6).[5] During
the second half of the 1980s, however, the Asian NICs experienced a
relative decline in their trade surplus with the United States owing to
the real appreciation of their currencies vis-à-vis the dollar. At the same
time, the NICs' trade deficits with Japan increased, despite the real depreciation of their currencies against the yen. As a consequence, in the
early 1990s they began running overall trade deficits (figure 11.5).

Structural factors explain the differences in behavior of NIC net exports to the United States and Japan. During the 1980s, the NICs trade
balance with the U.S., either in total trade or in manufactures, fluctuated considerably and was very elastic with respect to changes in real
exchange rates, whereas the trade balance with Japan did not fluctuate
but rather shifted steadily in favour of Japan throughout the 1980s,
despite the appreciation of the yen (tables 11.5 and 11.6; Figure 11.5).
This is because the increase in the NICs' exports to Japan was matched
by an almost equal increase in dependence on Japan for imports of
highly price-inelastic, technology-intensive products and capital goods
(Park and Park 1991; Guerrieri 1994). This dependence explains why
the NICs' deficit with Japan continued to be very high in the 1980s
despite the rapid growth of their exports to Japan and the real depreciation of their currencies vis-à-vis the yen.

To sum up, in the second half of the 1980s, the rapid growth of Asian
trade and the intensification of intra-Asian trade did not substantially
modify the triangular trade pattern that characterized Asian trade flows
from 1970 to 1985. At the beginning of the 1990s, Asian countries still
depended heavily on exports to the United States and Europe and imported more and more heavily from Japan, with most Asian countries
running large trade deficits with Japan and symmetrical trade surpluses
with the United States and Europe. Under this persistent triangular
pattern of trade, the high growth of Asia's exports has created serious
adjustment problems for countries outside the region. This has then
led to increasing trade tensions and fears that the multilateral trade
framework might be jeopardized (Sandholtz et al. 1992).

The evidence reviewed here does not support the contention that
Asia is evolving into an exclusive trading bloc centred around Japan,
with the risk of increasing discrimination against outsiders. On the contrary, our analysis of Asian import and export flows over the last twenty
years reveals not only that Asian trade has been heavily dependent upon
western industrial countries in the past, but also that this extraregional
trade dependency, particularly on the U.S. and Europe, remains critical to Japanese and Asian trade. The data suggest that trade relationships within Asia and between Asia and the rest of the world are organ-

ized in unique ways but certainly not along the lines of a self-contained bloc. Our analysis reveals that Asian integration remains firmly situated within a powerful triangle of trade and that this integration in fact grows out of that pattern of trade (Riedel 1991). Japan was the dominant force of this trade network. On the other hand, the bilateral trade relationships between the NICs and ASEAN increased significantly in the second phase, signalling the emergence of a new potential intraregional economic pole.

ASIAN TRADE INTEGRATION: A REVIEW
OF THE DETERMINANTS

The data presented here offer a very different view of Asian trade patterns from those of the two most prominent explanations in the literature. The data do not show the formation of an exclusive bloc, not even an emerging one. They do show that rapid economic growth and geographic proximity cannot by themselves explain the growth or distinct patterns of Asia's intraregional trade. And the data delineate a unique trade and production arrangement with far-reaching strategic consequences for the world economy.

Certainly, there are various political and economic forces responsible for the gradual increase in the regionalization of Asian trade. First, one should notice that Asian trade integration has not been propelled by any formal political or trade agreements, in contrast to European and American integration. The main players in the process of Asian integration have been firms and their private agreements, which have led to what has been called a *de facto* trade integration.

This feature of the regionalization trade pattern in Asia led many authors to interpret it along the *product cycle model*, in which Japan plays the role of the leading innovative country and the NICs and other Asian countries follow as second- and third-tier countries on the ladder of comparative advantage.[6] According to this model, as Japan produces and exports more technology-intensive manufactured products, it moves production capabilities in simpler technology, labour-intensive goods to Asian NICs. And as the NICs increase their competitiveness in these products and upgrade their production capabilities into more capital- and technology-intensive lines, more of their labour-intensive production will move to ASEAN and Chinese producers, which in turn will increase their domestic market shares and, eventually, export to Japan and the NICs. This model has been frequently summed up by the well-known image of wild geese flying in their V-formation.[7]

Foreign direct investment has played a major, if not dominant, role in this shift of production from Northeast Asia to Southeast Asia, which attracted a disproportionately large share of FDI to developing areas in the 1980s. In particular, there was a new upsurge of investment from Japan, first into NICs and then, in the second half of the 1980s, into ASEAN countries, when the substantial rise of the yen made Japanese firms more interested in investing in the region to cut production costs (Urata 1993). This rapid expansion of Japanese investment in the Asian Pacific region reinforced the trend towards greater trade integration.

Though it is a plausible construct, there is still too little evidence to support the product cycle hypothesis. To interpret the changing patterns of trade and industrialization in Asia according to the product cycle theory, the key hypothesis is that Japan must be the lead economy both in terms of demand and supply in the region. Yet, as shown above, Japan has been, and still is, a weak absorber of other Asian exports. In fact, even the recent increase in imported manufactured products from other Asian countries has been very slight (tables 11.3 and 11.4). Asia's dependency on markets outside the region for its exports, as previously noted, has continued to be very high through the early 1990s. That could change, but the most recent data evidence no change. The demand side is still a very different structure from the one called for by a regional product cycle model. Thus, although the "flying geese" hypothesis might be useful for interpreting a few sectoral trade patterns in Asia, it cannot be used as a general explanation for the increase in the regionalization of Asian trade. Some explanation other than the product cycle hypothesis or trade on the basis of revealed comparative advantage must be ventured. And this explanation could be related to FDI patterns in the region.

Japanese FDI has no doubt contributed significantly to shaping the new regional trade pattern, since a large proportion of trade integration is derived from intra-company transactions (Park and Park 1991; Urata 1993). Part of this investment, in line with the product cycle theory, aimed at taking advantage of local natural resources, skills, and relatively low wage costs (Bollard and Mayes 1992). But the same Japanese multinational companies that set up as "footloose" industries are now pursuing a more lasting involvement in the region. In other words, interest in the region is no longer motivated only by the search for new low-wage locations. The expansion of Japanese FDI, subcontracting, and outsourcing have in fact created new regional production networks,[8] often embodying global production strategies (Lim and Siddall 1993). The growing importance of intra-industry trade within the region also seems attributable largely to an increasing division of labour within multinational companies (Park and Park 1991), and Japan has developed a large network within the region (Borrus 1993).

Some authors have optimistically predicted that Japanese FDI and outsourcing would increase the share of East Asian exports to Japan enough to reduce East Asian dependence on North American and European markets (Urata 1993). This has not yet happened to any significant extent. Clearly, Japanese multinationals have assumed a greater role in Japan's trade in recent years. There is also evidence that part of the exports by Japanese multinational parent companies have been replaced by the production of their overseas affiliates and subsidiaries.

On the other hand, since the mid-1980s Japan's FDI has been allocated mainly to Asian export-oriented industries, primarily to create production and export bases aimed at expanding sales in third countries.[9] In other words, many Japanese overseas affiliates in Asia were concentrated in export-oriented industries and shipped their products to third countries rather than to Japan, linking up components and final production for export outside the region towards the U.S. and Europe.[10] This trend in Japan's FDI has indeed exacerbated trade imbalances between the U.S. and Europe, on the one hand, and the U.S. and Asia, on the other.[11]

The tendency is being reinforced by the Asian NICs, which have been following the example of Japanese multinational enterprises in developing production systems based on the division of labour in the Asian Pacific region. Foreign direct investment from the NICs in the ASEAN countries grew markedly in the second half of the 1980s and actually surpassed the flow of Japanese FDI to ASEAN in 1990 (JETRO 1992).[12]

In this regard, the rapid growth of Japanese and other Asian FDI in the region has been contributing to the growth in the regional production system.

CONCLUDING REMARKS

This paper has argued that while intraregional trade has significantly increased in Asia, this increase has not led to a self-contained bloc, nor even to an emergent one. But it has shown that rapid economic growth of the countries within the region and their relative geographic proximity cannot by themselves explain the growth or the distinctive patterns of Asia's intraregional trade. Instead, increased intraregional trade has, up to now, reinforced a production and trade arrangement that presumes asymmetrical trade between Asia and the rest of the world.

Asian trade has been integrating, not through political pacts as in Europe and North America, but according to corporate strategies of industrial restructuring and production reorganization. This development of regional production networks in Asia extended integration to both factor and product markets, with strong interactions between the two. The rapid growth of Asian trade and the intensification of intra-

Asian trade in the second half of the 1980s, however, did not substantially modify the basic feature of the triangular trade pattern that had characterized Asian trade flows in the past. At the beginning of the 1990s, Asian countries still depended heavily on exports to the United States and Europe, and their imports were heavily dependent on Japanese technology, tools, and components, with most Asian countries running large trade deficits with Japan and compensating trade surpluses with the U.S. and Europe. This unique trade configuration has continued to enlarge the trade imbalance within Asia and worsen trade conflicts between Asia and the rest of the world.

Regionalism is usually an issue of great debate because it is interpreted as an obstacle in the path towards the goal of multilateral free trade. In the case of East Asia, the real problem is strong extraregional export linkages – not intraregional linkages. A move towards stronger regionalism by developing a dynamic regional domestic market more able to absorb Asian production and exports could make multilateral agreement easier rather than more difficult to achieve. There are some early implications of movement in this direction. In this case, regionalism would be desirable.

APPENDIX

Data on trade flows of Asian countries selected above were aggregated by using an original trade database (SIE [Systems de Informacion Empresaria] World Trade database) derived from the OECD as well as United Nations trade statistics (see Guerrieri 1992, 1993). The SIE World Trade database provides detailed information on export and import of eighty-three countries with respect to 400 product groups. The database includes trade statistics with respect to the twenty-four OECD countries, the newly industrializing countries, the other developing countries, and the former CMEA countries, and makes it possible to examine and analyse the entire world trade matrix. The source for the basic trade statistics of the SIE World Trade is the official publications of the OECD and the United Nations provided on magnetic tapes. The SIE database is organized in different product group classifications at various levels of disaggregation (400 product groups, 98 sectors, 25 categories, 5 branches), according to the three Standard International Trade Classifications (SITC), Revised, Revision 2, and Revision 3, defined by the Statistical Office of the United Nations as to the periods 1961–75, 1978–87, and 1988 on. Thus, the main advantage of the SIE World Trade database lies in the fact that it allows us to use extremely disaggregated time series for products groups, given its system of correspondence between the SITC Revised, the SITC Revision 2, and the SITC Revision 3.

Table 11.1
Shares of Various Regions in the Total Exports and Imports of Asia* (per cent)

	Exports					
	1970	*1975*	*1980*	*1985*	*1991*	*1992*
North America	31.1	23.3	24.9	36.4	26.9	26.9
United States	28.6	21.3	23.3	34.1	25.2	25.1
Asia	29.6	31.6	33.8	32.5	39.0	39.8
Asia (except Japan)	22.3	21.7	23.0	23.5	30.4	31.7
APEC	64.1	58.2	61.4	71.8	67.9	68.8
Europe	17.2	16.9	17.8	13.9	17.3	17.1
EU-12	14.2	13.8	15.3	11.7	14.7	14.8
Rest of the world	18.8	24.9	20.8	14.3	14.8	14.1
	Imports					
	1970	*1975*	*1980*	*1985*	*1991*	*1992*
North America	27.4	22.1	20.6	20.3	20.1	19.3
United States	23.9	18.9	18.2	17.8	18.2	17.4
Asia	27.7	29.6	32.5	39.0	43.3	45.1
Asia (except Japan)	13.9	16.6	19.8	24.0	27.7	29.1
APEC	62.0	57.8	57.6	64.0	67.4	68.1
Europe	15.3	12.3	10.7	12.6	13.3	13.1
EU-12	12.8	10.3	8.8	10.3	10.4	10.4
Rest of the world	22.7	29.9	31.8	23.4	19.3	18.8

*Asia comprises Japan, the Asian NICs (Hong Kong, Singapore, South Korea, and Taiwan), the ASEAN economies (Indonesia, Malaysia, Philippines, and Thailand), and China.

Sources: UN and OECD trade data from SIE World Trade database.

Table 11.2
Shares of Various Regions in the Total Manufactured Exports and Imports of Asia*
(per cent)

	Exports					
	1970	*1975*	*1980*	*1985*	*1991*	*1992*
North America	35.2	25.1	28.6	41.8	29.4	29.2
United States	32.2	22.7	26.6	39.0	27.6	27.2
Asia	24.0	24.7	26.0	25.6	35.4	36.2
Asia (except Japan)	22.0	21.8	23.0	22.7	30.1	31.3
APEC	62.9	53.6	57.4	70.5	66.9	67.6
EUROPE	15.9	17.4	19.1	14.8	18.6	18.2
EU-12	12.6	13.8	16.1	12.3	15.9	15.7
Rest of the world	21.1	28.9	23.5	14.7	14.4	14.2

	Imports					
	1970	*1975*	*1980*	*1985*	*1991*	*1992*
North America	27.8	24.3	25.0	22.6	19.6	18.5
United States	26.8	23.2	23.9	21.6	18.7	17.8
Asia	35.8	41.4	44.7	47.6	50.6	52.4
Asia (except Japan)	7.0	10.1	14.3	19.3	28.2	29.9
APEC	65.5	67.5	70.9	71.2	71.1	71.8
EUROPE	29.4	27.2	22.9	21.1	16.5	16.1
EU-12	24.7	22.7	18.7	17.4	12.8	12.7
Rest of the world	5.1	5.4	6.2	7.7	12.4	12.1

*Asia comprises Japan, the Asian NICs (Hong Kong, Singapore, South Korea, and Taiwan), the ASEAN economies (Indonesia, Malaysia, Philippines, and Thailand), and China.

Sources: UN and OECD trade data from SIE World Trade database.

Table 11.3
Shares of Various Regions in the Imports and Exports of Japan, the Asian NICs, and
ASEAN (per cent)

		North America	Europe	Imports from Asia (except Japan)	Japan	China	Apec	Rest of World
Japan	1970	34.4	10.8	14.3		1.3	57.6	31.6
	1975	24.4	7.9	19.5		2.6	52.0	40.2
	1980	20.9	7.2	22.4		3.1	48.9	44.0
	1985	24.0	8.8	25.9		5.1	56.3	34.9
	1991	26.2	16.3	29.2		6.1	61.4	22.3
	1992	26.1	16.2	30.4		7.3	62.3	21.5
Asian NICs	1970	19.3	16.7	16.7	31.2	6.9	70.1	13.2
	1975	22.1	13.5	15.5	26.9	6.4	67.3	19.2
	1980	20.2	12.6	17.7	25.7	6.3	65.9	21.5
	1985	18.9	13.8	21.7	24.0	9.9	67.8	18.4
	1991	18.4	11.5	27.0	23.9	14.9	72.2	16.3
	1992	17.5	11.6	28.3	23.5	15.8	72.1	16.3
ASEAN	1970	20.4	23.7	10.9	29.2	1.5	65.5	10.8
	1975	16.7	20.5	12.4	27.8	2.7	61.8	17.7
	1980	17.8	16.0	17.7	24.1	2.8	63.8	20.2
	1985	17.5	17.5	22.4	23.4	2.7	67.3	15.2
	1991	14.9	12.5	22.5	26.1	2.7	67.1	20.4
	1992	14.8	13.5	24.9	26.0	2.5	69.4	17.1

		North America	Europe	Exports to Asia (except Japan)	Japan	China	Apec	Rest of World
Japan	1970	34.1	15.4	23.8		2.9	61.7	22.9
	1975	22.3	15.3	24.5		4.0	50.7	34.0
	1980	26.3	17.1	25.7		3.9	55.2	27.8
	1985	40.2	14.5	24.1		7.1	67.9	17.7
	1991	31.6	21.9	32.0		2.7	66.0	12.0
	1992	30.5	21.2	33.0		3.5	65.9	12.9
Asian NICs	1970	36.5	20.2	11.1	13.2	0.6	63.8	16.1
	1975	31.5	22.5	12.5	14.5	0.4	62.1	15.3
	1980	29.8	21.1	16.7	11.1	2.2	60.4	18.5
	1985	41.7	13.6	18.4	10.4	7.4	73.1	13.3
	1991	28.8	15.8	24.1	11.5	10.2	66.5	17.7
	1992	28.9	15.1	25.9	10.2	12.4	67.1	17.8
ASEAN	1970	20.9	17.6	22.7	27.9	0.5	73.5	8.9
	1975	22.4	14.5	17.2	33.3	0.6	74.0	11.5
	1980	19.1	14.7	19.5	34.5	0.8	74.9	10.3
	1985	20.5	13.0	23.9	30.8	1.3	76.8	10.1
	1991	19.4	13.8	26.9	22.9	2.3	71.1	15.1
	1992	22.9	17.7	28.9	21.9	2.4	75.8	6.5

Sources: UN and OECD trade data from SIE World Trade database.

Table 11.4
Shares of Various Regions in the Imports and Exports of Manufactures of Japan, the
Asian NICs, and ASEAN (per cent)

		North America	Europe	Imports from Asia (except Japan)	Japan	China	Apec	Rest of World
Japan	1970	50.2	33.8	7.5		1.7	59.4	6.8
	1975	39.9	33.6	18.3		3.2	60.1	6.3
	1980	40.3	30.7	21.6		3.7	62.6	6.8
	1985	42.6	26.5	22.8		4.7	66.1	7.4
	1991	30.8	29.8	32.9		7.6	64.6	5.6
	1992	29.8	29.4	35.3		9.9	66.1	4.5
Asian NICs	1970	17.7	23.0	8.4	43.9	4.8	71.4	5.6
	1975	22.7	19.7	9.4	40.9	4.4	74.2	6.1
	1980	21.4	18.5	12.9	39.0	5.8	74.4	7.1
	1985	19.1	18.6	16.8	34.5	8.6	71.2	10.1
	1991	17.3	12.3	27.6	29.8	16.5	75.5	12.2
	1992	17.0	12.1	29.2	28.8	17.4	75.7	12.2
ASEAN	1970	18.7	29.6	5.8	39.6	0.9	67.2	3.1
	1975	18.9	27.9	6.9	38.6	0.9	66.9	5.2
	1980	20.4	22.9	10.6	38.1	1.8	71.5	5.5
	1985	19.0	23.5	14.8	34.2	1.1	69.9	6.7
	1991	15.9	13.5	19.1	32.6	2.1	69.1	17.4
	1992	14.9	15.5	22.4	32.5	2.1	71.2	13.3

		North America	Europe	Exports to Asia (except Japan)	Japan	China	Apec	Rest of World
Japan	1970	34.5	14.9	23.3		3.0	61.7	23.4
	1975	22.2	15.0	24.1		4.1	50.3	34.7
	1980	26.6	17.0	25.2		4.0	55.0	28.0
	1985	40.4	14.6	23.5		7.1	67.7	17.7
	1991	31.9	22.2	31.3		2.7	65.6	12.2
	1992	30.8	21.5	32.2		3.5	65.4	13.1
Asian NICs	1970	44.2	19.1	10.9	9.3	0.2	67.3	13.6
	1975	37.6	25.3	10.4	10.6	0.1	61.7	13.0
	1980	35.9	23.2	14.2	8.0	2.2	60.0	16.8
	1985	47.8	14.7	17.1	6.7	8.1	73.8	11.5
	1991	31.5	17.3	22.7	9.2	10.3	65.6	17.1
	1992	31.1	16.3	24.6	8.2	12.3	66.4	17.3
ASEAN	1970	30.1	12.2	35.1	5.2	0.0	72.5	15.4
	1975	26.2	19.8	32.1	8.3	0.0	72.2	8.0
	1980	25.4	23.8	30.2	7.4	1.0	66.3	9.9
	1985	34.8	18.0	27.8	7.6	1.2	72.8	9.2
	1991	25.7	16.7	27.8	12.4	1.6	67.4	15.8
	1992	29.2	21.2	29.9	11.4	1.6	72.1	6.7

Sources: UN and OECD trade data from SIE World Trade database.

Table 11.5
Overall and Bilateral Cumulative Trade Balances of Asia, Japan, and the Asian NICs
(current U.S. dollars, millions)

a) Cumulative trade balances from 1980 to 1992

Export Import	World	Asia	Japan	Asian NICs	ASEAN	North America	Europe
Asia	773,358		(193,198)	366,753	(80,704)	802,143	326,770
Japan	680,865	193,198		278,551	(76,663)	435,599	264,141
Asian NICs	(1,807)	(366,753)	(278,551)		(4,283)	327,910	77,044

b) Cumulative trade balances from 1980 to 1985

Export Import	World	Asia	Japan	Asian NICs	ASEAN	North America	Europe
Asia	130,138		(30,140)	90,974	(46,294)	206,290	87,391
Japan	114,646	30,140		73,706	(49,360)	118,950	79,810
Asian NICs	(13,276)	(90,974)	(73,706)		727	87,046	16,690

c) Cumulative trade balances from 1986 to 1992

Export Import	World	Asia	Japan	Asian NICs	ASEAN	North America	Europe
Asia	643,220		(163,057)	275,780	(34,410)	595,852	239,379
Japan	566,219	163,057	0	204,845	(27,303)	316,649	184,331
Asian NICs	11,469	(275,780)	(204,845)	0	(5,010)	240,864	60,354

Sources: UN and OECD trade data from SIE World Trade database.

Table 11.6
Cumulative Manufactured Trade Balances of Asia, Japan, and the Asian NICs (current U.S. dollars, millions)

a) Cumulative trade balances from 1980 to 1992

Export	Import	World	Asia	Japan	Asian NICs	ASEAN	North America	Europe
Asia		2,010,251		(512,921)	352,146	173,148	1,117,782	332,361
Japan		2,004,057	512,921		321,306	138,943	701,912	312,681
Asian NICs		274,927	(352,921)	(321,306)		31,714	411,807	89,540

b) Cumulative trade balances from 1980 to 1985

Export	Import	World	Asia	Japan	Asian NICs	ASEAN	North America	Europe
Asia		649,470		(169,477)	80,619	68,557	311,247	68,901
Japan		707,239	169,477		88,483	51,256	217,580	89,604
Asian NICs		85,449	(80,619)	(88,483)		15,795	111,777	13,657

c) Cumulative trade balances from 1986 to 1992

Export	Import	World	Asia	Japan	Asian NICs	ASEAN	North America	Europe
Asia		1,360,781	0	(343,444)	271,528	104,591	806,536	263,460
Japan		1,296,817	343,444	0	232,823	87,687	484,332	223,077
Asian NICs		189,479	(271,528)	(232,823)	0	15,919	300,030	75,883

Sources: UN and OECD trade data from SIE World Trade database.

Figure 11.1
Trade Balance in Overall Merchandise Trade of Asia*

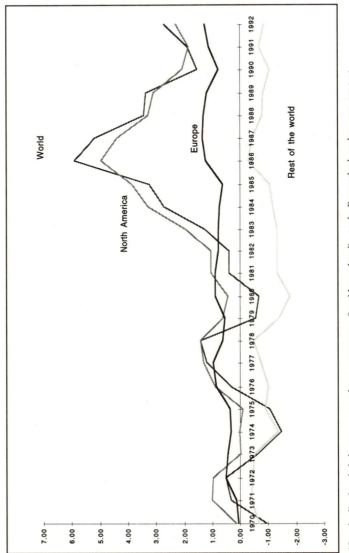

*Standardized trade balances expressed as a percentage of world merchandise trade. For methods and sources, see text.

Figure 11.2
Trade Balance in Total Manufactures of Asia*

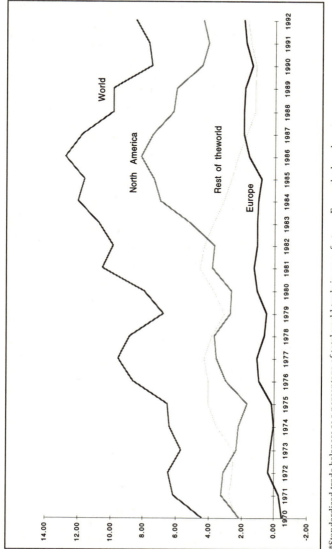

*Standardized trade balances as a percentage of total world trade in manufactures. For methods and sources, see text.

Figure 11.3
Trade Balance in Overall Merchandise Trade of Japan*

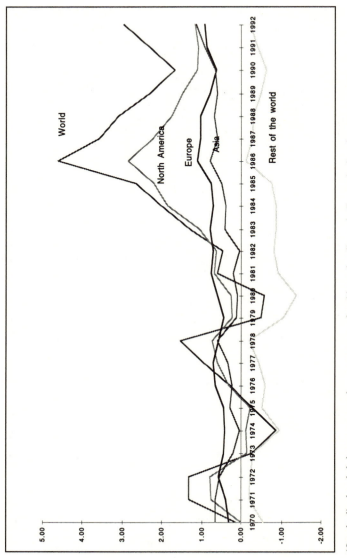

*Standardized trade balances expressed as a percentage of world merchandise trade. For methods and sources, see text.

Figure 11.4
Trade Balance in Total Manufactures of Japan*

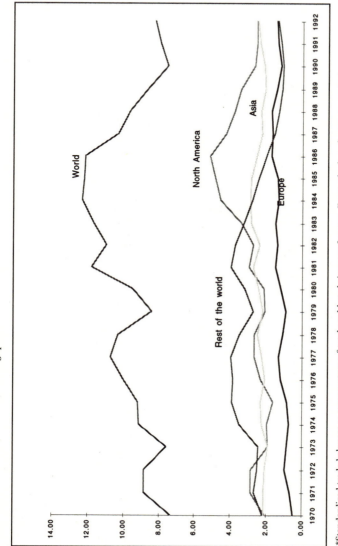

*Standardized trade balances as a percentage of total world trade in manufactures. For methods and sources, see text.

Figure 11.5
Trade Balance in Overall Merchandise Trade of the Asian NICs*

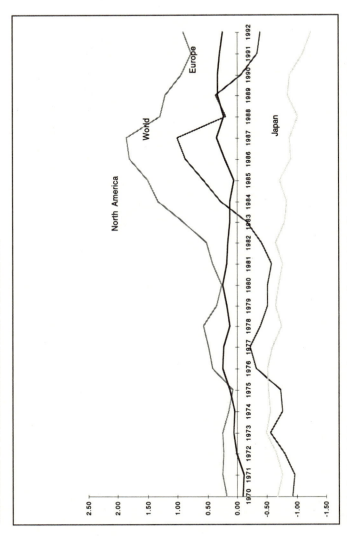

*Standardized trade balances expressed as a percentage of world merchandise trade. For methods and sources, see text.

Figure 11.6
Trade Balance in Total Manufactures of the Asian NICs*

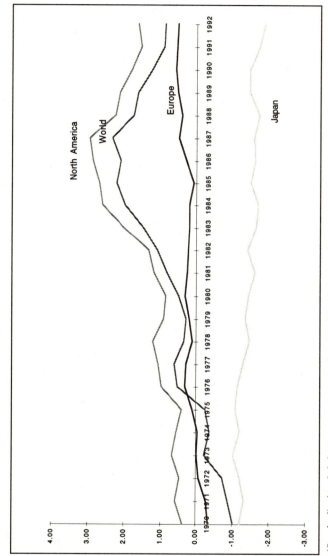

*Standardized trade balances as a percentage of total world trade in manufactures. For methods and sources, see text.

Figure 11.7
Trade Balance in Merchandise Trade of the ASEAN Countries*

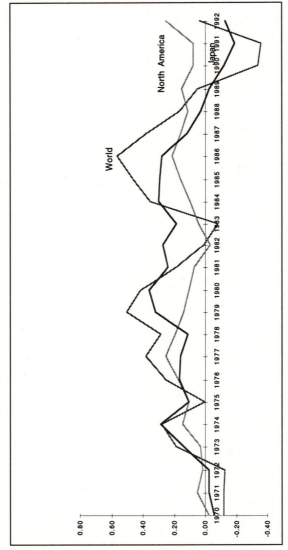

*Standardized trade balances expressed as a percentage of world merchandise trade. For methods and sources, see text.

Figure 11.8
Trade Balance in Total Manufactures of the ASEAN Countries*

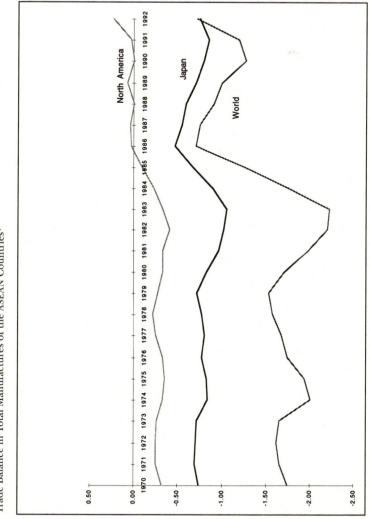

*Standardized trade balances as a percentage of total world trade in manufactures. For methods and sources, see text.

NOTES

Author's Note: The research leading to this paper was supported by the Alfred P. Sloan Foundation, the Center for Global Partnership, and the Italian CNR (National Research Council) within the project "Technological Change and Industrial Growth."

1 For a survey of this literature, see Hicks (1990).
2 The term "Asia" will be used throughout to refer to Japan, the four Asian NICs (Hong Kong, Singapore, South Korea, Taiwan), the four ASEAN economies other than Singapore and Brunei (namely, Indonesia, Malaysia, the Philippines and Thailand), and China.
3 See, for example, Dornbusch (1990), Krause (1990), and Nishikawa (1992).
4 See Frankel (1991), Lawrence (1991a), and Schott (1991).
5 For a detailed presentation of the database that the SIE World Trade used in its paper, see Guerrieri (1992, 1993) and the appendix of this chapter.
6 The standardized trade balance (STB) highlights the international distribution over time of trade surpluses and deficits among countries in each group of products. Trade balances are normalized by total world trade in the same group of products (CEPII 1989). The evolution of trade balance distribution permits highlighting competitiveness patterns of single countries in a certain group of products. For each country (j) the indicator is given by

$$STB = \frac{X_i - M_i}{WT_i}$$

Xi = total exports of country (j) in the product group (i); Mi = total imports of country (j) in the product group (i);_ WTi = total world exports (imports) in the product group (i).
7 On the trilateral pattern of East Asia's trade, see Park and Park (1991), Fouquin et al. (1991).
8 Under this pattern, the Asian NICs have developed production structures vertically integrated with Japan, by importing intermediate goods as well as capital goods from Japan, then exporting the finished goods to destinations outside the region, in particular, to the United States (Calder 1991; Park and Park 1991).
9 More generally, Japan's own low ratio of manufactured imports to GNP has always been much lower than that of the United States and Germany, for example, and it did not change substantially during the past two decades; see Lawrence (1991b) and Kreinin (1993).
10 Japan and the NICs share the common characteristic of having a poor resource endowment dependent on imported oil and other raw materials. In order to pay for this net import they must obtain a surplus in their

trade in manufactures with other countries. The ASEAN economies, on the other hand, have a rich resource base and have traditionally maintained a trade deficit in their manufactured trade with Japan and the other NICs (see Table 11.6).

11 In fact, the ASEAN Preferential Trading Agreement, although set up in 1977, is only a limited trade agreement (Yam, Toh, and Low 1992) and is not comparable to the trade arrangements in Europe or even in North America.

12 Among the more recent studies that propose the product cycle model are Ohkita (1986), Park (1989), and Yamazawa (1990).

13 See Yamazawa (1990) and the classic Akamatsu (1961).

14 It is true, as sceptics of the integration trend in Asia observe, that the share of Japanese direct investment in Asia has been much lower than that in the United States. However, nearly 40 per cent of Japanese investment in Asia is in manufacturing compared with a quarter in the world as a whole (Bollard and Mayes 1992).

15 Criticism of the flying geese model as an explanation of East Asian regional growth is also in Park and Park (1991) and Hobday (1993).

16 One should also add that this increase in direct investment has been supported by large amounts of Japanese foreign aid that aims at creating the necessary infrastructure for Japanese multinationals (Orr 1990).

17 Conditions for network strategies are particularly favourable, for example, in the car industry and in the electronics (computer) industry (see Ernst and O'Connor 1992; Ernst 1993), given the high degree of international standardization and the possibilities for splitting up production processes.

18 See, for example, Petri (1992a), whose results show, among other things, that in the case of Japanese direct investment in Thailand, Japanese affiliated firms tend to contribute to Asian "triangular trade," in other words, Thai trade deficits with Japan, and surpluses with other countries. As is well known, in the 1970s Japan's investment in Asia were in raw materials extraction and processing, and a minor part in manufacturing for the local markets.

19 Not only finished products, but also cheap components to Japanese subsidiaries in Europe and America.

20 See Petri (1992b), which confirms this relationship between FDI in East Asia and growing large trade imbalances.

21 One of the main factors determining this sharp increase in FDI in other Asian countries in the second half of the 1980s was the sharp appreciation of Asian NICs' currencies. This, together with sharply rising labour costs and growing domestic labour shortages, determined a substantial relocation, especially of labour-intensive production, to lower-cost neighbouring countries whose currencies depreciated with the dollar.

Much of the new investment has been in manufacturing for exports to world markets rather than in raw material extraction and processing or import substitution (Lim and Siddall 1993).

REFERENCES

Akamatsu, K. 1961. "A Theory of Unbalanced Growth in the World Economy." *Weltwirtschaftliches Archiv* 86 (2).

Bollard, A., and D. Mayes. 1992. "Regionalism and the Pacific Rim." *Journal of Common Market Studies* 30 (2).

Borrus, M. 1993. "The Regional Architecture of Global Electronics: Trajectories, Linkages and Access to Technology. In P. Gourevitch and P. Guerrieri, eds, *New Challenges to International Cooperation: Adjustment of Firms, Policies, and Organizations to Global Competition.* San Diego: University of California.

Calder, K.E. 1991. *Japan's Changing Role in Asia: Emerging Co-Prosperity?* New York: Japan Society Publication.

CEPII (Centre d'Etudes Prospectives et d'Information Internationales). 1989. *Commerce international: la fin des avantages acquis.* Paris: Editions Economica.

Dornbusch, R.W. 1990. "Policy Options for Freer Trade: The Case for Bilateralism." In R.Z. Lawrence and C.L. Schultze, eds, *American Trade Strategy: Options for the 1990s.* Washington, D.C.: Brookings Institution.

Ernst, D. 1993. "Network Transactions, Market Structure and Technology Diffusion – Implications for South-South Cooperation." Study prepared for OECD, Development Centre, Paris.

Ernst, D., and D. O'Connor. 1992. *Competing in the Electronics Industry: The Experiences of Newly Industrializing Economies.* Paris: OECD.

Fouquin, M., E. Dourille-Feer, and J. Oliveira-Martins. 1990. *Pacifique: Le Recen-trage Asiatique.* Paris: Editions Economica.

Frankel, J.A. 1991. "Is a Yen Bloc Forming in Pacific Asia?" In *Finance and the International Economy* Vol. 5, *The AMEX Bank Review Prize Essays,* edited by R. O'Brien. New York: Oxford University Press.

Guerrieri, P. 1992. Technological and Trade Competition: The case of US, Japan and Germany." In M. Harris, ed., *Linking Trade and Technology Policies: An International Comparison.* Washington, D.C.: National Academy Press.

– 1993. "Patterns of Technological Capability and International Trade Performance: An Empirical Analysis." In M. Kreinin, ed., *The Political Economy of International Commercial Policy: Issues for the 1990s.* London and New York: Taylor & Francis.

– 1994. "Trade Integration and Changing Specialization Patterns in the East Asian Electronics Industry." Mimeo, BRIE (Berkeley Roundtable on International Economics), University of California, Berkeley.

Hicks, G. 1990. "Explaining the Success of the Four Little Dragons: A Survey." In Seiji Naya and Akira Takayama, eds, *Economic Development in East and Southeast Asia*. Honolulu: Resource System Institute, East-West Center.

Hobday, M. 1993. "Economic Development of the Four Tigers: An Assessment of the Flying Geese Model of East Asian Progress." Science Policy Research Unit working paper, January, University of Sussex, U.K.

JETRO (Japan External Trade Organization). 1992. *Vision for the Economy of the Asia-Pacific Region in the Year 2000 and Tasks Ahead*. Tokyo: JETRO.

Krause, L. 1990. "Trade Policy in the 1990s: Good-bye Bipolarity, Hello Regions." *World Today* 46 (5).

Kreinin, M.E. 1993. "Super-301 and Japan-A Dissenting View." In M.E. Kreinin, ed., *The Political Economy of International Commercial Policy: Issues for the 1990s*. London and New York: Taylor & Francis.

Lawrence, R.Z. 1991a. "Emerging Regional Arrangements: Building Blocs or Stumbling Blocs?' In *Finance and the International Economy* Vol. 5, *The AMEX Bank Review Prize Essays*, edited by R. O'Brien. New York: Oxford University Press.

– 1991b. "How Open Is Japan?" In Paul Krugman, ed., *Trade with Japan: Has the Door Opened Wider?* Chicago and London: National Bureau of Economic Research and University of Chicago Press.

Lim, L.Y.C., and N.S. Siddall. 1993. *Foreign Investment, Trade and Technology Linkages in Asian Developing Countries in the 1990s*. New York: United Nations Centre on Transnational Corporations.

Nishikawa, J. 1992. "The Tri-polarization of the World Economy and Asian Economic Development." Waseda Economic Papers, 31. Tokyo, Japan.

Noland, M. 1990. *Pacific Basin Developing Countries: Prospects for the Future*. Washington, D.C.: Institute for International Economics.

Ohkita, S. 1986. "Pacific Development and Its Implications for the World Economy." In W. Morley, ed., *The Pacific Basin: New Challenges for the United States*. New York: Academy of Political Science.

Orr, R.M. 1990. *The Emergence of Japan's Foreign Aid Power*. New York: Columbia University Press.

Park, Y.C. 1989. "Little Dragons and Structural Change in Pacific Asia." *World Economy* 12 (2).

Park, Y.C. and Won-Am Park. 1991. "Changing Japanese Trade Patterns and the East Asian NICs." In Paul Krugman, ed., *Trade with Japan: Has the Door Opened Wider?* Chicago and London: National Bureau of Economic Research and University of Chicago Press.

Petri, P. 1992a. "Platform in the Pacific: The Trade Effects of Direct Investment in Thailand." *Journal of Asian Economics* 3 (2).

– 1992b. "One Bloc, Two Blocs or None? Political-Economic Factors in Pacific Trade Policy." In K. Okuizumi, K.E. Calder, and G.W. Gong, eds,

The US-Japan Economic Relationship in East and Southeast Asia: A Policy Framework for Asia-Pacific Economic Cooperation. Significant Issues series. Washington, D.C.: Center for Strategic and International Studies.

Porges, A. 1991. "US-Japan Trade Negotiations: Paradigm Lost." In Paul Krugman, ed., *Trade with Japan: Has the Door Opened Wider?* Chicago and London: National Bureau of Economic Research and University of Chicago Press.

Riedel, J. 1991. "Intra-Asian Trade and Foreign Direct Investment." *Asian Development Review* 9 (1).

Sandholtz, W., M. Borrus, J. Zysman, and S. Weber. 1992. *The Highest Stakes.* Oxford and New York: Oxford University Press.

Schott, J.J. 1991. "Trading Blocs and the World Trading System." *World Economy* 14 (March).

Urata, S. 1993. "Changing Patterns of Direct Investment and the Implications for Trade and Development." In C.F. Bergsten and M. Noland, eds, *Pacific Dynamism and the International Economic System.* Washington, D.C.: Institute for International Economics.

Yam, T.K., M.H. Toh, and L. Low. 1992. "ASEAN and Pacific Economic Cooperation." *ASEAN Economic Bulletin* 8 (3).

Yamazawa, I. 1990. *Economic Development and International Trade: The Japanese Model.* Honolulu: East-West Center, Resource Systems Institute.

12 Stabilization, Structural Adjustment, and Labour Market Performance after NAFTA: The Mexican Experience

DIANA ALARCÓN AND EDUARDO ZEPEDA

Although fifteen years have passed since radical economic reforms were initiated, Mexico is still confronting the difficult challenge of establishing conditions for stable long-term development. In recent years, the social sustainability of the reform process has been repeatedly called into question because reform has failed to deliver economic growth, job expansion, or opportunities to improve the standard of living of large sectors of Mexican society. In a largely urban country like Mexico, the possibilities of improving standards of living and creating greater social mobility – indeed, social and political cohesion – critically depend on generating productive employment for a growing labour force.

The objective of this chapter is to assess the impact that structural reforms and the integration of Mexico into the North American region have had on employment creation. In the first section, some theoretical aspects of economic integration are discussed. Next, we provide a brief summary of macroeconomic policies implemented during the period of structural adjustment. In the third section, we discuss available data on employment and unemployment trends that point to a deterioration of employment in Mexico. In the following section, we present more detailed information on the manufacturing sector. Using different data sources, we hope to show how employment trends have been affected by trade liberalization and a more pronounced export orientation. In the fifth section, we evaluate the argument that the lack of flexibility in labour markets is an important constraint to the creation of employment during the period of economic reforms. We close this chapter with a brief discussion of policy options that could improve the creation of employment in Mexico in the context of Mexico's greater integration with the other two economies North America.

ECONOMICS OF LIBERALIZATION AND INTEGRATION

With the signing of the North American Free Trade Agreement (NAFTA) in late 1993, the Mexican government ratified its plan to proceed further into the process of domestic market liberalization and greater economic integration with North America. Any process of economic reform is associated with transitional costs of adjustment where some sectors of society benefit while others lose. Mexico, as the small partner in the North American Free Trade Agreement, was expected to be the largest beneficiary of the integration of regional markets, but it was also the country that was expected to face the largest costs of adjustment. The problem, however, is that *a priori* it is difficult to predict the long-term welfare costs of reform. In general, the social, political, and economic costs of Mexico's greater integration with the United States and Canada largely depend on the flexibility of the Mexican economy in adapting but also on the set of policy decisions that initiate the process of integration.[1] Thus, government policies, whether by decision or by omission, play an important role in shaping the process of adjustment and distributing the costs and benefits of economic restructuring.

In Mexico, liberalization of trade had started in the mid-1980s, representing an opportunity to overcome the limitations and inefficiencies accumulated during years of protected industrialization. A more open economy would be able to stimulate production by overcoming the restrictions of a narrow domestic market. Dynamic employment creation associated with the growth of both exporting and importing sectors would have beneficial effects on income distribution and poverty reduction. Both are badly needed outcomes in a country where large inequality and poverty have been endemic.

The actual distributional impact of such integration, however, is contingent upon a larger set of factors. There is a growing literature that discusses the effect of economic reform on different indicators of welfare. Results, it is argued, often depend upon the characteristics of the exporting sectors. Peasant agricultural goods, labour-intensive commodities in agriculture or manufacture, or sectors with interlinkages between larger and smaller producers may reap welfare benefits from trade reform. By contrast, trade liberalization in countries that export mineral resources, that have capital-intensive manufacturing, or that produce agricultural commodities with minimal labour input may reduce overall welfare.

Benefits from trade also depend upon the flexibility with which countries can adapt to the new realities of more open markets. In their search to expand external markets and/or remain competitive in their own domestic markets, economic agents are exposed to greater competition from international producers. The liberalization of trade involves important changes in the relative prices of goods and services purchased by domestic firms and households. Sectors that are already pricing competitively by international standards are further stimulated by the expansion of regional markets, but firms and sectors that are unable to compete with more efficient international competitors may face large losses. Thus, the benefits of trade liberalization depend on the ability of the economy to reallocate resources to their most efficient use. Successful resource reallocation across sectors is a process that requires dynamic, fast growth to ensure that investment flows to the sectors where the country has a comparative advantage.

Macroeconomic policy plays a critical role in shaping the process of reform. Economic policy that emphasizes stabilization, rather than structural reform, may actually block the transformation of the structure of production by inducing long and costly recessions. Alternatively, economic policy may play an important role in facilitating the transition to a more competitive, fast-growing economy. Most recent research in the area emphasizes that government should intervene in the economy to help resolve the coordination and market failures typical of developing countries (Rodrik 1995). Within this perspective, governments must go beyond their current overwhelming preoccupation with macroeconomic stability, to play a more active role in the provision of social and productive infrastructure. This may involve the promotion of specific sectors and activities where dynamic comparative advantages can be developed or where investment in human capital, or the development of sectors and activities with large, positive externalities, can be fostered.

MACROECONOMICS OF REFORM AND TRADE LIBERALIZATION

The intense period of liberalization in Mexico took place under the assumption that strong stabilization was a prerequisite for sustained growth. In the context of a more comfortable debt negotiation in 1989, policymakers raised the expectation that policies in support of stability would be successful this time. They were ready to accept heavy social costs, perceived as short lasting. Negotiations under the Brady plan in 1989 brought little debt relief but played a significant role in renewing large capital inflows from international financial markets. In 1989 the economy started to show some signs of recovery. Large flows of foreign capital attracted by high interest rates and the government's commitment to a stable nominal exchange rate led to average rates of GDP (gross domestic product) growth of 4.5 per cent in 1989–91. Inflation was brought down after 1989 through the successful negotiation of wage-price controls and the government's commitment to keep a stable nominal exchange rate.[2] Growth was further accelerated by greater government spending in 1994 in preparation for that year's presidential election. The stability of growth, however, was seriously threatened by continuous overvaluation of the exchange rate, deterioration of the trade account, and a fragile position in the balance of payments.[3]

Economic growth, however, continued to be unstable (see Figure 12.1). Critics of macroeconomic policies implemented during those years defined them as a strategy of no-growth. Between 1989 and 1994, the average rate of growth of GDP was 3.8 per cent, or 1.8 per cent in per capita terms. Social tensions were heightened owing to persistent high levels of unemployment and underemployment, which weakened aggregate demand.

Policies that would have facilitated the transformation of the economy were postponed. These could have included reforms to the financial sector to increase the availability of capital at competitive interest rates; assistance for the traditional producers in rural areas in the pursuit of export sales; the promotion of backward and forward production linkages among industries; and investment in human capital formation. Instead, economic policy reforms were limited to controversial privatization – as in the banking and road infrastructure – and deregulation of markets.

EMPLOYMENT TRENDS

Economic reform on the scale undertaken in Mexico in the 1980s and 1990s is intended to generate important changes in the structure of employment. One problem with evaluating the overall changes, however, is that the structural adjustment in Mexico occurred in the context of severe macroeconomic restrictions generated by tight stabilization policies and several external shocks. Economic growth was fairly unstable and several recessions accompanied the process of adjustment. So, when analysing employment trends, one needs to be careful in making the distinction between cyclical and trend patterns.

In general, the employment situation in Mexico has deteriorated since the 1982 debt crisis. At least two indicators clearly point to such a conclusion: an increase in part-time employment and the growth of the informal sector.

In a country that does not have a system of unemployment insurance, unemployment is a luxury that few workers can afford. Therefore, open unemployment figures are typically of little use for assessing employment performance, particularly if one is interested in longer-term trends. Rates are frequently too low and changes are, consequently, too small to be meaningful. During most of the 1980s, for example, average annual unemployment rates for Mexico City ranged from 3.9 to 6.0 per cent, with very little relation to business cycles. In more recent years, however, improved estimates of open unemployment allow us to track the relationship between unemployment and business fluctuations. The unemployment rate did, for example, follow the downturn of 1988, peaking at 4.0 per cent that year. It decreased to about 3 per cent in the following years before going up again to 7.4 per cent during the sharp recession of the economy in 1995 (see Figure 12.2).

Given the difficulties in producing more accurate estimates of unemployment, fluctuations in part-time employment and changes in the conditions of employment are frequently used to evaluate the performance of labour markets in developing countries. The numbers of people working less than thirty-five hours a week increased from 23.3 per cent of the labour force in 1987 to 25.3 per cent in 1996 (see Figure 12.3). Similarly, the proportion of those working less than fifteen hours a week increased from 4.1 per cent to 4.9 per cent over the same period (INEGI, ENEU, 1987–97). Among part-time workers in 1996, only 6.3 per cent explicitly chose to work part time. The great majority of them had no other option. Some 9.8 per cent worked part time owing to the contraction of market demand, and part-time employment was the regular schedule of 66.3 per cent of them. These figures indicate that part-time employment in Mexico is largely involuntary and that the proportion of involuntary part-time employment has increased over time.

A second indicator of the deterioration of employment in Mexico is the growth of the informal sector. The heterogeneity that characterizes this sector prevents any accurate evaluation of its performance. There are, however several indicators of the growth of this sector in the last few years. Looking at general urban labour conditions as reported by the National Survey of Urban Employment (Encuesta Nacional de Empleo Urbano – ENEU), one sees a definite increase in the proportion of people working in micro enterprises (less than five workers) – a proxy for informality. Looking at the proportion of waged workers without fringe benefits (*prestaciones*) as yet another indicator of labour informality, one also observes a clear upward trend from around 20 per cent in the early 1990s to about 25 per cent in more recent years (see Figure 12.4).

Estimates from the regional office of the ILO (International Labour Organization) for Latin America calculate informality in Mexico at 57 per cent of total non-agricultural employment in 1994, with an increasing trend throughout the 1990s. A more accurate estimation of informality comes from an ad hoc survey conducted by the National Office of Statistics (Instituto Nacional de Estadistica, Geografia e Informatica – INEGI) that attempts to capture the specific characteristics of this sector. INEGI also reports an increase in the proportion of people engaged in informal-sector activities. In 1989 the informal sector absorbed one-fourth of total employment in urban areas; in 1992 that proportion increased to one-third; and by 1994, 35.3 per cent of total urban employment was in the informal sector. Such increase of informality in the urban sector corresponds to an increase in the proportion of employees, mostly prime-age male workers in business services, commerce, and manufacturing production.[4] The profile of the average worker involved in informal-sector activities is an indication of the severity of the employment problem in Mexico. The informal sector is not primarily made up of women and young workers looking for ways to compensate decreased family income. The large proportion of male workers in the prime employment age range also found in the informal sector is an indicator of the inability of the formal modern sector of the economy to expand employment opportunities. Lack of employment creation has forced a large proportion of the labour force into lower productivity, mostly unregulated, low-income sectors.

Employment statistics clearly point to the deterioration of employment in Mexico. How much of the decline in employment is related to the contraction of the economy and how much of it is associated with the particular pattern of production that is emerging out of structural adjustment are relevant questions with important policy implications. If the deterioration of employment conditions is the consequence of the contraction of the economy, the solution is fairly straightforward. The prompt restoration of growth would re-establish the conditions for employment creation. The difficulty would lie in generating growth that is dynamic enough to (1) re-establish the level of formal-sector employment lost during the last fifteen years and (2) provide employment opportunities for a growing labour force. However, available data suggest that more than simply cyclical changes are reflected in the increasing part-time employment. This is, indeed, a more complex situation, one that calls for serious, far-reaching remedies.

EMPLOYMENT IN MANUFACTURING

The liberalization of trade and economic reform were expected to improve overall employment conditions in Mexico, particularly in the manufacturing sector. The rapid growth of manufacturing exports was a key component of the economic strategy implemented in the last fifteen years. Indeed, manufacturing exports rose dramatically, from 51 per cent of total exports in 1987 to 75 per cent in 1996. The rapid growth of manufacturing exports, however, has not been matched by a corresponding growth of employment in manufacturing.

The number of persons occupied in manufacturing increased during the period. Calculations based on data from the National Survey of Urban Employment suggest an increase in manufacturing employment of about 20 per cent between 1987 and 1993. Throughout these years, employment in such diverse sectors as machinery and equipment and wood products clearly expanded.[5] From 1990 to 1993, employment in food and chemical industries also increased (see Figure 12.5).

Such an increase in manufacturing employment, however, was not strong enough to increase the share of manufacturing in urban employment. The proportion of manufacturing in total urban employment actually fell from about 25 per cent in 1987–88 to around 23 per cent in 1993–94 – it was 21 per cent in the crisis years of 1995–96.

In the Mexican case, the manufacturing sector is integrated by three major components: large and medium-sized nationally integrated firms; the *maquiladora* sector; and small and micro enterprises. The prototype of the new manufacturing enterprise would be a highly productive firm with adequate investment in human and physical capital, able to compete in international markets. In order to reach an optimum scale of production, firms need to be relatively large. These firms would have a higher probability of success in export markets and/or in retaining domestic markets vis-à-vis competition from imports. Similarly, in a process of industrial restructuring, these firms would also be able to constitute networks of suppliers for large exporting firms. At the risk of being simplistic, we identify these agents of modernization with medium-sized and large firms that would be more or less integrated with the national economy.

A large proportion of manufacturing exports from Mexico originate in mostly foreign-owned, in-bound export plants known as *maquiladoras*.[6] As early as the mid-1960s, these plants began to locate along the Mexican border with the United States. However, it was not until the 1980s that these plants proliferated along the northern border and even in locations further south. Employment creation in *maquiladoras* has been impressive. In 1980 some 114,000 persons worked in these manufacturing plants, but by 1993 there were about 514,000. The share of these plants in total manufacturing jobs increased from 6 to 17 per cent between 1980 and 1993. Although *maquiladoras* have made an undeniable contribution to the expansion of exports and employment, they constitute a second-best option for promoting outward-oriented industrialization. Despite the many programs designed to encourage national firms to supply inputs to these plants and despite the arrival of more integrated plants, as described by the literature on the "new *maquiladora*,"[7] the national input content of *maquiladora* production remains unchanged at 2 per cent on average since the early 1980s. Thus, the output and employment multipliers of this type of production are very small.

A third component of manufacturing firms are small and micro enterprises. As size decreases, the economic conditions of these firms become rather marginal. These segments of the labour market are highly unregulated, with low levels of income. Business turnover is high; productivity and the scale of production are low. Access to financing is frequently restricted to informal markets at very high rates. Thus, few exports can be expected from these firms and little success can be foreseen in their confrontations with competition from imports.

We have roughly estimated that large and medium-sized nationally integrated firms accounted for about 41 per cent of total manufacturing employment in 1988 (see Table 12.1). *Maquiladoras* represented at the time 15 per cent of these jobs. Small and micro firms accounted for the remaining 44 per cent: 15 per cent in small firms and 29 per cent in establishments with less than sixteen employees. By 1993 the share of each of these sections of the labour market had changed dramatically. Large and medium-sized integrated firms accounted for only 29 per cent of total employment in manufacturing. *Maquiladoras* and smaller firms, on the contrary, had increased from 17 to 54 per cent of total employment respectively. In absolute numbers, manufacturing employment had a net increase of about 624,000 jobs. The *maquiladoras* added 161,000, small firms some 286,000, and micro or very small firms about 272,000. Employment in large integrated firms decreased by 77,000 workers.

Thus, employment creation in manufacturing has been largely concentrated in marginal small and micro enterprises and *maquiladora* firms during the period of adjustment. The problem with the latter, however, is the low level of integration with the rest of the economy. As employment shifts towards these types of jobs, the outlook for a strong and sustainable industrialization that would entail the creation of many "good jobs" becomes gloomy.

MEDIUM-SIZED AND LARGE MANUFACTURING FIRMS

In a dynamic process of adjustment, medium-sized and large non-*maquiladora* manufacturing firms should play an important role.[8] In this section, we turn to analyse employment creation in this sector according to the level of exposure to international markets.

After years of protection for domestic producers, trade liberalization was intended to remove the restrictions to exports, promote growth, and introduce greater efficiency in production. Mexico, a country largely endowed with labour resources, would arguably enhance its competitiveness by shifting resources towards the production of more labour-intensive products in a liberalized trade region. Employment would grow and workers, particularly the less skilled, would benefit from higher wages. By contrast, we find that there is no evidence within the manufacturing sector to support the claim that trade liberalization has, so far, induced a reduction in the capital-intensive structure of production that has been characteristic of import substitution industrialization. Nor has liberalization increased the relative wages of the unskilled and thereby improved income distribution. The most dynamic exporting sectors in manufacturing are those linked to international production networks with a large content of intrafirm trade,[9] many of them the same firms that once benefited from import substitution policies.

This emerging pattern of specialization is immediately apparent from export figures, even at the aggregate two-digit level. Between 1989 and 1992, almost 75 per cent of the increase in manufacturing exports (excluding *maquiladoras*) came from sectors producing machinery and equipment with an annual rate of growth of 15.6 per cent. Another 14 per cent increase in total exports came from the chemical industry. Textiles increased by 5 per cent only.[10]

Between 1987 and 1995, employment in all large and medium-sized non-*maquiladora* sectors decreased in absolute terms. Manufacturing employment fell 2.9 per cent during these years, with the sharpest reductions occurring in sectors with relatively low export activity, such as steel (6.7 per cent), textiles (5.1 per cent), and wood (4.9 per cent). Exporting sectors had relatively low employment reductions. In the sector producing machinery and equipment, for example, employment decreased by 3 per cent and chemicals recorded a contraction of 2.3 per cent. Among medium-sized and large non-*maquiladora* firms, thus, an export orientation seems to have helped to halt employment reduction somewhat.[11]

A more precise picture of the employment dimensions of trade specialization can be obtained by looking at large and medium-sized firms in four-digit manufacturing sectors. The data in Table 12.2, the data confirm that exports tend to originate in capital-intensive sectors and are concentrated in just a few sectors.[12] Looking at the shares in non-*maquiladora* exports, we identify the following sectors as leading exporters: the auto industry; electric and electronic items; machinery and parts; plastics; and some chemicals. These sectors accounted for 53 per cent of average non-*maquiladora* exports between 1991 and 1993, 30 per cent of employment, and 36 per cent of the value of production generated by medium-sized and large firms.

In Figure 12.6, we plot employment levels for leading exporting sectors, weak exporting sectors, and non-exporting sectors for the years between 1987 and 1995. The graph confirms the reduction of employment in medium-sized and large firms, including those in the leading exporting sectors. Of a total reduction of 201,000 jobs in 1987–95, leading exporting sectors accounted for 20 per cent. Employment in weak exporting sectors decreased, while employment in non-exporting sectors remained constant.

Thus, despite of the rapid increase in manufacturing exports, the expansion of employment among leading exporting sectors was not fast enough to reverse the overall contraction of manufacturing employment. One of the reasons that comes to mind is the low level of integration of exporting sectors with the rest of the economy. As mentioned above, *maquiladora* plants import 98 per cent of inputs used in production. But even among non-*maquiladora* exporting firms, there is a low level of integration with the rest of the economy. A study that looked at the interindustry linkages of exporting sectors with the rest of the economy (Alarcón and Tapia 1993) found that once account is taken of direct and indirect employment creation, exporting sectors have one of the lowest employment multiplier effects in Mexico.

Another indicator of the low level of integration of exporting sectors with the rest of the economy is the sharp increase of imports that followed the liberalization of trade. While exports were growing at average rates of 12 per cent a year between 1987 and 1994, the growth of imports was 23 per cent. A large portion of these imports came as inputs for non-*maquiladora* exporters and domestically oriented firms, in a process of import substitution. Increasing the imported content in manufacturing production has reduced the employment multiplier effects of Mexico's export orientation.

PRODUCTIVITY AND TECHNOLOGY

Arguments in favour of liberalization in Mexico have often pointed to the remarkable increase in productivity that is claimed to have accompanied the transformation of manufacturing. To the extent that a solid increase in productivity becomes the foundation of the newly outward-oriented process of industrialization, it could be argued that the strategy is sustainable. The poor employment record so far documented in this chapter could be explained, at least partially, as a short-term transitional cost of greater efficiency. In this section, we first qualify the strength of the productivity increase by looking at the underlying changes in employment and the value of production by sector among medium-sized and large firms. Then, we turn to analyse the technological characteristics of the various sectors in an attempt to clarify the link between productivity and technology.

Figure 12.7 shows productivity in medium-sized and large firms increasing steadily from 1989 to 1995. Moreover, the enhancing effect of outward orientation is highlighted by the fact that the more export-intensive manufacturing sectors are those with the highest levels of productivity.

In Table 12.3 we show average annual changes in productivity, output, and employment for medium-sized and large firms in manufacturing classified according to their export performance. The increase in productivity is slightly faster in sectors with few exports compared to the leaders, but in both cases the increase in productivity was much larger than that for non-exporting sectors. In all cases, increasing productivity was the result of a contraction of employment, especially among weak exporting sectors, where an increase in productivity seems to be more associated with employment reduction than with output expansion. The modest increase in productivity among non-exporting sectors reflects the conditions of sectors in economic distress, since output increased by 1.6 per cent a year while employment contracted by 1.9 per cent. The increase in productivity among leading exporting sectors was relatively stronger, as it was based on a larger increase in output, although it was also associated with a smaller contraction of employment. Again, the benefits of the process of restructuring seem to be restricted to a small group of firms.

Turning to the link between technology and productivity, we are interested in assessing whether the superior performance of outward-oriented sectors can be related to the intensity of the use of technology. By way of illustrating the use of technology, Table 12.4 shows the average number of computerized machinery and robots per establishment and the proportion of workers involved in innovative labour and production processes. It is apparent from the table that leading exporting sectors make more intensive use of technology as measured by these three indicators. Weak exporting sectors do not, however, have a stronger technological position compared to non-exporting exports. These two facts suggest that success in the select group of leading exporters is based on higher technology use, but they also suggest that beyond this élite group the link between technology and access to exports markets is not clear.

Table 12.4 also includes expenditures in research and development (R&D) as percentages of total sales, a traditional indicator of the intensity of technology. According to these figures, there is not much difference among the three groups in the proportion of sales allocated to R&D. In the context of Mexico, not much can be concluded from these results. Firms in Mexico may use relatively new technology, but not much innovation is taking place, since these firms are highly dependent on imported technology.

MANUFACTURING EMPLOYMENT AND COMPETITIVE IMPORTS

Trade liberalization actually started when Mexico joined GATT (General Agreement on Tariffs and Trade) in 1986 and there followed a unilateral reduction of tariffs. Import-weighted tariffs decreased from 13.3 per cent in 1985 to 5.6 in 1987 (later they increased to 11.1 in 1991), and imports restricted by quota decreased steadily from 35.1 per cent in 1985 to 9.1 per cent in 1991. The liberalization of trade gave rise to a large increase in imports, amplified by economic recovery in 1988–91 and the electoral year of 1994. Imports were also stimulated by a continuous appreciation in the real exchange rate in the period from 1990 to 1994. Not surprisingly, soaring imports had a strong impact on employment.

In order to assess this issue, we organize manufacturing sectors according to the indicated degree of competition from imports.[13] We identify a group of twenty-six sectors facing significant competitive pressures from imports. The remaining sectors are grouped into export- and domestically oriented sectors according to the percentage of exports in total sales. In Figure 12.8, we plot employment levels in medium-sized and large firms for these three groups of sectors. Employment trends in import-competing sectors are most discouraging. The number of jobs in these sectors declined continuously throughout the period at an average rate of 3.9 per cent. As many as 133,000 jobs disappeared, representing two-thirds of the net employment reduction in medium-sized and large firms.

To summarize, we have identified three main employment trends. First, during the period of adjustment – identified in this case as the period between 1987 and 1995 – manufacturing employment in large enterprises declined throughout, though more strongly in the early 1990s when trade liberalization was accompanied by increasing overvaluation in the exchange rate. Second, rapid expansion of manufacturing exports did not generate an equivalent expansion in employment, although employment losses in leading exporting sectors were less pronounced. Finally, contraction of employment was large in import-competing sectors where the combination of trade liberalization and the overvalued exchange had the largest impact.

Overall, the capacity of manufacturing production to generate employment has decreased. The elasticity of employment in response to output growth in the manufacturing sector illustrates this tendency. If employment creation is measured as the proportionate increase in employment that corresponds to output growth, the manufacturing sector made a decreasing contribution to employment creation. In 1975–80 the elasticity of employment in manufacturing was 0.49 per cent, but if we take the period 1975–92, it was a low 0.14: that is, every 1 per cent increase in the value of output in this period led to just 0.14 per cent increase in employment.

LABOUR MARKET FLEXIBILITY

The degree of flexibility in labour markets plays an important role in the process of stabilization. The effect of fiscal, monetary, and exchange-rate policy depends, to a large extent, on the degree of flexibility in nominal wages (Agénor and Montiel 1996). In addition, the degree of flexibility in the operation of labour markets is thought to be essential to the successful transformation of the structure of production. The explicit objective of structural adjustment is to alter the composition of production through the transfer of resources from the less competitive to the more competitive sectors, a process that enhances the comparative advantage of the country in international markets and leads to a more efficient structure of production.

Obviously, the successful transformation of the economy requires a high degree of flexibility to facilitate the transfer of resources throughout the economy. If there are restrictions to the mobility of capital, labour, and financial resources, then the mobilization of resources through the economy will be limited. One of the arguments that has been made to explain the poor performance of programs of structural adjustment undertaken in developing countries is that rigidities in labour markets prevent the dynamic transformation of the economy.

According to this view, labour market regulations that protect employment (such as legislation for minimum wages, taxation, and rules to resolve labour disputes) and the existence of large and powerful unions are said to increase the cost of labour and restrict the mobility of workers. On the basis of this argument, the Mexican government, business representatives, and unions have engaged in a long process of reform of Mexico's labour legislation and the mechanisms to resolve disputes with the aim of increasing the flexibility of the labour market. The most recent expression of this process is the signature of the "new codes of conduct" early in 1996.

However, the argument that Mexico's economic restructuring has been hampered by lack of flexibility in labour markets is controversial. Labour market flexibility can be examined by three indicators: (1) price or wage flexibility to induce changes in output and employment; (2) quantitative flexibility to facilitate the mobility across sectors; and (3) flexibility within the firm to improve the efficiency of labour use, especially during periods of rapid technological change and/or rationalization of production within the firm. Although further research in this area is required, studies on the subject and available evidence point to the existence of fairly flexible labour markets in Mexico during the period of adjustment (Covarrubias 1996; El Colegio de México; Félix 1996; Zapata 1995).

Policies of structural adjustment have been associated with the sharp contraction of wages in real terms. Severe wage restrictions (eventually formalized in the numerous *pactos* signed by the government, business representatives, and unions) have been a key element in the anti-inflationary strategy of the Mexican government since the outbreak of the debt crisis. Average remuneration per worker (taking into account the number of hours actually worked) has declined substantially, especially among blue-collar workers. In 1989, when the economy started to grow, wages showed a slight improvement in real terms, but for blue-collar workers, wages never returned to the level they had been in 1980. Such slight improvement in average earnings was quickly reversed by the 1995 crisis. Since 1982, average earnings for manufacturing workers have clearly lagged behind productivity growth. Moreover, according to calculations provided by the World Employment Report 1996/97, there is a clear inverse relationship between real wages and unemployment rates in the case of Mexico, suggesting the existence of fairly flexible labour markets, at least with respect to wages.

Restrictions on the mobility of workers in response to changes in demand may be another element of labour market rigidity. Severance payments or other restrictions to the mobility of workers across sectors may constrain the process of reform. Employment creation in the manufacturing sector has lagged far behind the growth of manufacturing output. As shown in Table 12.3, despite the expansion of output in all manufacturing sectors, employment contracted in all of them. Thus, there is no evidence to support the claim that business firms are facing restrictions in their ability to adjust employment to market fluctuations. Quite the contrary, as Table 12.3 indicates, employment in manufacturing has contracted throughout the period, even at times of expansion in output. Similarly, research about the conditions of particular labour markets suggests the existence of a high degree of employment flexibility. In the northern *maquiladora* plants, high turnover rates indicate the prevalence of highly flexible labour markets in one of the most dynamic exporting sectors (Félix 1996).

Although no conclusive evidence has been provided with respect to the third factor of labour market flexibility, namely, the ability of firms to reassign workers to perform different tasks, several studies have found a high degree of intrafirm mobility among production workers to accommodate changes in technology and management. This is especially the case of the most export-oriented sectors: automobiles, autoparts, electronics, and the *maquiladora* industry (Agénor and Montiel 1996).

In sum, available evidence suggests the existence of a high degree of wage and employment flexibility through the period of reform. Similar to the experience of other countries (Horton et al. 1994; Agénor and Montiel 1996; Collier 1996), labour market rigidity does not seem to be an issue in the process of adjustment in Mexico. But imperfect competition in product markets, rigidities in other factor markets (credit would be a prime candidate), bureaucratic restrictions to factor mobility and entrepreneurship, and lack of infrastructure for development to support the process of reform may become important constraints in the process of adjustment.[14] More substantial research is needed in this area.

FINAL REMARKS

Mexico has adopted far-reaching economic reforms in an attempt to re-establish the conditions for long-term sustainable growth. Closer integration with North America was perceived as an opportunity to expand markets for exports and initiate the structural transformation required. However, the poor performance of the Mexican economy during the period of adjustment has generated an intense debate about the direction and sustainability of the reform process. At the centre of that debate is the employment question. In this regard, serious concerns have been raised about the continuous deterioration of employment conditions evidenced by the expansion of precarious jobs and stagnant or declining "good jobs."

As illustrated above, the strong export performance of manufacturing sectors has not been able to generate an equivalently strong impact on employment. Even in the few segments of the manufacturing exporting sectors where there has been a net addition of employment – *maquiladoras* and leading exporting firms – higher reliance on imported inputs restricts the multiplier effects of increasing production for exports.

Closer integration in North America indeed represents for Mexico an opportunity to expand production for exports and generate employment and better labour conditions, but recent experience in Mexico illustrates the importance of shaping the integration process with a strategic view of the development process. What needs to be carefully evaluated is the industrial policy that leads the process of liberalization. There are at least five areas that, in our view, deserve attention:

1. There is the need to increase the integration of *maquiladora* firms with the rest of the industrial sector by stimulating production of inputs by domestic firms.
2. The export base should be expanded in order to overcome the current concentration of exports in a few firms. There are strong grounds on which to argue for the implementation of policies intended to stimulate exports production in a larger number of sectors, including agricultural products.
3. A third area of concern is the need to re-establish the interlinkages of exporting sectors with the other manufacturing and economic sectors. The liberalization of trade and the large presence of international firms among exporting sectors have increased the import content of exports production, delinking those sectors from the rest of the economy. Experience in other countries, where greater integration with the world economy was successfully translated into strong economic growth, employment creation, and improved welfare, emphasizes the importance of building strong backward and forward linkages between exporting sectors and the rest of the economy.
4. One of the sectors most affected by recent reforms is the import-competing sector represented by medium-sized and large enterprises. Given their importance as a source of employment creation, there seems to be a need to reverse the negative impact that trade liberalization has had so far. The restructuring of these firms could be supported by policies that expanded their access to credit; through competitive exchange rate policies that would not exacerbate the impact of more open markets; with effective enforcement of countervailing and anti-dumping policies that protect firms from unfair competition from imports; and through technical assistance to support the transition of these firms to higher levels of productivity.
5. Finally, given the structure of labour markets in Mexico, there seems to be an urgent need to increase production among small and micro enterprises by building production networks among them and strengthening their links with the formal manufacturing sector.

Table 12.1
Employment Composition in Manufacturing by Size and Type of Firm

	1988		1993	
	Number of Workers	Percentage	Number of Workers	Percentage
Medium-sized and large integrated firms[1]	945,622	40.69	850,201	28.84
Maquiladora plants[2]	353,552	15.21	514,161	17.44
Medium -sized[3]	0	0.00	26,230	0.89
Small[4] (51–100 workers)	65,136	2.80	275,191	9.34
Small[5] (16–50 workers)	279,774	12.04	329,881	11.19
Micro[5] (1–15)	680,105	29.26	952,030	32.30
Total[6]	2,324,189	100.00	2,947,694	100.00

[1]Average employment in medium-sized and large non-*maquiladora* firms as reported by EIM a monthly industrial survey that collects information on non-*maquiladora* firms ranked by value of production up to 80 per cent of total output in each six-digit industrial sector.
[2]Average employment in *maquiladora* plants collected by SECOFI and reported in Banco de Datos del Instituto Nacional de Estadistica (BDINEGI).
[3]These figures partially correspond to total employment in establishments of 101 to 250 workers as estimated from the ENEU database.
[4]Figures for 1993 partially correspond to total employment in establishments of 51 to 100 workers as estimated from the ENEU database and fully represent figures for 1988.
[5]Figures fully correspond to total employment in establishments of 16 to 50 and 0 to 15 workers as estimated from the ENEU database.
[6]As estimated from the ENEU database.
Note: See methodology in text note 12.

Sources: Own calculations based on *Encuesta Industrial Mensual,* BDINEGI, and ENEU.

Table 12.2
Manufacturing Exports, 1991–1993 (thousands of dollars)

Sector Groups	Total		Average 1991–93 Non Maquiladora		Maquiladora	
	$000s	%	$000s	%	$000s	%
Total	46,923	100.00	28,134	100.00	18,789	100.00
Manufacturing	36,085	76.90	17,307	61.51	18,778	99.94
Leading exporting sectors	18,299	39.00	9,169	32.59	9,130	48.59
3,841 Auto	7,599	16.20	6,286	22.34	1,313	6.99
Electronics	8,699	18.54	1,606	5.71	7,093	37.75
3,823 computers	651	1.39	479	1.70	172	0.91
3,831 machinery and parts	5,211	11.11	873	3.10	4,338	23.09
3,832 radio and TV sets	2,837	6.05	254	0.90	2,583	13.75
Chemicals	2,000	4.26	1,277	4.54	724	3.85
3,512 basic chemicals	979	2.09	908	3.23	72	0.38
3,522 plastic	189	0.40	188	0.67	1	0.01
3,560 other chemicals	832	1.77	181	0.64	651	3.46
Weak exporting sectors	6,539	13.93	3,651	12.98	2,888	15.37
Non-exporting sectors	11,247	23.97	4,487	15.95	6,760	35.98

Source: Own calculations based on Banco de Mexico, *Indicadores del Sector Externo,* and BDINEGI.

Table 12.3
Changes in Output, Employment, and Productivity of Medium-Sized and Large
Manufacturing Firms, 1987–1994 (per cent)

Sector Groups	Output	Employment	Productivity
Manufacturing	3.39	-2.23	5.76
Leading exporting sectors	6.55	-1.08	7.71
Weak exporting sectors	2.19	-5.14	7.73
Non-exporting sectors	1.60	-1.90	3.57

Note: Productivity is measured as value of production per employee. *Maquiladora*
plants are not included.

Source: Own calculations based on *Encuesta Industrial Mensual,* BDINEGI, and INEGI (Instituto
Nacional Estadistica Geografia e Informatica).

Table 12.4
Technology in Manufacturing in Medium-Sized and Large Firms, 1989–1992 (percentages in all firms)

Sector Groups	Innovative Computerized Machinery	Innovative Labour Processes	Production Processes	Research and Development
Manufacturing	1.94	31.02	5.58	3.55
Leading exporting sectors	4.28	49.58	7.90	3.54
Weak exporting sectors	0.43	27.83	3.64	4.41
Non-exporting sectors	1.37	24.29	5.11	3.34

Notes: "Research and Development" refers to average percentage of sales income spent in research and development in 1989 and 1991.
"Computerized Machinery" refers to average number of computerized machinery and robots per establishment in 1992.
"Innovative Labour Processes" refers to number of workers involved in innovative labour processes, implemented from 1989 or after, as percentage of total employment.
Innovative production processes refers to number of workers involved in innovative production processes as percentage of total employment in 1992.
Maquiladora plants are not included.

Sources: Own calculations based on a firm survey "Encuesta Nacional de Empleo, Salarios, Tecnología y Capacitación en el Sector Manufacturero," 1992, STPS (Secretaria del Trabajo y Prevision Social), INEGI, and OIT.

Figure 12.1
Economic Growth (annual percentage change in GDP)

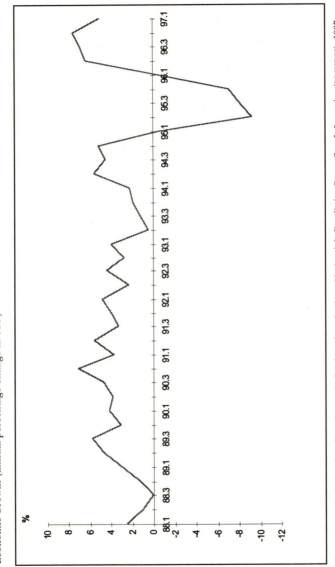

Source: Own calculations based on electronic data base from Instituto Nacional de Estadística Geografía e Informatica (BDINEGI), 1997.

Figure 12.2
Open Unemployment (percent of total economically active population)

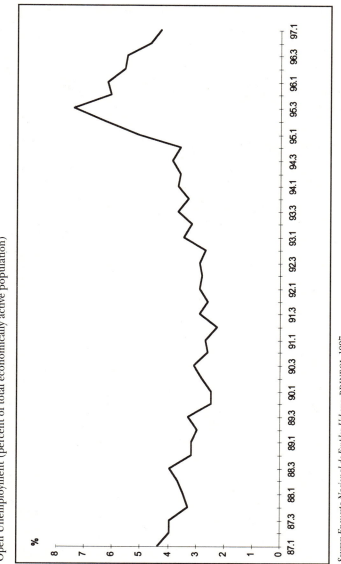

Source: Encuesta Nacional de Empleo Urbano, BDINEGI, 1997.

Figure 12.3a
Part-Time Employment (percent of people working less than 35 hours per week)

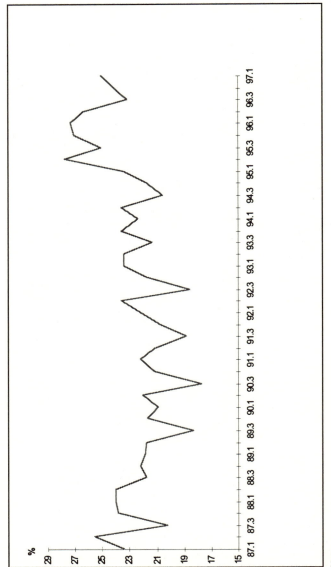

Notes:
[1]Per cent of people working less than 35 hours per week.
[2]Per cent of people working less than 15 hours per week.
Source: Encuesta Nacional de Empleo Urbano, BDINEGI, 1997.

Figure 12.3b
Part-Time Employment (percent of people working less than 15 hours per week)

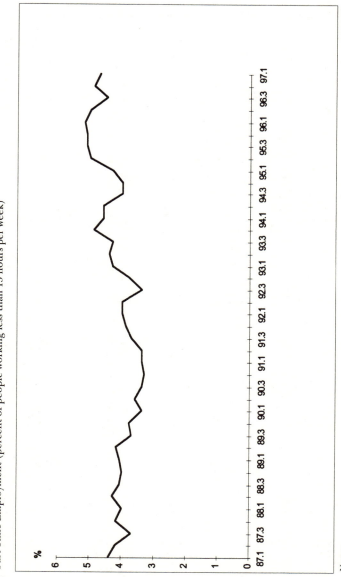

Notes:

[1]Per cent of people working less than 35 hours per week.
[2]Per cent of people working less than 15 hours per week.
Source: Encuesta Nacional de Empleo Urbano, BDINEGI, 1997.

Figure 12.4
The Informal Sector (percent of total employment)

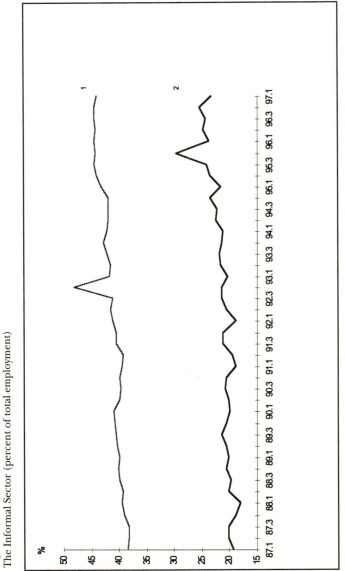

Notes:
[1]Occupation in businesses with 5 or less workers.

[2]Salaried workers with no benefits.

Source: Encuesta Nacional de Empleo Urbano, BDINEGI, 1997.

Figure 12.5
Employment in Manufacturing by Sector (thousands of persons)

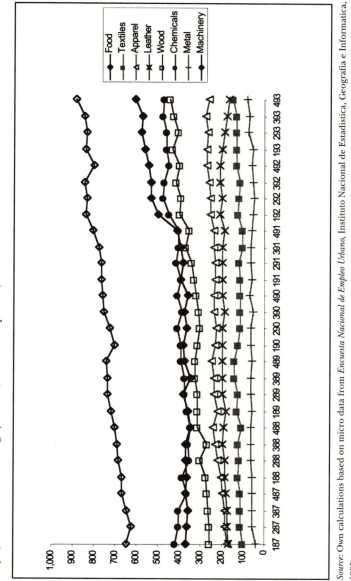

Source: Own calculations based on micro data from *Encuesta Nacional de Empleo Urbano*, Instituto Nacional de Estadisitca, Geografia e Informatica, 1995.

Figure 12.6a
Employmnent in Manufacturing: Medium and Large Firms (thousands of workers)

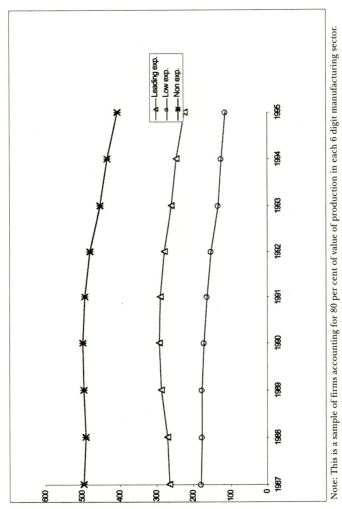

Note: This is a sample of firms accounting for 80 per cent of value of production in each 6 digit manufacturing sector. Included firms are medium (100-250 workers) and large (more than 250 workers). *Maquiladora* plants are excluded.

Source: Own calculations based on *Encuesta Industrial Mensual*, BDINEGI, 1997.

Figure 12.6b
Employment in Manufacturing: Medium and Large Firms (thousands of workers)

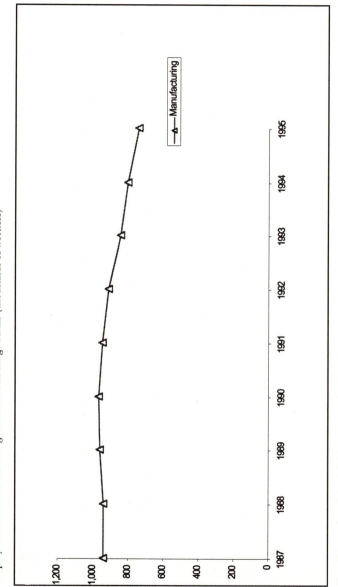

Note: For sample and size definition see note on Figure 12.6a.
Source: Own calculations based on *Encuesta Industrial Mensual,* BDINEGI, 1997.

Figure 12.7
Productivity in Manufacturing: Medium and Large Firms (output over employment)

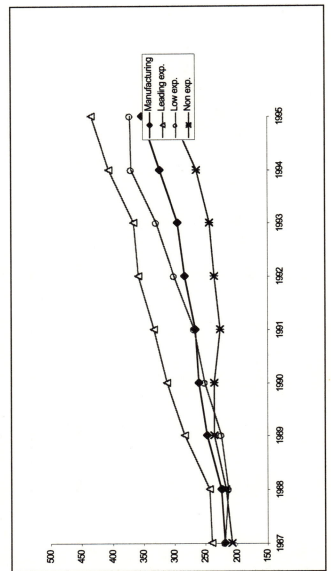

Note: For sample and size definition see note on Figure 12.6a.
Source: Own calculations based on Encuesta Industrial Mensual, BDINEGI, 1997.

Figure 12.8
Employment in Manufacturing: Medium and Large Firms (thousands of workers)

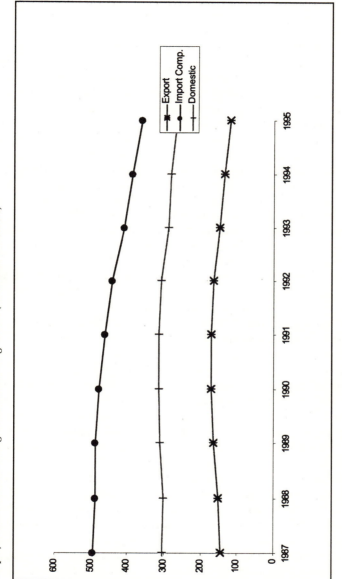

Note: For sample and size definition see note on Figure 12.6a.
Source: Own calculations based on *Encuesta Industrial Mensual,* BDINEGI, 1997.

NOTES

1 This is an issue emphasized by Sidney Weintraub's chapter in this volume.

2 In the context of South Korea and Taiwan, Rodrik (1995) argues that one of the most important factors explaining the economic miracle in these countries was the active role governments played in both cases, coordinating investment decisions in sectors that were key in the process of development but would not had been created in the absence of government intervention.

3 Since 1988, the Mexican government has negotiated several agreements (*pactos*) with business representatives and unions that have included tight wage and price controls as well as certain targets for nominal exchange rates.

4 Close observers of the Mexican economy had been warning about the risk of collapse given the large margins of overvaluation accumulating from the early 1990s (Dornbusch and Werner 1994; 1995).

5 Capital flows in that period came to Mexico on very short-term bases. Portfolio investment accounted for 10 per cent of total capital flows, 73 per cent in 1992, and 87 per cent in 1993.

6 See, for example, Dornbuch and Werner (1994) and Krugman (1995).

7 There were at least three distinctive troughs, in 1988, 1993, and 1995.

8 More recently, in an attempt to take into account the peculiarities of the Mexican labour market, official statistics provide a series of alternative measures of unemployment, including the number of hours worked and the income level of workers. These rates, however, produce trends very similar to the more traditional measure of open unemployment.

9 Figures for the informal sector in 1989 are not directly comparable to those for 1992 and 1994 because of a change in the methodology used for the collection of data. Data for 1992 and 1994 are fully comparable (Instituto Nacional de Estadistica, Geografia e Informatica, (INEGI), 1989 Encuesta Nacional de Economía Informal; INEGI, 1992 and 1994 Encuesta Nacional de Micronegocios).

10 In 1989 about 66 per cent of workers in the informal sector were self-employed. That proportion decreased to 59 per cent in 1992 and 57 per cent in 1994, with a corresponding increase in the share of employed workers, from 16 to 23 and 25 per cent in the corresponding years. In terms of age structure, in 1994, 61.3 per cent of workers were between twenty-five and fifty-four years old and only 25.2 per cent were younger than twenty-four years of age. Male workers accounted for 64 per cent of total workers in the informal sector. In terms of their distribution by sector of production, 37.6 per cent of the total were employed in business services, 34 per cent in trade and services, and 20.1 per cent in manufacturing (INEGI, ibid.).

11 Other observers also find worsening employment conditions. See, for example, Garcia (1988), Rendon and Salas (1993), and Samaniego (1997).

12 These figures refer only to exports from manufacturing firms and exclude exports from in-bound export plants. Historically, exports of manufactures began to increase since the second half of the 1970s; however, it was after the large devaluation following the 1982 debt crisis that export growth accelerated. Towards the turn of the decade, exports of manufactured goods accelerated again.

13 Sectors are grouped at two-digits.

14 *Maquiladora* exports increased from $2,600 billion in 1980 to $9.7 billion in 1987 and $24.1 billion in 1994. See Mendiola (1996).

15 Refer to Carrillo (1989) and Wilson (1989).

16 No single survey provides information about the structure of employment in Mexico. Figures discussed here are rough estimates of the proportion of employment by size of establishment. They were obtained by comparing employment data in three surveys: (1) EIM (monthly industrial employment), which provides data for the largest non-*maquiladora* firms; (2) employment in *maquiladoras* as reported by SECOFI, the Ministry of Commerce; (3) ENEU, (national survey of urban employment), a household survey that provides estimates of total employment in urban areas.

17 Employment in medium-sized and large firms as reported by EIM decreased throughout the 1980s. From 1988 to 1993, the accumulated reduction in employment was about 10 per cent. Although jobs in these firms have been shrinking throughout the 1980s, recent reductions are sharper. Employment was reduced by about 8 per cent between 1980 and 1988 as compared to a 10 per cent reduction between 1988 and 1993. Not surprisingly, the share in manufacturing employment for these firms was reduced from 48 in 1980 to 41 and 29 per cent in 1988 and 1993, respectively.

18 See, for example, Alarcón and McKinley (1997) and Zepeda and Ghiara (1996).

19 For a discussion of intra-industry and intrafirm trade in Mexico, see Buitelaar and Padilla (1996), Mattar and Schatan (1993), and Mercado and Godinez (1995).

20 Exports from *maquiladoras* also concentrate in machinery and equipment (73 per cent in 1990) and textiles (13 per cent in 1990) (Inegi Cuentas Nacionales, CD Rom 1996).

21 These figures refer to medium-sized and large non-*maquiladora* manufacturing sectors only; thus, they are different from those presented in preceding sections.

22 Other observers have found similar patterns of specialization. See Casar (1993), Capoenilie, Cimoli, and Dutrenit (1996), and Unger (1993).

23 Concentration of exports also applies to firms, as only a few of them account for a large volume of exports.
24 See, for example, Sánchez, Fernández, and Pérez (1994).
25 INEGI, *Encuesta Industrial Mensual, 1994.*
26 For a discussion on exports and technology, see Dutrenit and Capdevielle (1993), and Unger (1993).
27 For further discussion on this, see Ross (1995).
28 This classification makes use of INEGI's Encuesta Nacional de Empleo, Salarios, Tecnologia y Capacitacion en la Industria Manufacturera (1992), specifically in a question where managers were asked to rank the intensity of competition from imports.
29 In a study of the process of reform in Latin America, Edwards (1995) argues that in "most countries, the deregulation of labour did not form part of the reform program. In many ways, labour was the forgotten sector."
30 Helleiner (1994) argues that lack of infrastructure development and the retrenchment of the government from its role in the economy have in fact blocked the dynamic transformation of African countries. This issue deserves attention in the Latin American context.

REFERENCES

Agénor, Pierre-Richard, and Montiel, Peter J. 1996. *Development Economics*, chap. 2. New Jersey: Princeton University Press.
– 1997. Development Macroeconomics. New Jersey: Princeton University Press.
Alarcón, Diana, and Terry McKinley. 1997. "The Paradox of Narrowing Wage Differentials and Widening Wage Inequality in Mexico." *Development and Change* 28:505–30.
Buitelaar, Rudolf, and Ramon Padilla. 1996. "El Comercio Intra-industria en Mexico con sus Principales Socios Comerciales." *Estudios Economicos*, El Colegio de Mexico, January–June, 77–116.
Carrillo, Jorge. 1989. "Transformaciones en la Industria Maquiladora de Exportacion." In Bernardo Gonzalez and Rocio Barajas, eds, *Las Maquiladoras: Ajuste Estructural y Desarrollo Regional.* Mexico: colef-Fundacion Ebert.
Capoenilie, Mario, Mario Cimoli, and Gabriela Dutrenit. 1996. "Specialization and Technology in Mexico: A Virtual Pattern of Development and Competitiveness?" *Nota Di Lavora*, September.
Casar, Jose. 1993. "La Competitividad de la Industria Manufacturera Mexicana 1980–1990." *El Trimestre Economico*, 113–183.
Collier, Paul. 1996. "Recent African Economic Performance and Its Implications." Background paper for The World Employment Report, 1996/1997. Geneva: International Labour Office.

Covarrubias, Alex. 1996. "Actitudes Obreras y Compromiso Organizacional en la Industria Automotriz Mexicana: Transformaciones Bajo Sistemas de Producción Flexibles." Seminario Internacional: Globalizacao, Restructuracao Productiva e Transformacao nas Relacoes Capital Trabalho no Complejo Automobilistico, Centro Brasileiro de Analise e Planejamento, Sao Paulo, 26–28 August 1996.

Dipartimento Di Science Economiche. Universita La Foscari Di Venezia.

Dornbusch, Rudiger, and Manfred Werner. 1994. "Mexico: Stabilisation, Reform, and No Growth." In *Brookings Papers on Economic Activity*, vol. 1. Washington, D.C.: Brookings Institute.

Dutrenit, Gabriela, and Mario Capdevielle. 1993. "El Perfil Tecnológico de la Industria Mexicana y su Dinámica Innovadora en la Década de los Ochenta." *Trimestre Económico* 60 (239): 643–74.

Edwards, Sebastian. 1995. *Crisis and Reform in Latin America*, chap. 8. Washington D.C.: World Bank.

El Colegio de México, Fundación Ebert and Colegio de la Frontera Norte. 1992. *Ajuste Estructural, Mercados de Trabajo y TLC.*

Félix, Gustavo. 1996. "La Rotación de Personal en la Maquiladora y sus Determinantes Laborales y Productivos." Documento de Trabajo 2. Instituto de Economía Regional, Universidad Autónoma de Coahuila.

Garcia, Brigida. 1988. *Desarrollo Economico y Absorcion de Fuerza de Trabajo en Mexico.* Mexico: El Colegio de Mexico.

Helleiner G. 1994. "From Adjustment to Development in Sub-Saharan Africa: Consensus and Continuing Conflict." *From Adjustment to Development in Africa.* New York: St Martin's Press.

– 1995. *Manufacturing for Export in the Developing World: Problems and Possibilities.* New York: Routledge.

Horton, S., R. Kanbur, and D. Mazumdar, eds. 1994. *Labor Markets in an Era of Adjustment.* Vols 1 and 11. Washington, D.C.: World Bank.

INEGI (Instituto Nacional de Estadistica, Geografia e Informatica). 1989. *Encuesta Nacional de Economía Informal.*

– 1994. *Encuesta Industrial Mensual.*

– 1992. *Encuesta Nacional de Empleo, Salarios, Tecnologia y Capacitacion en la Industria Manufacturera.*

– 1992 and 1994. *Encuesta Nacional de Micronegocios.*

Inegi Cuentas Nacionales. CD Rom 1996.

Krugman, Paul. 1995. "Dutch Tulips and Emerging Markets." *Foreign Affairs,* July–August.

Mattar, Jorge, and Claudia Schatan. 1993. "El Comercio Intraindustrial e Intrafirma México–Estados Unidos: Autopartes, Electrónicos y Petroquímicos." *Comercio Exterior,* February, 103–24,

Mendiola, Gerardo. 1996. *Tendencias Recientes de la Estructura Productiva, la Especializacion Industrial y los Flujos Comerciales en la Industria Maquiladora*

Mexicana 1980–1994. Thesis, Facultad de Economia, Universidad Nacional Autonoma de Mexico.

Mercado, Alfonso, and Alberto Godinez. 1995. "El Comercio Intraindustrial de Bienes en la Frontera de Mexico: El Caso de Baja California." *Fontera Norte* 14 (Mexico).

Rendon, Roberto, and Rafael Salas. 1993. "El Empleo en Mexico en los Ochentas: Tendencias y Cambios." *Comercio Exterior* 43 (8): 717–30.

Rodrik, Dani. 1995. "Getting Intervention Right: How South Korea and Taiwan Grew Rich." In *Growth Policy*, 55–104.

Ross, Jaime. 1995. "Trade Liberalisation with Real Appreciation and Slow Growth: Sustainability Issues in Mexico's Trade Policy Reform." In Helleiner (1995).

Samaniego, Norma. 1997. "El Mercado de Trabajo en Mexico." *El Economista Mexicano* 2:53–74.

Sánchez, Fernando, Manuel Fernández, and Eduardo Pérez. 1994. *La Política Industrial ante la Apertura.* Mexico: Fondo de Cultura Económica.

Unger, Kurt. 1993. "Productividad, Desarrollo Tecnologico y Competitividad Exportadora en la Industria Mexicana." *Economia Mexicana* 2 (1): 183–237.

Wilson, Patricia. 1989. "The New Maquiladoras: Flexible Production in Low Wage Regions." Working paper no. 9. Community and Regional Planning, University of Texas, Austin.

Zapata, Francisco. 1995. "El Sindicalismo Mexicano Frente a la Restructuración." Paper, El Colegio de México.

Zepeda, Eduardo, and Ranjeeta Ghiara. 1996. "Returns to Education and Economic Liberalisation." *Documentos de Investigacion 4.* Instituto de Economia Regional, Universidad Autonoma de Coahuila, Mexico.

13 Sustainable Development and Technological Innovation in North America

ROBERTO A. SANCHEZ

This chapter explores the relationship between sustainable development and technological innovation in North America with a view to fostering further discussion on the topic. It focuses on the feasibility of achieving a process of sustainable development in the region and on the potential role of innovation in this process.

SUSTAINABLE DEVELOPMENT

Sustainable development has a wide variety of definitions. These range from a strategy loosely defined as the search for a way to conserve natural resources and protect the environment, to a more comprehensive social approach that seeks both intra- and intergenerational equity. Although a common element in most definitions is the relationship between economic growth and environmental protection, there is still a significant gap among them in the type of actions and policies needed to make the transition from rhetoric to concrete programs in the real world.

The search for more suitable patterns of environmental management has been suggested in the literature since the late 1960s. Among others, Boulding (1966) introduced the concept of "spaceship earth" and Sachs (1976) advocated ecological development. In 1987 the Brundtland Commission (formally titled World Commission on Environment and Development) opted for the concept of sustainable development, a term that has become a popular slogan. What these views have in common is that environmentally bounded possibilities for using natural resources are taken as a starting-point for the development and refinement of economic theory.[1]

The Brundtland Commission defines sustainable development as "a process of change in which the exploitation of resources, the direction of investments, the orientation of technological development, and institutional change are all in harmony and enhance both current and future potential to meet human needs and aspirations" (World Commission 1987). This definition has been later enriched by other contributions emphasizing the importance not only of intergenerational equity, but also of income distribution or intragenerational equity (Elliot 1994; Reppeto 1992; ECLAC 1991).

Contributions to the meaning of sustainable development from the point of view of economic theory are relevant to the discussion of North America, given the economy's role as the driving force in structural changes in all North American societies. Most mainstream economists see sustainable development as a process in which the natural resource base is not allowed to deteriorate. They emphasize the unappreciated role of environmental quality and environmental inputs in the process of raising real income and improving the quality of life (Pearce and Warford 1993). Efforts focused on finding technical solutions to environmental problems, including ways of costing environmental losses, do not address key elements of the sustainable development concept. John Pezzey's economic analysis of sustainable development illustrates this problem. Pezzey (1992) uses several economy-environment models in an effort to quantify sustainable development. He suggests the definition and enforcement of property rights to the environment as a way of alleviating poverty and improving the environment. The operation of property rights is problematic in developing countries, however, because of the existence of considerable social unbalances. Although Pezzey does not altogether recognize this problem, he is aware of the difficulty of making sustainability operational at the project level. Even conceptually, he notes the difficulty, observing that "system sustainability cannot be desegregated into project rules in the same way that system optimality can be desegregated into rules for cost-benefit analysis of projects" (48). In his analysis, he also questions the definition, distribution of costs, and feasibility of intergenerational compensation projects and recognizes the difficulty in addressing income distribution and intergenerational equity in quantitative and qualitative terms.

Other economists follow different approaches. Herman Daly brings key concepts of thermodynamics to the debate over the relationship between the economy and the environment and questions mainstream economists' obsession with growth (Daly 1993, 32). He supports the concept of a steady-state economy where the central issue is the stock of wealth, not the flow of income and consumption. He also emphasizes reducing demands on environmental resources while increasing social equity: "sustainable development must be development without growth – but with population control and wealth distribution – if it is to be a serious attack on poverty (Daly 1993, 268)."[2]

Along the same lines, Townsend (1993) draws attention to the incompatibility of exponential economic growth with a biosphere that is finite in its capacity to yield material and energy resources and to absorb economic wastes. Georgescu-Roegen (1993, 81) offers a similar argument: "the economic process is solidly anchored to a material base which is subject to definite constraints." Boulding (1966) developed the important vision of the economy as an open system that maintains some structure in the midst of an entropic flow of throughput.

The debate on the material base of economic growth is undoubtedly pertinent to the study of future alternatives for sustainable development in North America, given the path of consumption in the United States and Canada. These two countries are the two major per capita consumers of natural resources in the world, and the debate on sustainable development in them emphasizes the sustainable use of resources but not the development of society. The incorporation of Mexico as part of the North America free trade area, however, provides a different context for the debate of sustainable development in the region. Mexico is a country with serious social problems (income distribution, poverty, social justice, etc.). Challenges and opportunities for sustainable development in Mexico differ from those in Canada and the United States owing to the differences in economic resources and social well-being among these countries.

The debate over sustainable development in North America must take into account these differences. Contributions from the point of view of political economy that conceptualize sustainable development within a North-South framework are useful in this regard. Michael Redclift and David Goodman (1991) refer to sustainable levels of both production and consumption and to the resource base itself and the livelihoods derived from it. They emphasize the importance of considering sustainable development within the contradictions imposed by the structural inequalities of the global system. They also emphasize the need to specify greater equity, or the reduction of poverty, as a primary objective of sustainable development before the question of environmental quality can be fully addressed. By the same token, Elliot (1994) emphasizes the need for the concept of sustainable development to include an understanding not only of the patterns of development but also of the patterns of underdevelopment and the processes underlying them.

From this brief review of sustainable development concepts, several issues appear to be worth further consideration. First, there is the need for a better working definition of sustainable development, one that would provide a fuller understanding of those things that need to be sustained, how and where we might do this more effectively, and what actions foster development with equity.

Second, decisions about what to sustain and about the strategies that would ensure sustainability must be taken with the goal of accomplishing intragenerational and intergenerational equity according to the needs and resources of each society. This suggests the need to define equity between and among generations in North America. To this end, it is worth remembering that sustainable development actions cannot be considered to be unidimensional. Programs oriented to achieving this goal in one country may cause negative consequences in neighbouring societies because of fundamental social and economic differences among them. This is particularly relevant in the case of Mexico, and in some instances in that of Canada too, given the enormous weight of the neighbouring U.S. economy and its pattern of consumption in the region.

A third issue concerns differences in the level of development among Canada, the United States, and Mexico. Because of these differences, Canada and the U.S., two developed societies, tend to emphasize the sustainability side of the concept, while Mexico gives priority to the development side. The usefulness of the sustainable development concept, even for developed countries, is based on a balanced relationship between its two components, sustainability and development. Opportunities for regional cooperation programs fostering sustainable development in North America will depend on the political will of the three countries to bridge their differences in development levels and on finding an agreeable working definition of sustainable development under which suitable strategies for the three countries could be defined. A loose definition of sustainable development would cause confusion and misunderstanding among social sectors. The lack of a clear working definition would facilitate the invocation of the concept to legitimize actions that are bereft of any potential to enhance intragenerational and intergenerational equity. Potential links between sustainable development and technological innovation would also be lost on account of this problem. I will come back to this issue in the second part of the chapter.

The role of institutions is fourth, relevant to the question of sustainable development in North America. The extent to which cooperation among countries and among social sectors fosters sustainable development in North America will depend heavily on the role of current and future institutions in this process. The Commission for Environmental Cooperation (CEC), the North American institution created under the North American Free Trade Agreement (NAFTA) to foster environmental cooperation among Canada, the U.S., and Mexico, is perhaps the most suitable candidate to assume a leading role in this direction. While the CEC has achieved some success in promoting cooperation in critical environmental areas (transboundary air pollutants, migratory species, environmental information) during its first three years of existence, the commission is vulnerable to political vagaries in the three countries. The CEC has not yet assumed a specific commitment to the promotion of sustainable development in the region, and it is unclear how far political will in the three countries would support such a role for the commission. There are several other binational institutions with environmental mandates in North America (the International Joint Commission between Canada and the U.S., the International Boundary and Water Commission between Mexico and the U.S., etc.), but none of them has a trinational perspective or a specific mandate to promote sustainable development. A serious commitment to sustainable development in the region would reflect a commitment beyond the jurisdiction and scope of the current binational institutions.

On the basis of the arguments presented above, and for the purpose of discussion, I would argue that it is difficult to talk about sustainable development in North America under the current conditions. In spite of the concept's appeal, it would be more accurate and realistic to talk about a *transition* to sustainable development than about sustainable development as an end-product. The paradigms for development in the region could be defined in terms of realistic goals and actions in time and geographic space that are capable of making contributions to that transition. This would include actions linked not only to environmental protection, but also to economic development and the enhancement of social well-being.

TECHNOLOGICAL INNOVATION AND SUSTAINABLE DEVELOPMENT

In the brief discussion on sustainable development presented above, technological change is regarded as important to achieving significant advances in pollution reduction and the better management of those natural resources critical to the economy and social well-being, such as energy, water, biodiversity, and so on. As mentioned above, it is a matter of time before the carrying capacity of the environment is overloaded. The cumulative effect of pollution has already reached critical levels in parts of the three countries and the same could happen soon in others, given the frequent efforts to promote economic growth at all cost. I will limit my comments to technological innovation in pollution prevention.

All three countries in North America follow "command-and-control" approaches. Under this arrangement, the national government sets environmental quality goals based on available scientific data, determines the methods to achieve them, and stipulates the deadlines for action, with penalties for non-compliance. However, rising concern over the limitations and costs of pollution control policies and increasing conflict over natural resource programs have led to consideration of a diversity of new policy approaches in North America. Most of these approaches are being considered in earnest or are being implemented in the U.S., but they are also emerging as part of discussion, debate, and policy reform in Canada and Mexico.

Technological changes in the United States that are intended to improve environmental protection have been oriented during the last years to the substitution of materials used as inputs in industrial production, process redesign, and final product reformulation, in order to reduce pollution. Such changes are known as pollution prevention, source reduction, waste reduction, or clean technology. They distinguish themselves from end-of-pipe pollution control technology, used in the command-and-control approach, that reduces – but does not eliminate – the emission or discharge of pollutants.

In 1990 the U.S. Congress enacted the nation's first federal law aimed at curbing pollution at its source. The Pollution Prevention Act, which puts a premium on preventing, rather than cleaning up, pollution, was designed to expand the level and quality of information available to industry and regulators. Largely voluntary, the law directs the Environmental Protection Agency (EPA) to establish standard methods of measurement and audits for industrial pollution prevention goals (Kraft 1996). The Pollution Prevention Act's success has yet to be demonstrated. Some basis for optimism is the reduction in releases of toxic chemicals by major industrial sources (recent data show a decrease of about 43 per cent between 1988 and 1993). The U.S. government has collaborated with major corporations in designing pollution prevention programs, and environmental organizations in the U.S. have initiated pollution prevention strategies, with both industry and citizen cooperation.

The most notable Canadian initiative for pollution prevention is called Accelerated Reductions/Elimination of Toxics (ARET), a process involving industries that are engaged in large-scale emission, federal and provincial officials, and professional organizations. The goal of this process is by the year 2000 to reduce by 90 per cent the 1988 pollution levels of some fourteen substances and by 50 per cent another eighty-seven substances (Environmental Policy Unit 1996). To date there has been no independent assessment of the effectiveness of the ARET process. Mexico has not created a similar waste reduction program so far. Pollution prevention initiatives have concentrated on a few sectors only. Despite these achievements, an enormous quantity of toxic chemicals continues to be released into the air, water, and soil in all three countries.

The success of pollution prevention efforts will depend largely on the motivation of industry to implement technological changes in industrial production. What are the driving forces of technological innovation in environmental protection? Some scholars document the functional relationship, motivated by profit, that can exist between innovator and innovation: "Innovating users appear to be motivated by considerations of increased profits they may obtain by having better equipment than that available to competitors" (von Hippel 1988, 8). In the case of the environment, some scholars present evidence that indicates a competitive advantage in firms engaged in improving their environmental performance (Porter and van der Linde 1995). Other authors indicate that a "greening" strategy is being actively pursued by many corporations across the spectrum of manufacturing sectors through industry initiatives and partnerships that operate in advance of, or outside of, formal policy requirements (Press and Mazmanian, 1996).

However, Ashford (1993) considers that innovation in environmental protection is still largely a response to regulation and public pressure rather than part of a firm's business strategy. He states that one potential obstacle to innovation is that public pressure on firms – "chiefly from what is being called the 'green' consumer" – for pollution reduction is diluted by their compliance with the current regime of regulation, designed in the early 1970s and at a level attainable by existing technology. Despite aggressive government intervention with clear and stringent regulations in the 1970s, "understandably, industry not only did not want to be forced to develop new technology, it did not want to be forced to make any technological changes that were costly and that compromised production efficiency" (289).[3] Studies on individual accomplishments in pollution prevention in industry discovered little fundamental technological change in U.S. industry (EPA 1992; Doyle 1991). These results tend to confirm Ashford's position, which stresses the importance to pollution prevention efforts of initiatives requiring stringent and specific regulatory demands (such as emission, effluent, or exposure standards, or product bans and phase-outs), explicitly designed with technological considerations in mind.

To what degree have technological changes in pollution prevention contributed to sustainable development in the U.S. and in the rest of North America? The evidence so far shows the encouraging developments in this area in the U.S. mentioned above, but these do not represent a substantial trend towards sustainable development. Cooperative agreements focus on large corporations, and they are generally oriented to specific processes and products, not across the full range of the corporations' activities. Reductions in the release of toxic chemicals have taken place in regulated environments, but to only a small extent can these be attributed to technological changes in pollution prevention. Voluntary pollution prevention programs have also taken place in regulated environments. Voluntary programs are attractive as an alternative to mandatory regulation when industry gains economically (for example, by avoiding the loss of valued by-products of manufacturing) or when there is a high public relations value to being seen as environmentally responsible. They may be much less useful where continued governmental monitoring is needed to ensure compliance or where competitive market forces are insufficient to induce companies to reduce pollution to an acceptable level.

There are other potential obstacles to innovation. These include: technological deficiencies, such as the poor performance capability of technology under certain economic requirements and process design standards, the lack of alternative substances for hazardous components, and poor processing flexibility; factors related to finance and to the labour force; poor regulatory compliance and regulatory focus on end-of-pipe technology; and consumer- supplier-, and manager-related factors (lack of top management commitment; lack of employee education, training, and motivation; and company reluctance to change) (OTA 1986).

It is likely that governments in the North American region will continue to employ a combination of regulatory and voluntary approaches to pollution control, despite the emphasis given to voluntary programs. The scepticism derives from the continued push by many corporations to weaken environmental protection statutes and to challenge perceptions about the severity of public and environmental health risks (thus raising questions about their commitment to environmental goals). Corporate actions tend to be governed by an emphasis on short-term economic gains and a neglect of long-term economic, health, and environmental benefits. It is unclear whether technological innovation will contribute significantly to sustainable development in the region. There are still questions that need to be addressed in the discussion of innovation and sustainable development in North America: Will voluntary pollution reduction programs be broadly embraced by the affected industries over time even if regulatory requirements are relaxed? Will these actions be sufficient to meet public health and environmental quality goals imbedded in sustainable development? Will innovation be restricted to the United States and Canada or could it also expand to Mexico? Is innovation limited only to big firms and certain sectors? Can we expect greater disparities in pollution levels among the three countries because of regional disparities in innovation technology?

A TRANSITION TO SUSTAINABLE DEVELOPMENT

North America excels as one of the leading regions in the world economy. The implementation of the North America Free Trade Agreement has led to the portrait of North America as one of the three leading economic blocs within the globalization process of the world economy. Economically, however, the region relies heavily on the indisputable power of the United States as the world's leading economy and the largest consumer market.

The international image of North America as an economic bloc contrasts, however, with the reality of a region divided by social, economic, political, and cultural differences among countries and within countries. A sustainable development process in North America has to take into account the differences and commonalties among the three countries at the national level and within each country at the local level. Efforts to foster sustainable development should recognize that it is impossible to separate socio-economic development issues from environmental issues – hence the importance of keeping a balanced relationship between its two components, sustainability and development.

Is sustainable development feasible in North America? There is no optimistic answer to this question. Current growth patterns in the region create considerable obstacles to regional sustainable development: the priority of a market economy over social and environmental issues, the deregulation of public institutions, a growing opposition to environmental priorities, and growing social inequalities and their linkage to environmental issues (different forms of environmental justice and environmental racism). Higher standards for environmental protection have been under attack in all three North American countries, and there is a significant political conflict between groups seeking lower environmental regulations and those seeking higher environmental standards. The pressure on all three governments has led to the implementation of voluntary compliance strategies, economic instruments, budget cuts on environmental agencies, and political battles over a misperceived conflict between economic growth and environmental protection.

Within this context and as mentioned in the first part of this chapter, it would be more realistic to talk about a transition to sustainable development than about sustainable development as an end-product. Steps to foster sustainable development in North America could be defined in terms of their role in that transition, with specific actions in time and geographic space. There are several advantages in this approach: goals can be set to obtain results in the short and middle term without creating unrealistic expectations; these goals could accommodate even small (but concrete) actions that represent a contribution to sustainable development; actions and programs could be evaluated by the participating organizations and their constituencies according to their contribution to a specific target in the transition process and not to an end goal of sustainable development; the transition process and its milestones could be adjusted more easily according to the availability of resources or with respect to new needs and demands owing to unexpected economic, social, or political changes. There are, however, at least two conditions that must be met in order to move from mere rhetoric to a concrete transition to sustainable development. First, the goals and actions of the regional and local levels must be coordinated, as much as possible, to ensure coherence; second, there must be a better understanding of, and agreement on, what to sustain and how this would interact with development goals.

Some efforts in North America could contribute to the creation of a transition process towards sustainable development. The most notable development in the United States in this regard has been the creation of the President's Council on Sustainable Development (PCSD) in 1993. The council, consisting of twenty-five leaders from industry, government, and the environmental community, was established to formulate a national action strategy for sustainable development. The parallel organization in Canada is the National Round Table on Environment and Economy established in 1991. In a similar manner, the Mexican Secretariat for the Environment (Secretaría de Medio Ambiente, Recursos Naturales y Pesca, SEMARNAP) created in April 1995 the National Consultative Council for Sustainable Development, which operates together with four regional consultative councils. The national council consists of forty representatives from the regional councils, Congress, universities, and research centres, business and industry, social organizations, non-government organizations (NGOs), and departments of the federal government. As is the case with the U.S. and Canadian councils, the Mexican's purpose is to procure cooperation and consensual decisions in environmental policies. An assessment on the strengths and limitations of these organizations is beyond the scope of this chapter, but these organizations appear to offer some potential for coordination if enough political will and momentum are built in each country. This momentum will depend on political pressure by domestic social organizations and the potential transnational alliances that could be created among them.

The Commission for Environmental Cooperation appears to be the best option to foster cooperation in the transition to sustainable development at the regional level in North America. As mentioned above, its secretariat has facilitated cooperation among Canada, the U.S., and Mexico. For example, all three governments recently agreed to phase out lead, mercury, and DDT in North America. Cooperative efforts in monitoring transboundary air pollution, migratory species, and pollution release inventories have also succeeded. The potential role of the CEC and its secretariat must be stressed. It is the only organization with a clear mandate at a regional level in North America, and it has the capacity to convene a broad range of actors, from public officials at the federal, state, or local level to local activists and representatives from the business community. These characteristics give the CEC secretariat a potentially leading role in coordinating the transition to sustainable development in North America.

The CEC secretariat could also provide opportunities to expand technological innovation in pollution prevention in North America. The CEC secretariat could convene trinational discussions and cooperation in the effort to establish specific regulatory demands to induce technological innovation in pollution prevention. A trinational forum might be critical for regional initiatives given the early stages of pollution prevention in Canada and in Mexico.

The CEC is, however, a young and fragile organization dependent on the political will of the three federal governments.[4] The CEC council and its secretariat are still seeking to define the CEC's niche in environmental protection and, hopefully, in sustainable development. There are, however, clear obstacles to the fulfilment of this potential. All three federal governments are jealous of their national sovereignty and want to revise the role of the CEC secretariat according to their perception of "the best national interest." The ill-defined national interest is often an excuse to avoid or limit compromising actions beyond the direct control of federal bureaucrats, including transboundary cooperation among states and communities. The three council members of the CEC, as well as environmental agencies in Canada, the U.S., and Mexico, are concerned that the secretariat might have "too much freedom." Efforts to micro-manage the work of the secretariat limit the possibility to construct a more ambitious working agenda with opportunities for a transition to sustainable development. A broader role of the CEC secretariat in regional sustainable development initiatives will depend on lobbying and political pressure from environmental groups, NGOs, and other social organizations in all three countries to counterbalance the limitations imposed by the three federal governments.

CONCLUSION

This chapter summarizes some of the obstacles to achieving sustainable development in North America, as well as a potential role of technological innovation in that process. It also discusses some opportunities to reach realistic policies leading to sustainable development. Challenges to achieving sustainable development include reconciling the ambitions and expectations of various interest groups and balancing present and future development aspirations. It is unclear at this point whether political challenges to environmental protection and social well-being would aggravate the patterns of growth in the region or if social participation would counterbalance these pressures, facilitating a regional transition to sustainable development. Any effort in this direction will have to take into account social and economic gaps among countries and within countries. It is also unclear whether innovations in pollution reduction technology will be able to contribute to a transition to sustainable development in the region. What is clear is the need for a new paradigm for development in North America in an era of globalization, the polarization of regions, the redefinition of the nation-state, and rapid and dramatic social and economic changes driven by the power and ideology of a market economy. Sustainable development could be a response to the search for this new paradigm if it includes the equity previsions mentioned at the beginning of this chapter.

NOTES

1 An overview of several approaches of economic theory on sustainable development is summarized in Dietz and van der Straaten (1992).

2 By the same token, Nicholas Georgescu-Roegen (1993, 77) states that from the point of view of thermodynamics, matter-energy enters the economic process in a state of low entropy and comes out of it in a state of high entropy.

3 For Daly, the earth ecosystem develops (evolves) but does not growth. Its subsystem, the economy, must eventually stop growing, but it can continue to develop.

4 The United States' population is three times larger than Mexico's and more than nine times larger than Canada's. The disparities in GDP are even greater. U.S. GDP in 1992 was twelve times that for Canada and seventeen times that for Mexico. Per capita GDP in the United States in 1992 was 1.12 times that in Canada but 6.7 times that for Mexico.

5 This is particularly evident in the border areas of North America, where there is a socio-economic interdependence and natural resources are

shared by two countries (fresh water, energy, air quality). For example, per capita consumption of shared fresh water resources is on average three to four times higher on the U.S. side than on the Mexican side of the border.

6 For example, the Natural Resources Defense Council is currently working with Amoco Petroleum, Dow Chemical, Monsanto, Rayonier, and the New Jersey Department of Environmental Protection on a Pollution Prevention Pilot Project (4P) that is expected to cut both production and environmental compliance costs while reducing pollution at chemical manufacturing plants. EPA's 33/50 initiative called for voluntary efforts by industry to reduce the use of seventeen priority toxic chemicals below the original 1988 TRI levels – 33 per cent by 1992 and 50 per cent by 1995. Despite significant achievements, some citizen groups have sharply criticized these voluntary efforts, and especially the 33/50 program, as insufficient to reduce the use of toxic chemicals to an acceptable levels (Kraft 1996).

7 Ashford points out that despite some improvements, equipment modifications, increasing recycling, input substitution, process redesign, and product reformulation were rare events. "They were rare events because environmental requirements were not stringent enough ... and/or because there was inadequate [regulatory mechanisms] to force technological change" (291).

8 It is important to distinguish between the two main bodies of this organization, the council and the secretariat. The council is the ruling body of the organization and is integrated by the environmental ministers of the three countries. The secretariat is integrated by an executive director and its staff. The secretariat is designed to propose an annual working program to the council and to carry it out once approved. A critical issue for the integrity and credibility of this institution is the relative independence of the secretariat from the council. This is likely to be a source of conflict and struggle within the institution.

REFERENCES

Ashford, N.A. 1993. "Understanding Technological Responses of Industrial Firms to Environmental Problems: Implications for Government Policy." In K. Fisher and J. Schot, eds, *Environmental Strategies for Industry: International Perspectives on Research, Needs, and Policy Implications.* Washington D.C.: Island Press.

Boulding, K.E. 1966. "The Economics of the Coming Spaceship Earth." In H. Jarret, ed, *Environmental Quality in a Growing Economy: Essays from the Sixth RFF Forum.* Baltimore: Johns Hopkins Press.

Daly, E.H. 1993. "Introduction to Essays toward a Steady-State Economy." In Daly and Townsend (1993).

Daly, E.H., and N.K. Townsend, eds. 1993. *Valuing the Earth: Economics, Ecology, Ethics.* Cambridge, Mass.: MIT Press.

Dietz, J.F., and J. van der Straaten. 1992. "Sustainable Development and the Necessary Integration of Ecological Insights into Economic Theory." In F.J. Dietz, U.E. Simonis, and J. van der Straaten, eds, *Sustainability and Environmental Policy.* Berlin: Edition Sigma.

Doyle, J. 1991. *Hold the Applause! A Case Study of Corporate Environmentalism as Practiced at DuPont.* Washington, D.C.: Friends of the Earth.

ECLAC. Economic Commission for Latin America and the Caribbean. 1991. *Sustainable Development: Changing Production Patterns, Social Equity and the Environment.* Santiago, Chile: United Nations.

Elliot, A.J. 1994. *An Introduction to Sustainable Development: The Developing World.* London: Routledge.

Environmental Policy Unit, Queen's University. 1996. *Lessons Learned from ARET: A Qualitative Survey of Perceptions of Stakeholders.* Kingston: Queen's University School of Policy Studies.

EPA (Environmental Protection Agency). 1992. *Improving Technology Diffusion for Environmental Protection: Report and Recommendations of the Technology and Economics Committee of the National Advisory Council for Environmental Policy and Technology (nacept).* Washington, D.C.: EPA.

Georgescu-Roegen, N. 1993. "The Entropy Law and the Economic Problem." In Daly and Townsend (1993).

Kraft, M.E. 1996. *Environmental Policy and Politics: Toward the Twenty-First Century.* New York: Harper Collins.

National Commission on the Environment. 1993. *Choosing a Sustainable Future: The Report of the National Commission on the Environment.* Washington, D.C.: Island Press.

OTA (Office of Technology Assessment). 1986. *Serious Reduction of Hazardous Waste.* Washington, D.C.: OTA.

Pearce, D., and J. Warford. 1993. *World without End: Economics, Environment and Sustainable Development.* Published for the World Bank. Oxford: Oxford University Press.

Pezzey, J. 1992. *Sustainable Development Concepts: An Economic Analysis.* Environment Paper no. 2. Washington, D.C.: World Bank.

Porter, M.E., and C. van der Linde. 1995. "Green and Competitive: Ending the Stalemate." *Harvard Business Review* 73:120.

Press, D., and D.A. Mazmanian. 1996. "The Greening of Industry: Achievement and Potential." In N.J. Vig and M.E. Kraft, eds, *Environmental Policy in the 1990s: Reform or Reaction?* Washington, D.C.: CQ Press.

Redclift, M., and D. Goodman. 1991. "Introduction." In D. Goodman and M. Redclift, eds, *Environment and Development in Latin America: The Politics of Sustainability.* Manchester: Manchester University Press.

Repetto, R. 1992. "Promoting Environmentally Sound Economic Progress: What the North Can Do." In K. Uner, ed, *Change: Threat or Opportunity for Human Progress.* New York: United Nations.

Sachs, I. 1976. *Ecodesarrollo.* Mexico: El Colegio de Mexico.

Townsend, N.K. 1993. "Steady State Economies and the Command Economy." In Daly and Townsend (1993).

von Hippel, E. 1988. *The Sources of Innovation.* Oxford: Oxford University Press.

World Commission on Environment and Development. 1987. *Our Common Future.* Oxford: Oxford University Press.

Contributors

Diana Alarcón, social development specialist, Inter-American Development Bank, New York.

John Alic, lecturer, Nitze School of Advanced International Studies, Johns Hopkins University, Washington, D.C., U.S.A.

Robert Anderson, professor, School of Communications, Simon Fraser University, Burnaby, British Columbia, Canada.

Stephen S. Cohen, professor, Department of City and Regional Planning and co-director, BRIE, University of California, Berkeley, California, U.S.A.

Theodore Cohn, professor, Department of Political Science, Simon Fraser University, Burnaby, British Columbia, Canada.

Charles Davis, NSERC-SSHRC-NB Power-Xerox Chair in the Management of Technological Change, Faculty of Business, University of New Brunswick at Saint John, Canada.

Chad Day, professor, School of Resource and Environmental Management, Simon Fraser University, Burnaby, British Columbia, Canada.

Henry Etzkowitz, associate professor, Department of Sociology, State University of New York at Purchase and Stony Brook, U.S.A.

Paolo Guerrieri, professor, Faculty of Economics, University of Rome, "La Sapienza," Italy.

Richard G. Harris, professor, Department of Economics, Simon Fraser University, Burnaby British Columbia, Canada.

Michael Howlett, associate professor, Department of Political Science, Simon Fraser University, Burnaby, British Columbia, Canada.

Catherine Murray, associate professor, School of Communications, Simon Fraser University, Burnaby, British Columbia, Canada.

Jorge Niosi, professor, Department of Administrative Science, University of Quebec at Montreal, Quebec, Canada.

Gilles Paquet, professor, Faculty of Administration, University of Ottawa, Ottawa, Ontario, Canada.

J. Carlos Ramírez, Centro do Investigacion y Docencia Economicas, Division de Economia, Carreteria Mexico-Toluca, Mexico DF, Mexico.

John Ravenhill, senior fellow, Department of International Relations, Research School of Pacific and Asian Studies, Australian National University, Canberra, Australia.

Roberto A. Sanchez, professor, Department of Environmental Studies, University of California, Santa Cruz, California, U.S.A.

Luc Soete, director, Maastricht Economic Research Institute on Innovation and Technology (MERIT), Faculty of Economics, University of Maastricht, Maastricht, The Netherlands.

Kurt Unger, Centro do Investigacion y Docencia Economicas, Division de Economia, Carreteria Mexico-Toluca, Mexico DF, Mexico.

Sidney Weintraub, professor, Lyndon B. Johnson School of Public Affairs, University of Texas, Austin, Texas.

Eduardo Zepeda, Center for U.S.-Mexican Studies University of California, San Diego, and Centro de Investigaciones Socio-Economicas, Universidad Autonoma de Coahuila, Mexico.